SWORD MASTER

WAR OF THE ANCIENTS

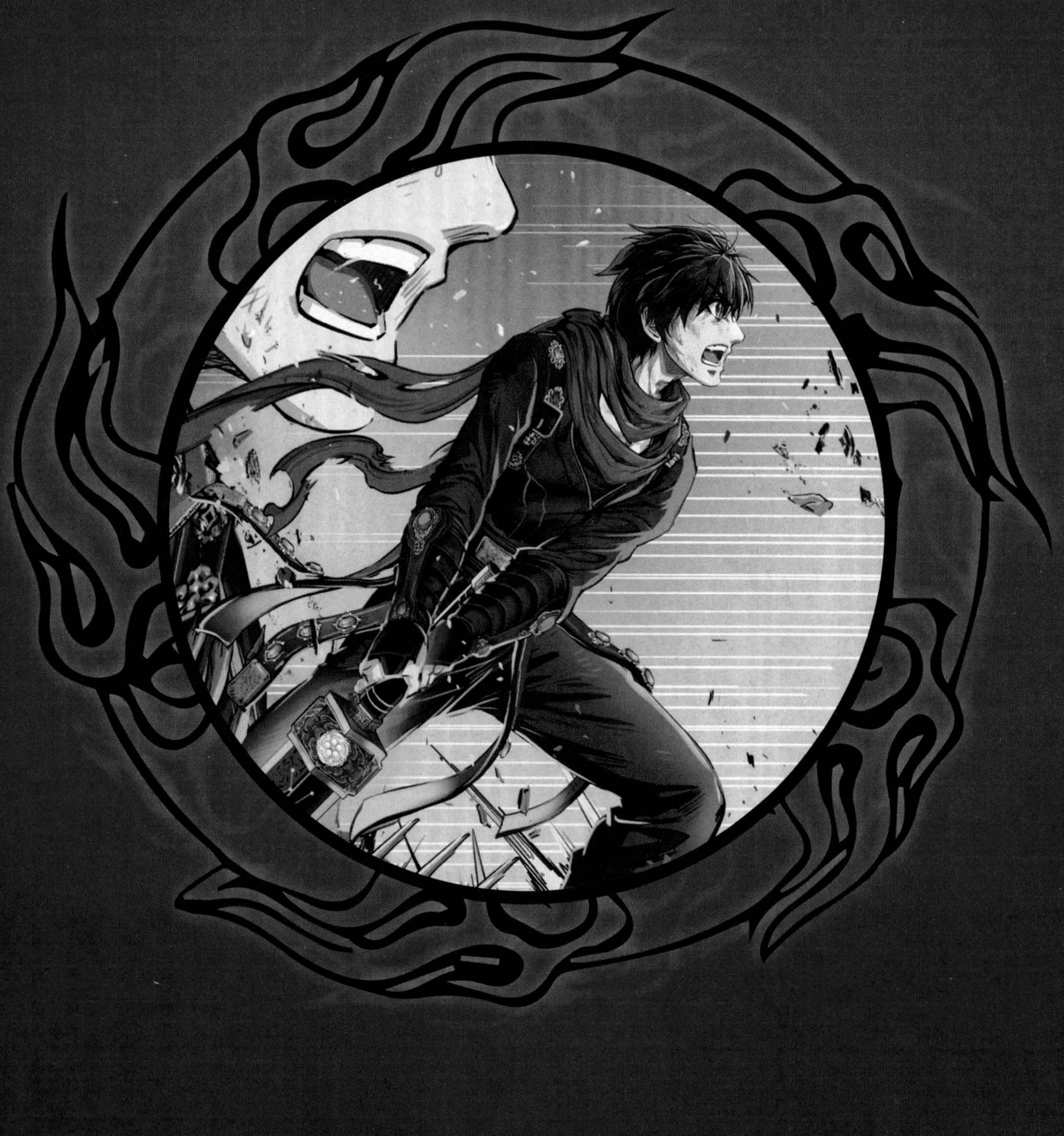

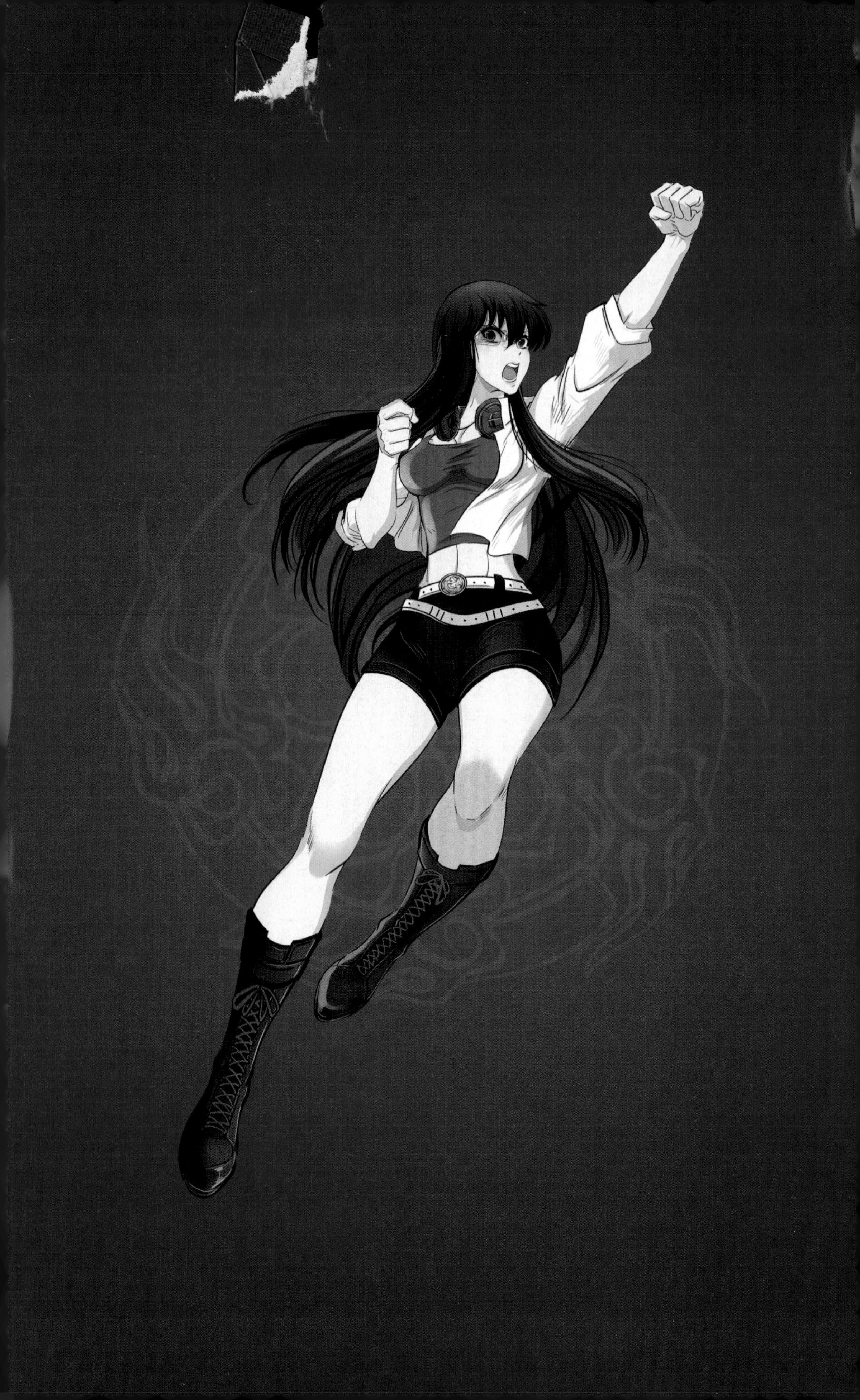

SWORD MASTER
WAR OF THE ANCIENTS

SHUIZHU
WRITER

GUNJI
ARTIST

GREG PAK
ADAPTATION

VC's TRAVIS LANHAM
LETTERER

GUNJI
COVER ART

CARLOS LAO
LOGO DESIGN

TOM GRONEMAN & LINDSEY COHICK
ASSISTANT EDITORS

MARK PANICCIA
EDITOR

SPECIAL THANKS TO
WINNI WOO & YIFAN JIANG

COLLECTION EDITOR JENNIFER GRÜNWALD
ASSISTANT MANAGING EDITOR MAIA LOY
ASSISTANT EDITOR CAITLIN O'CONNELL
EDITOR, SPECIAL PROJECTS MARK D. BEAZLEY
VP PRODUCTION & SPECIAL PROJECTS JEFF YOUNGQUIST
BOOK DESIGNER ADAM DEL RE
SVP PRINT, SALES & MARKETING DAVID GABRIEL
EDITOR IN CHIEF C.B. CEBULSKI

SWORD MASTER VOL. 1: WAR OF THE ANCIENTS. Contains material originally published in magazine form as SWORD MASTER (2019) #1-6. First printing 2019. ISBN 978-1-302-91948-1. Published by MARVEL WORLDWIDE, INC., a subsidiary of MARVEL ENTERTAINMENT, LLC. OFFICE OF PUBLICATION: 1290 Avenue of the Americas, New York, NY 10104. © 2019 MARVEL No similarity between any of the names, characters, persons, and/or institutions in this magazine with those of any living or dead person or institution is intended, and any such similarity which may exist is purely coincidental. **Printed in Canada.** KEVIN FEIGE, Chief Creative Officer; DAN BUCKLEY, President, Marvel Entertainment; JOHN NEE, Publisher; JOE QUESADA, EVP & Creative Director; TOM BREVOORT, SVP of Publishing; DAVID BOGART, Associate Publisher & SVP of Talent Affairs; Publishing & Partnership; DAVID GABRIEL, VP of Print & Digital Publishing; JEFF YOUNGQUIST, VP of Production & Special Projects; DAN CARR, Executive Director of Publishing Technology; ALEX MORALES, Director of Publishing Operations; DAN EDINGTON, Managing Editor; SUSAN CRESPI, Production Manager; STAN LEE, Chairman Emeritus. For information regarding advertising in Marvel Comics or on Marvel.com, please contact Vit DeBellis, Custom Solutions & Integrated Advertising Manager, at vdebellis@marvel.com. For Marvel subscription inquiries, please call 888-511-5480. Manufactured between 12/13/2019 and 1/14/2020 by SOLISCO PRINTERS, SCOTT, QC, CANADA.

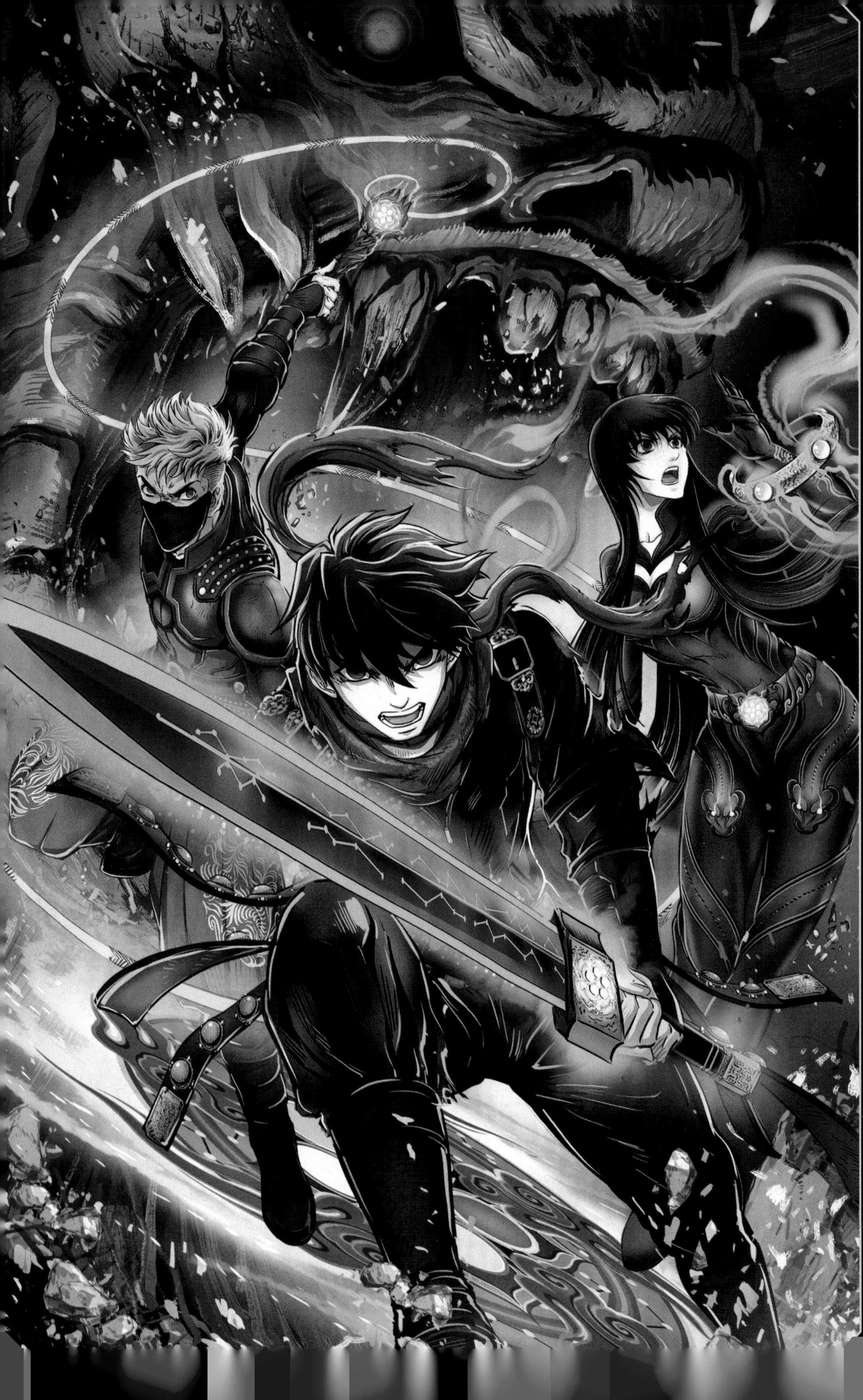

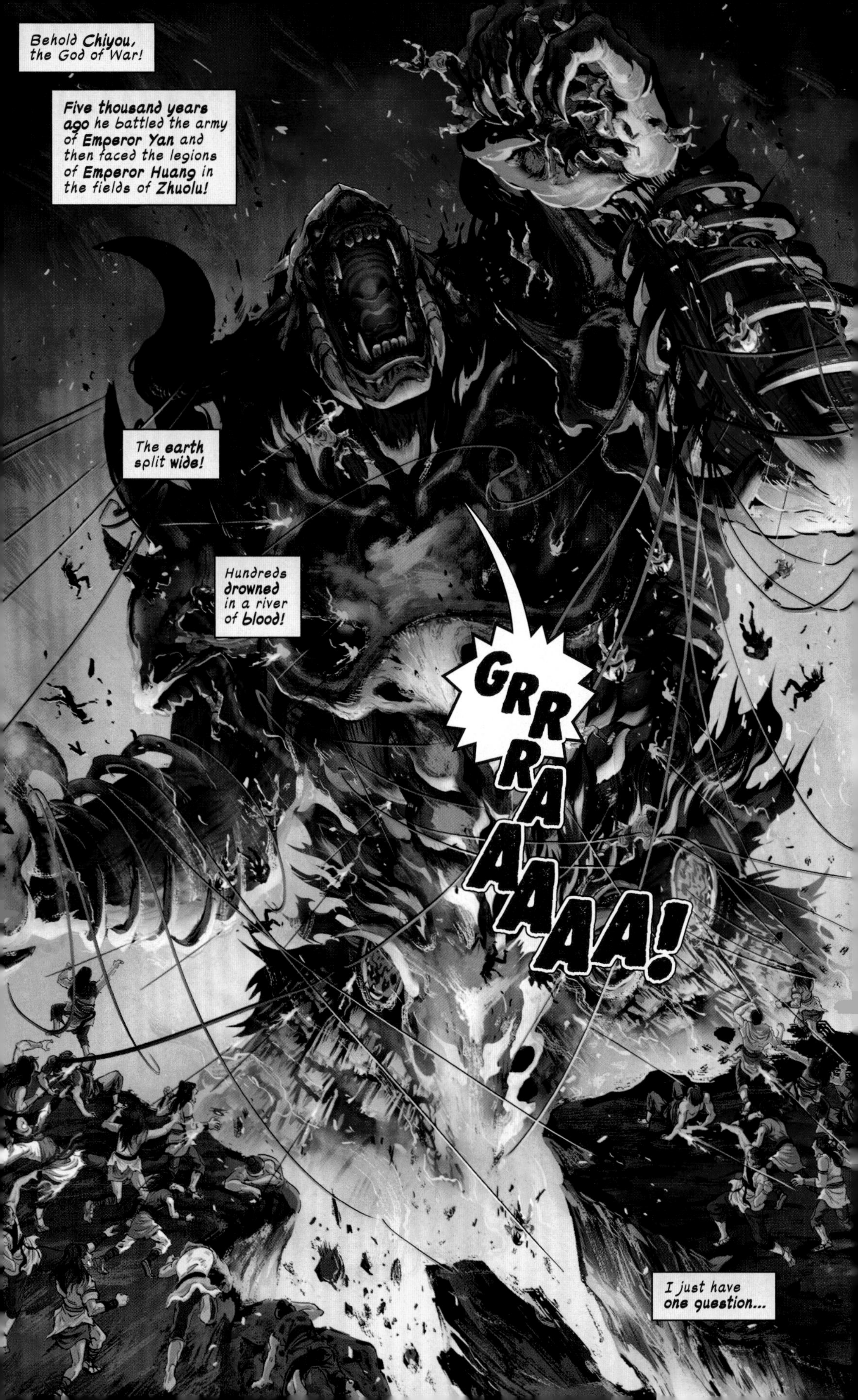
Behold Chiyou, the God of War!
Five thousand years ago he battled the army of Emperor Yan and then faced the legions of Emperor Huang in the fields of Zhuolu!
The earth split wide!
Hundreds drowned in a river of blood!
GRRRAAAAAA!
I just have one question...

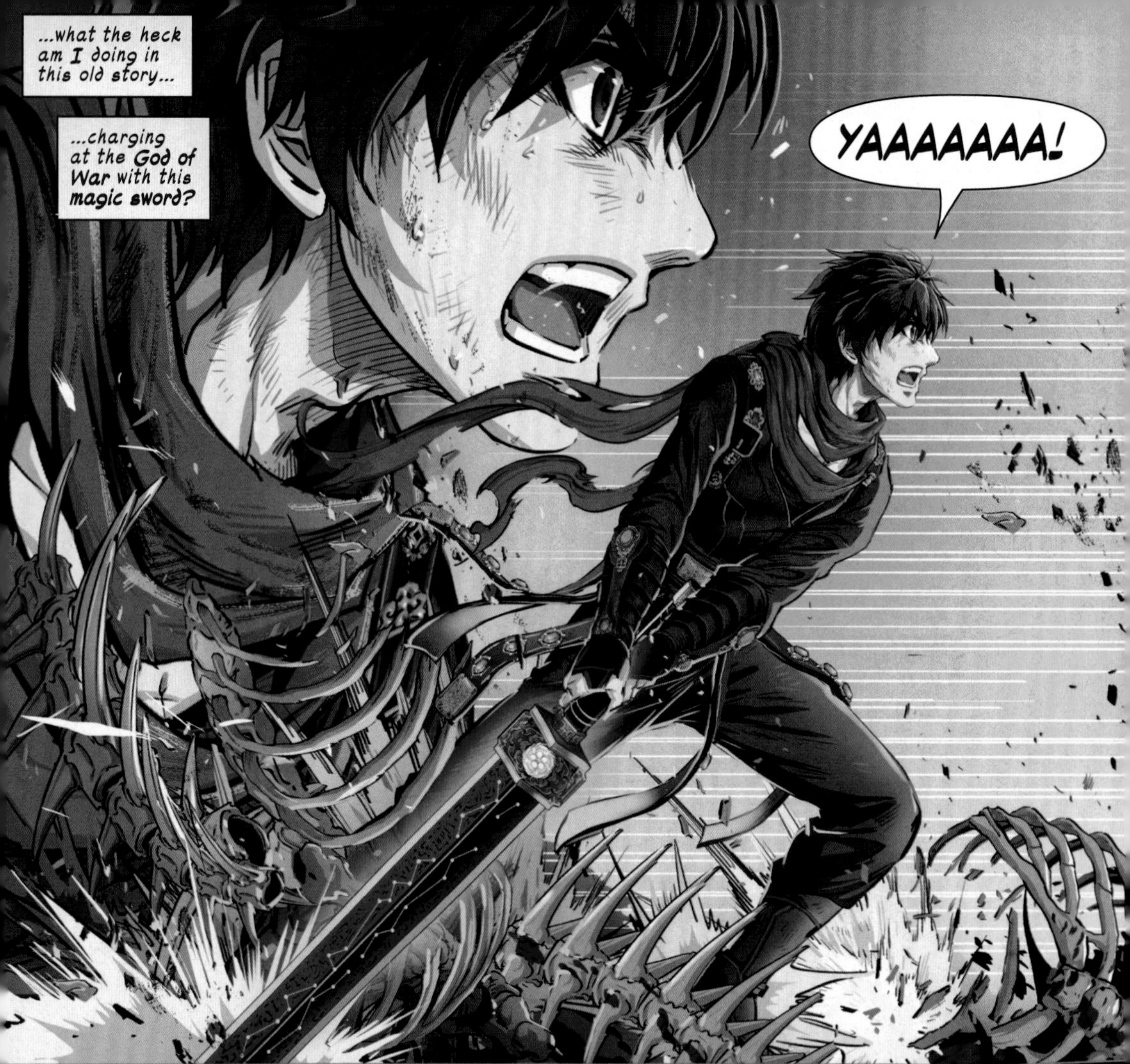
...what the heck am I doing in this old story...
...charging at the God of War with this magic sword?
YAAAAAAA!

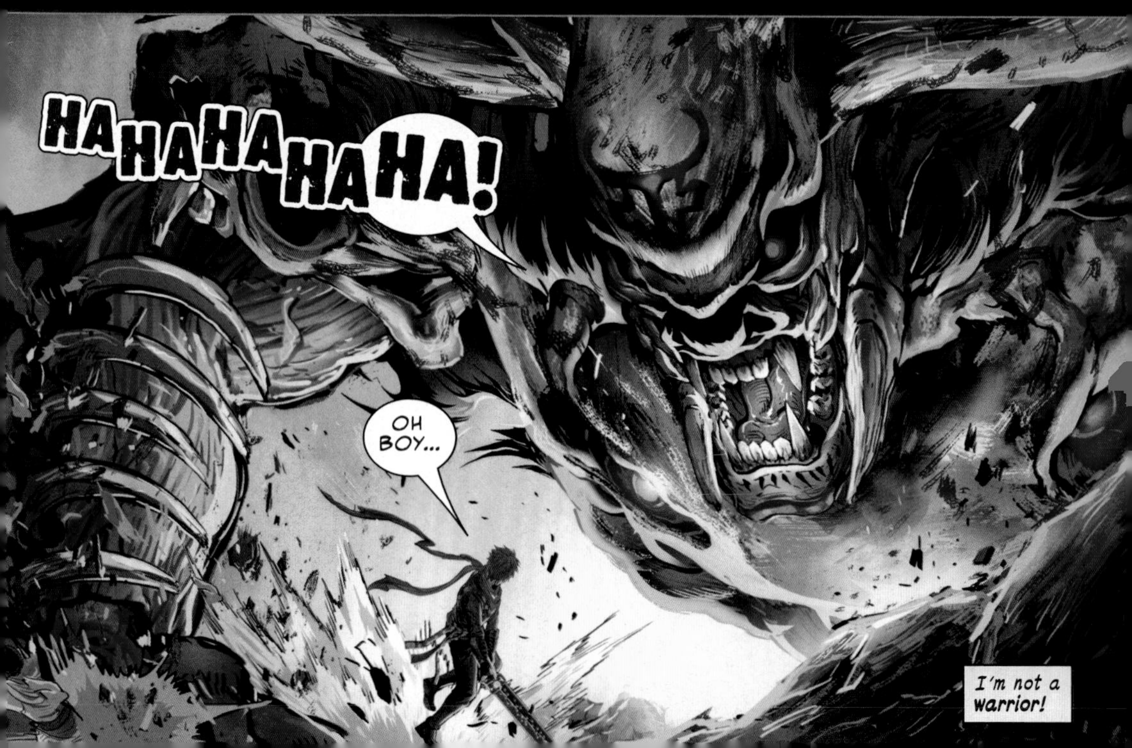
HAHAHAHAHAHA!
OH BOY...
I'm not a warrior!

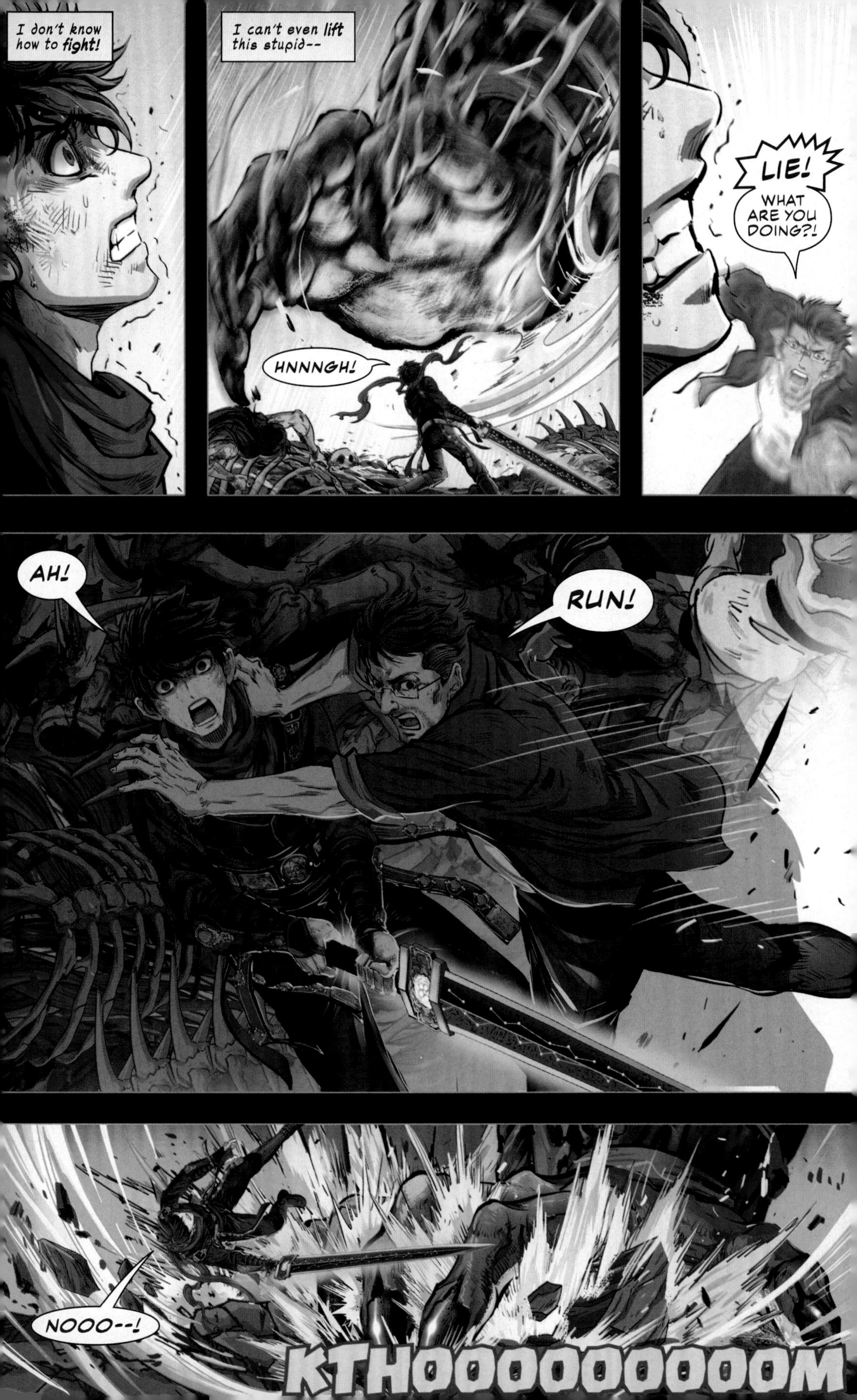
I don't know how to fight!
I can't even lift this stupid--
HNNNGH!
LIE!
WHAT ARE YOU DOING?!
AH!
RUN!
NOOO--!
KTHOOOOOOOOOOM

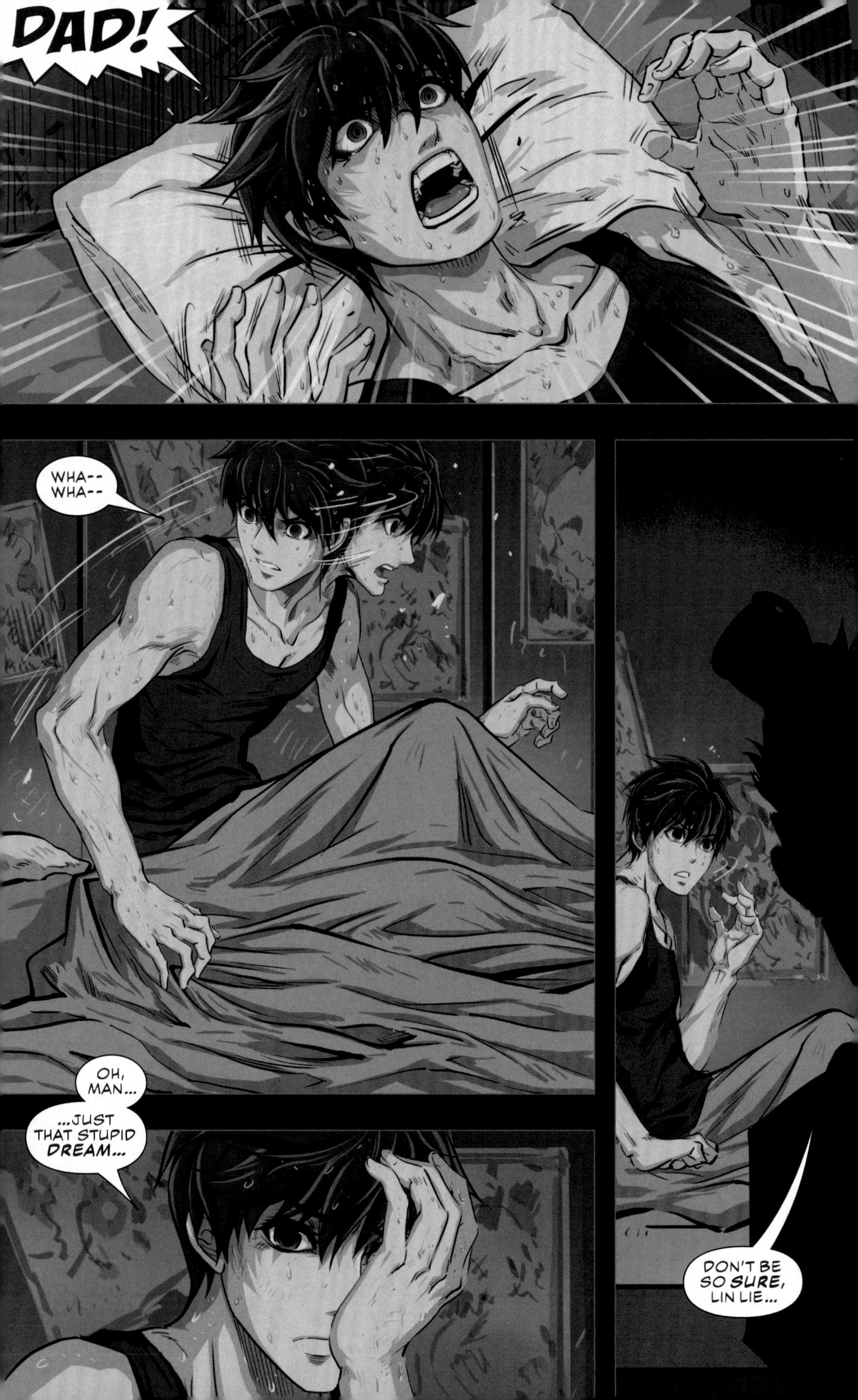
DAD!
WHA-- WHA--
OH, MAN...
...JUST THAT STUPID DREAM...
DON'T BE SO SURE, LIN LIE...

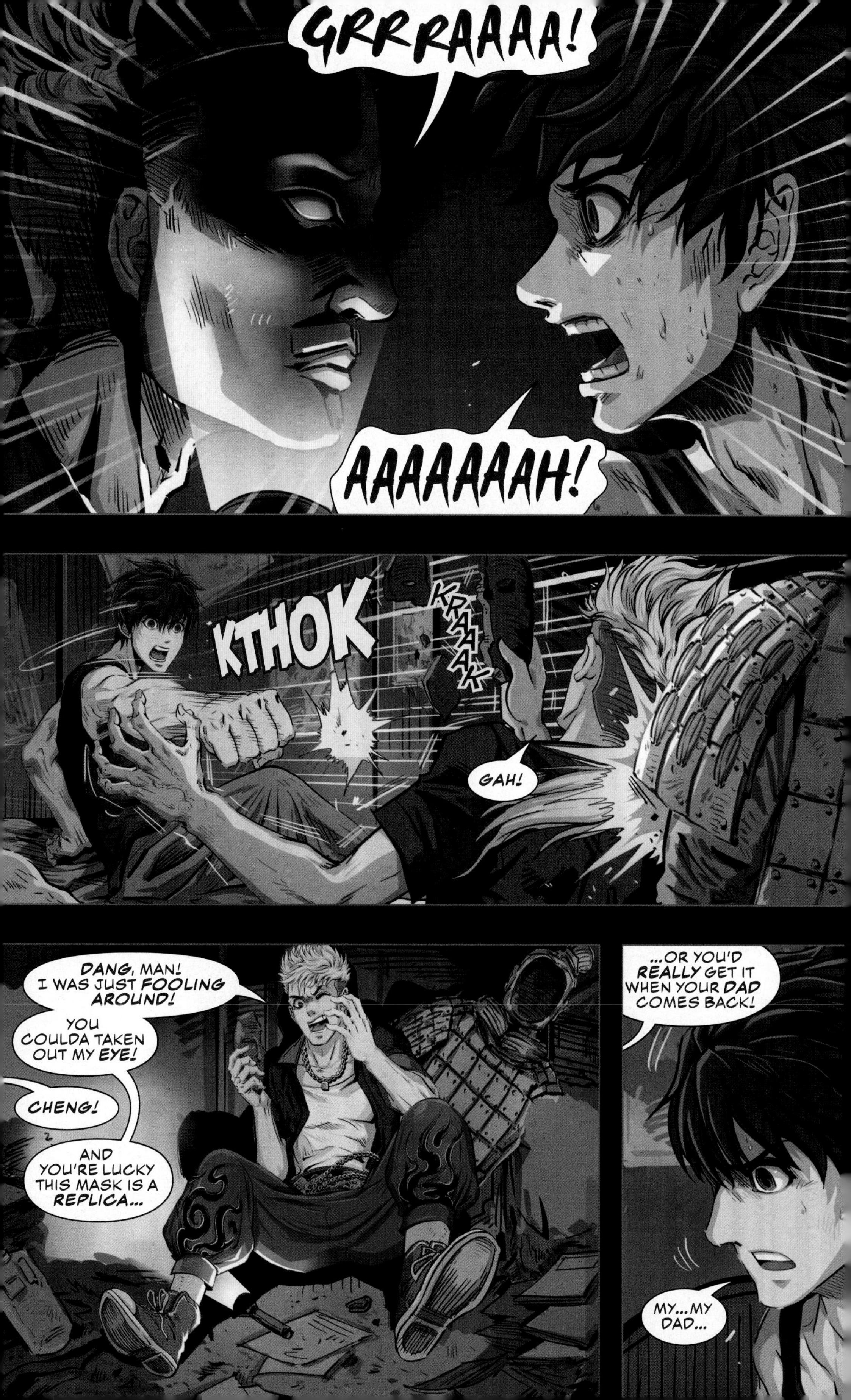
GRRRAAAA!
AAAAAAAH!
KTHOK
KRAAAK
GAH!
DANG, MAN! I WAS JUST FOOLING AROUND!
YOU COULDA TAKEN OUT MY EYE!
CHENG!
AND YOU'RE LUCKY THIS MASK IS A REPLICA...
...OR YOU'D REALLY GET IT WHEN YOUR DAD COMES BACK!
MY...MY DAD...

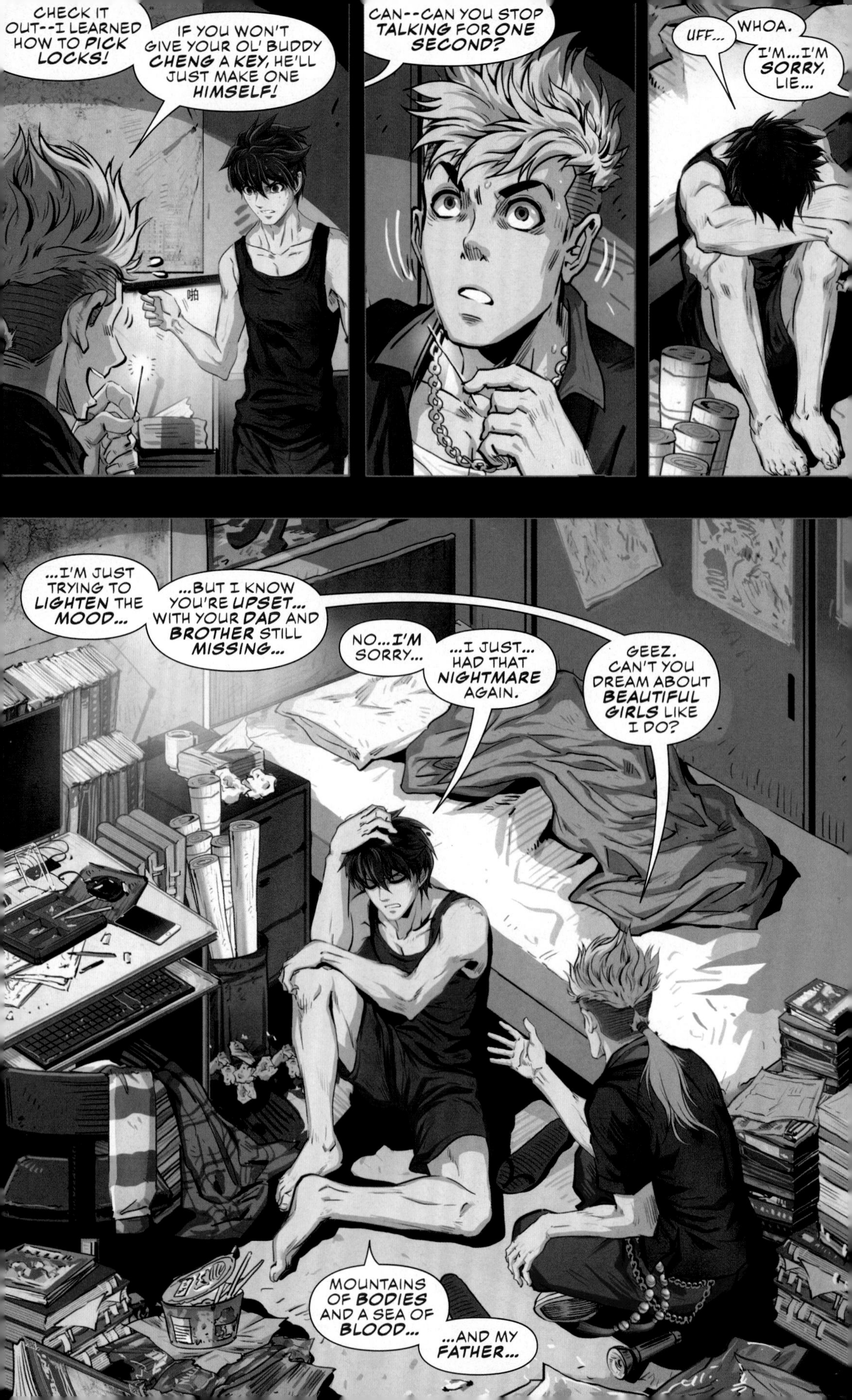
CHECK IT OUT--I LEARNED HOW TO PICK LOCKS!
IF YOU WON'T GIVE YOUR OL' BUDDY CHENG A KEY, HE'LL JUST MAKE ONE HIMSELF!
啪
CAN--CAN YOU STOP TALKING FOR ONE SECOND?
UFF...
WHOA.
I'M...I'M SORRY, LIE...
...I'M JUST TRYING TO LIGHTEN THE MOOD...
...BUT I KNOW YOU'RE UPSET... WITH YOUR DAD AND BROTHER STILL MISSING...
NO...I'M SORRY...
...I JUST... HAD THAT NIGHTMARE AGAIN.
GEEZ. CAN'T YOU DREAM ABOUT BEAUTIFUL GIRLS LIKE I DO?
MOUNTAINS OF BODIES AND A SEA OF BLOOD...
...AND MY FATHER...

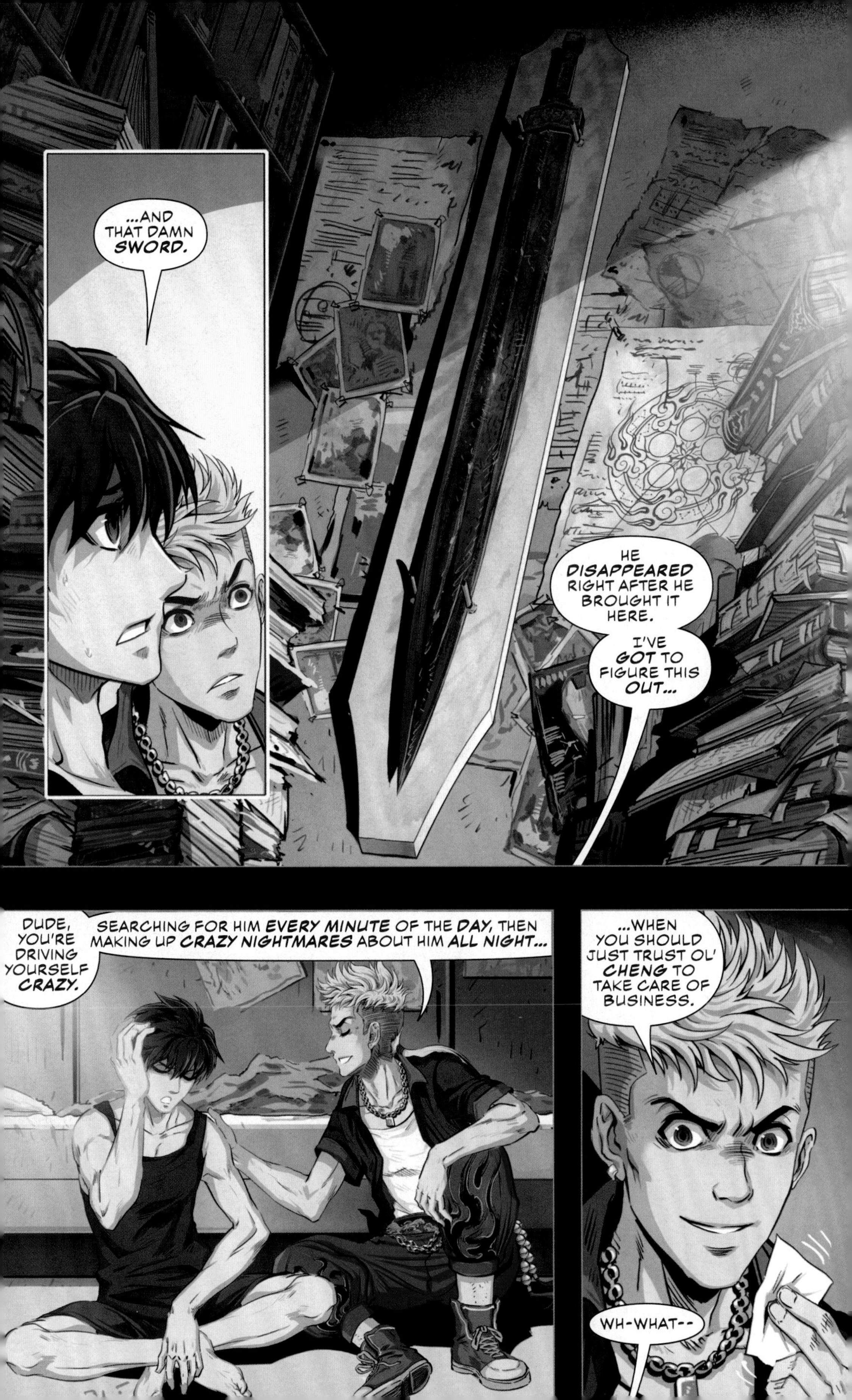
...AND THAT DAMN SWORD.
HE DISAPPEARED RIGHT AFTER HE BROUGHT IT HERE.
I'VE GOT TO FIGURE THIS OUT...
DUDE, YOU'RE DRIVING YOURSELF CRAZY.
SEARCHING FOR HIM EVERY MINUTE OF THE DAY, THEN MAKING UP CRAZY NIGHTMARES ABOUT HIM ALL NIGHT...
...WHEN YOU SHOULD JUST TRUST OL' CHENG TO TAKE CARE OF BUSINESS.
WH-WHAT--

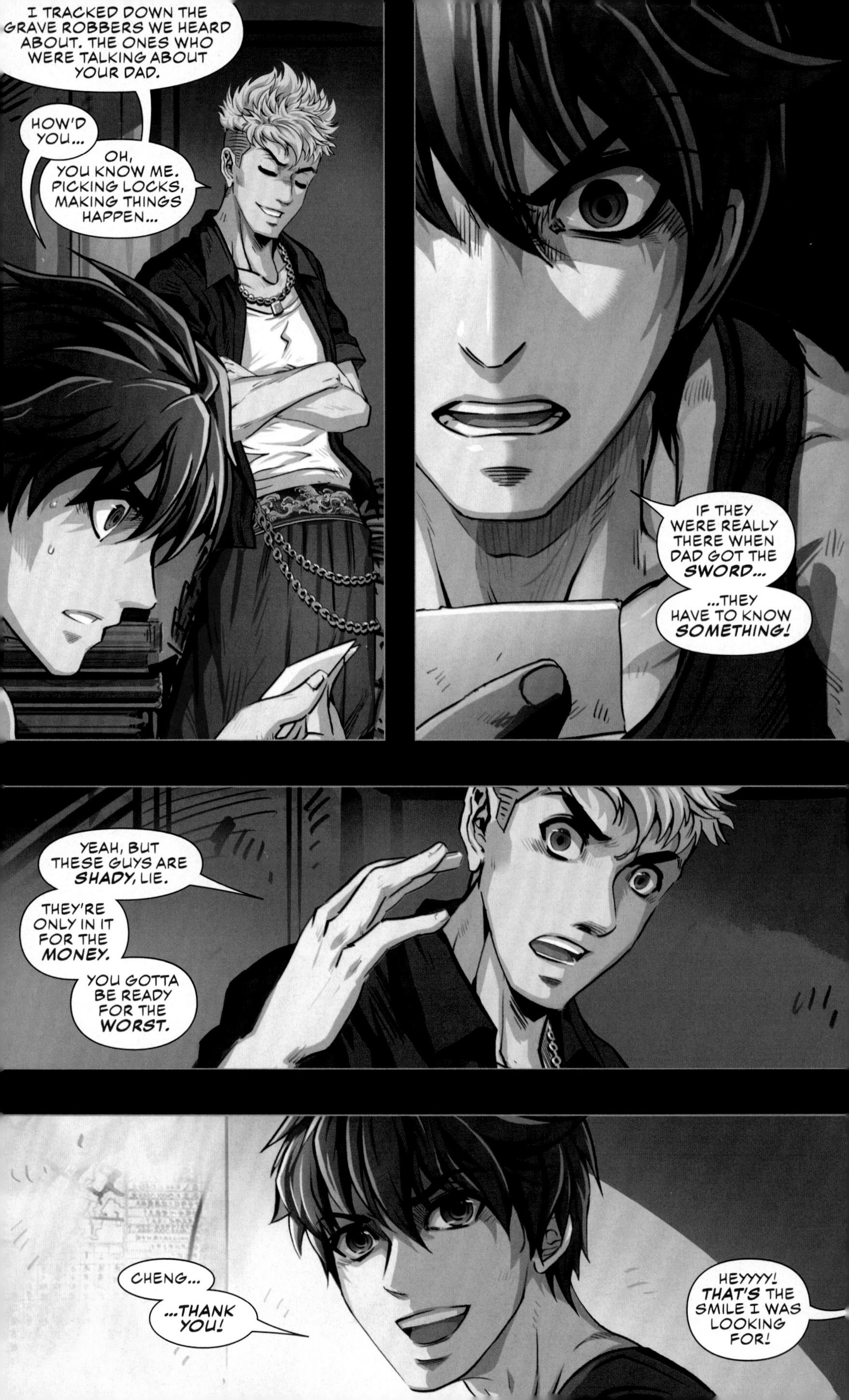
I TRACKED DOWN THE GRAVE ROBBERS WE HEARD ABOUT. THE ONES WHO WERE TALKING ABOUT YOUR DAD.
HOW'D YOU...
OH, YOU KNOW ME. PICKING LOCKS, MAKING THINGS HAPPEN...
IF THEY WERE REALLY THERE WHEN DAD GOT THE SWORD...
...THEY HAVE TO KNOW SOMETHING!
YEAH, BUT THESE GUYS ARE SHADY, LIE.
THEY'RE ONLY IN IT FOR THE MONEY.
YOU GOTTA BE READY FOR THE WORST.
CHENG...
...THANK YOU!
HEYYYY! THAT'S THE SMILE I WAS LOOKING FOR!

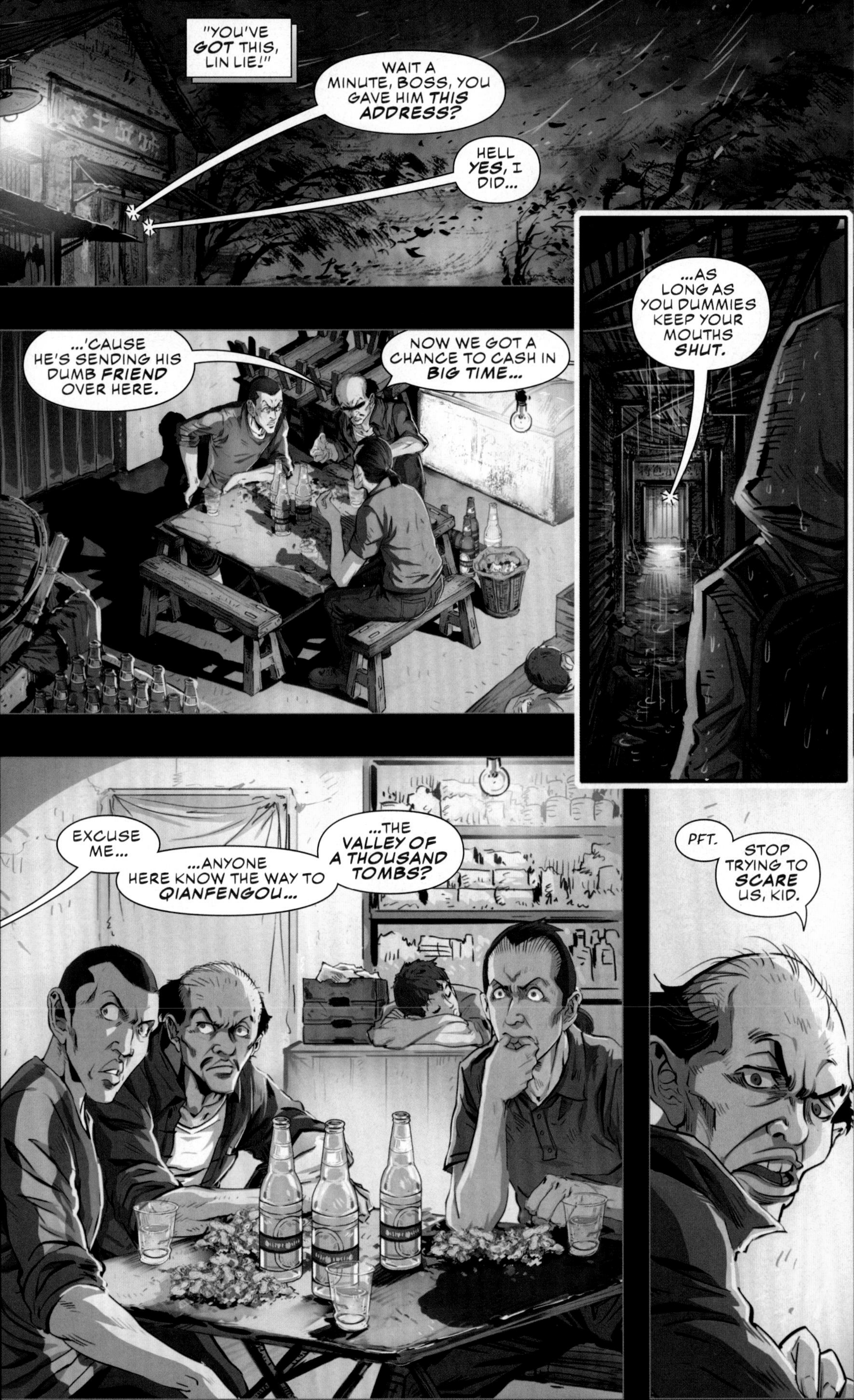
"YOU'VE GOT THIS, LIN LIE!"
WAIT A MINUTE, BOSS, YOU GAVE HIM THIS ADDRESS?
HELL YES, I DID...
...AS LONG AS YOU DUMMIES KEEP YOUR MOUTHS SHUT.
...'CAUSE HE'S SENDING HIS DUMB FRIEND OVER HERE.
NOW WE GOT A CHANCE TO CASH IN BIG TIME...
EXCUSE ME...
...ANYONE HERE KNOW THE WAY TO QIANFENGOU...
...THE VALLEY OF A THOUSAND TOMBS?
PFT.
STOP TRYING TO SCARE US, KID.

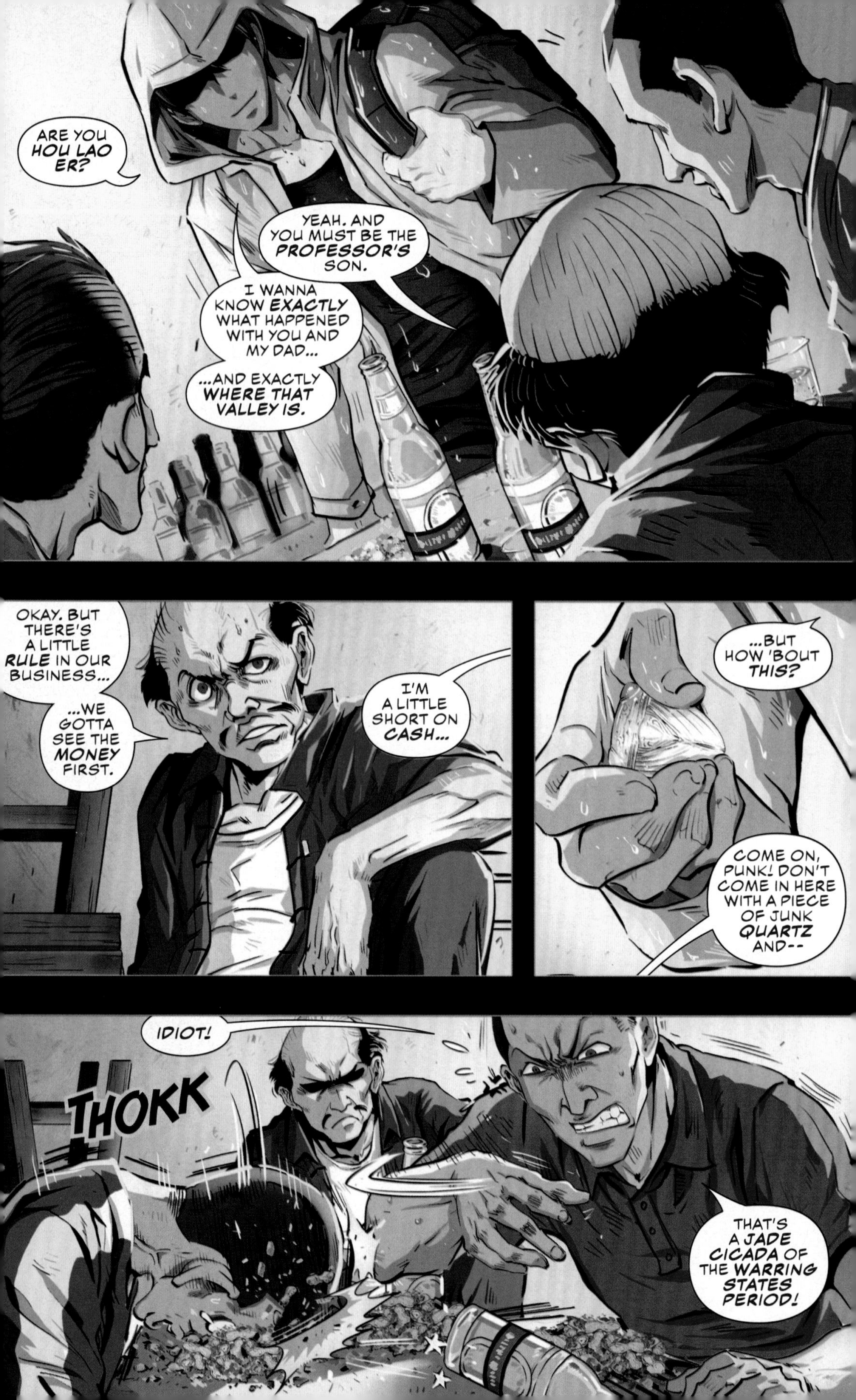
ARE YOU HOU LAO ER?
YEAH. AND YOU MUST BE THE PROFESSOR'S SON.
I WANNA KNOW EXACTLY WHAT HAPPENED WITH YOU AND MY DAD...
...AND EXACTLY WHERE THAT VALLEY IS.
OKAY. BUT THERE'S A LITTLE RULE IN OUR BUSINESS...
...WE GOTTA SEE THE MONEY FIRST.
I'M A LITTLE SHORT ON CASH...
...BUT HOW 'BOUT THIS?
COME ON, PUNK! DON'T COME IN HERE WITH A PIECE OF JUNK QUARTZ AND--
IDIOT!
THOKK
THAT'S A JADE CICADA OF THE WARRING STATES PERIOD!

ALL RIGHT, KID.
YOU GOT THE GOODS...
...SEE FOR YOURSELF.
HUH!
It's Dad!
In a red fog...
...with that sword?!
WHAT IS THIS?
WHAT HAPPENED?!
IT'S... IT'S PRETTY FREAKY, RIGHT?
WE HEARD ABOUT THIS TOMB...
...WHERE SOME GRAVE ROBBERS SUPPOSEDLY GOT KILLED...

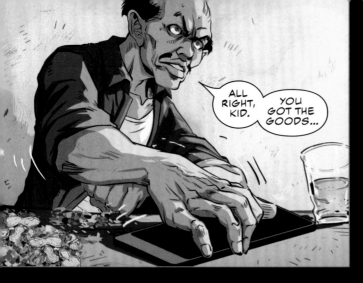

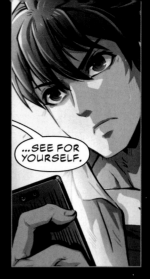

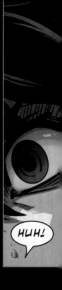

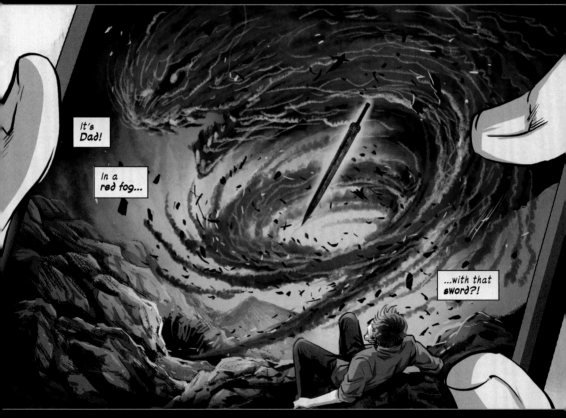

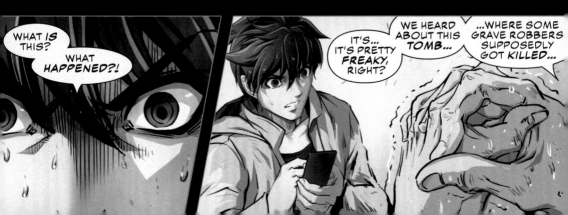

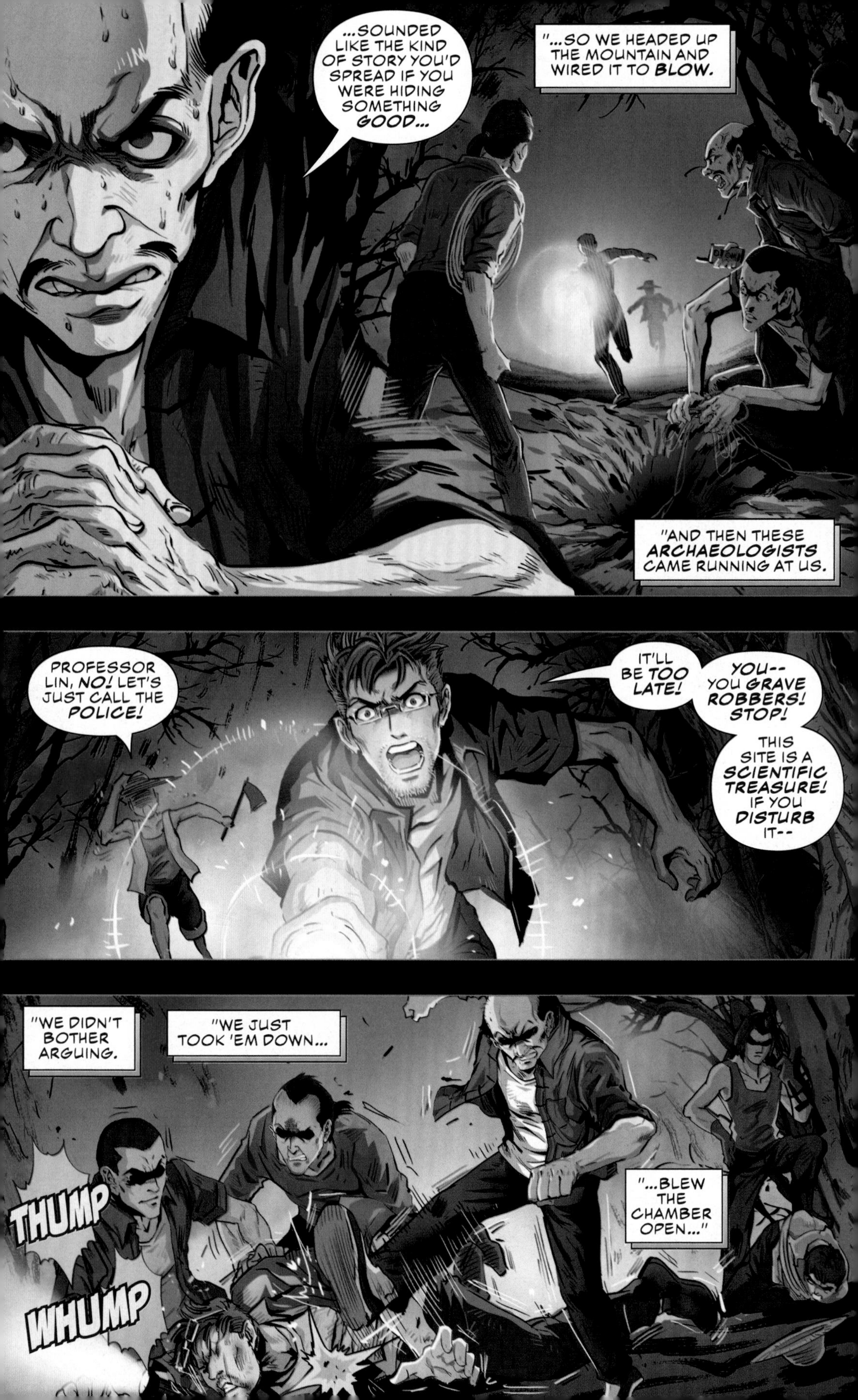
...SOUNDED LIKE THE KIND OF STORY YOU'D SPREAD IF YOU WERE HIDING SOMETHING GOOD...
"...SO WE HEADED UP THE MOUNTAIN AND WIRED IT TO BLOW.
"AND THEN THESE ARCHAEOLOGISTS CAME RUNNING AT US.
PROFESSOR LIN, NO! LET'S JUST CALL THE POLICE!
IT'LL BE TOO LATE!
YOU-- YOU GRAVE ROBBERS! STOP!
THIS SITE IS A SCIENTIFIC TREASURE! IF YOU DISTURB IT--
"WE DIDN'T BOTHER ARGUING.
"WE JUST TOOK 'EM DOWN...
THUMP
WHUMP
"...BLEW THE CHAMBER OPEN..."

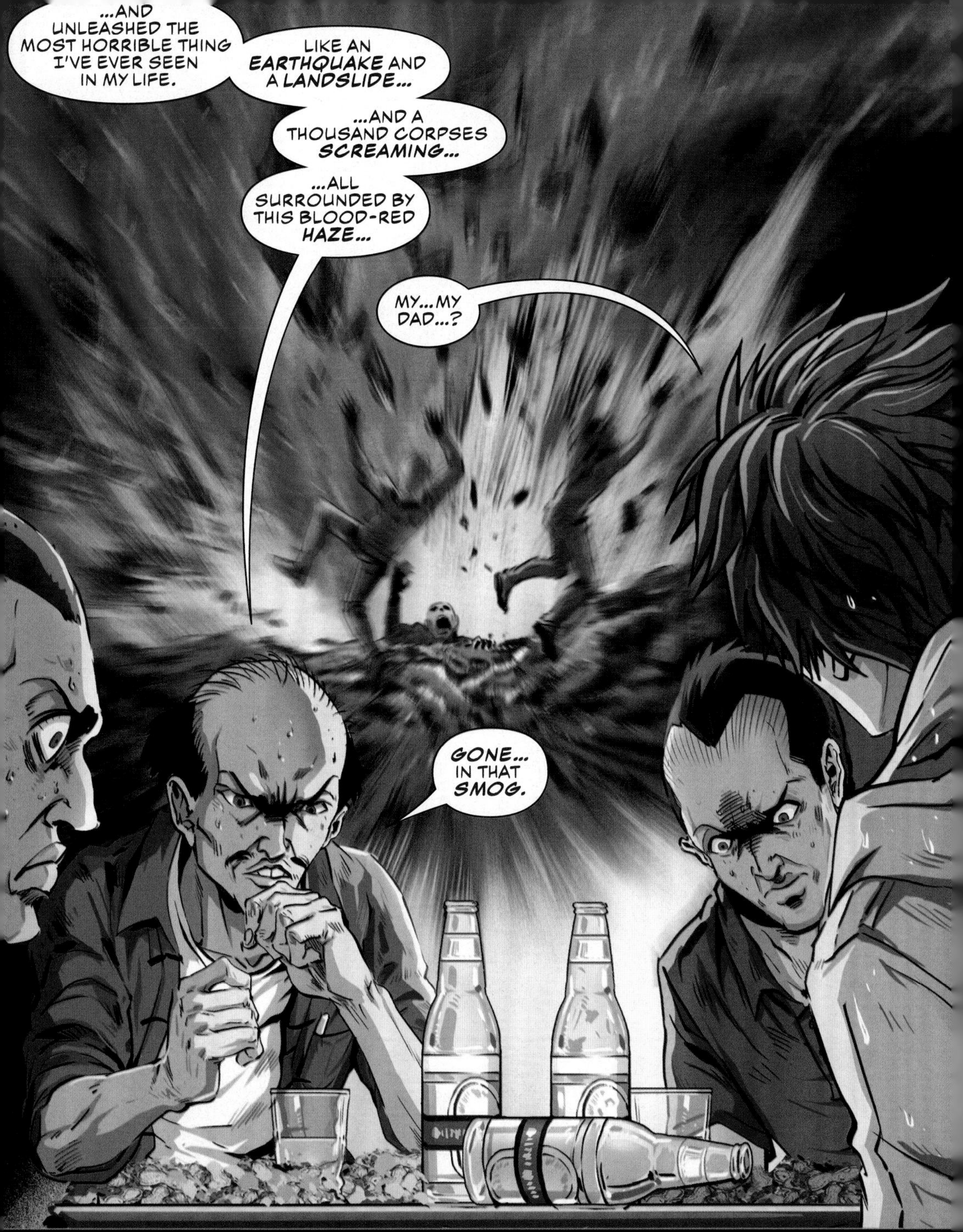
...AND UNLEASHED THE MOST HORRIBLE THING I'VE EVER SEEN IN MY LIFE.
LIKE AN EARTHQUAKE AND A LANDSLIDE...
...AND A THOUSAND CORPSES SCREAMING...
...ALL SURROUNDED BY THIS BLOOD-RED HAZE...
MY...MY DAD...?
GONE... IN THAT SMOG.

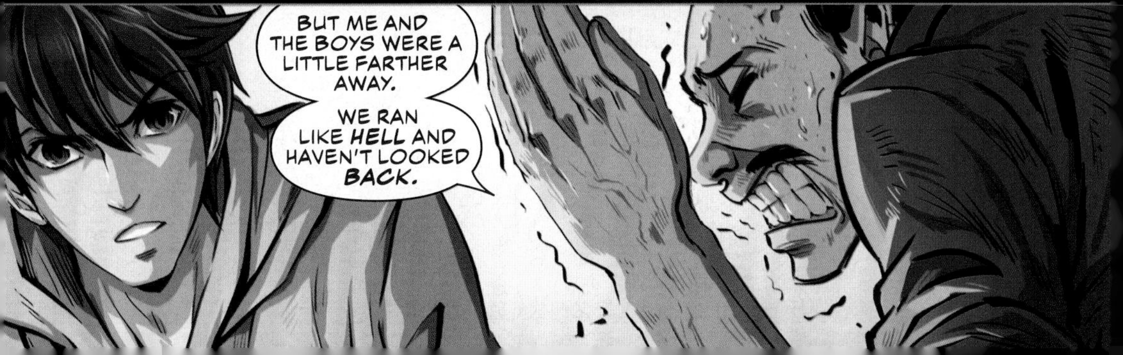
BUT ME AND THE BOYS WERE A LITTLE FARTHER AWAY.
WE RAN LIKE HELL AND HAVEN'T LOOKED BACK.

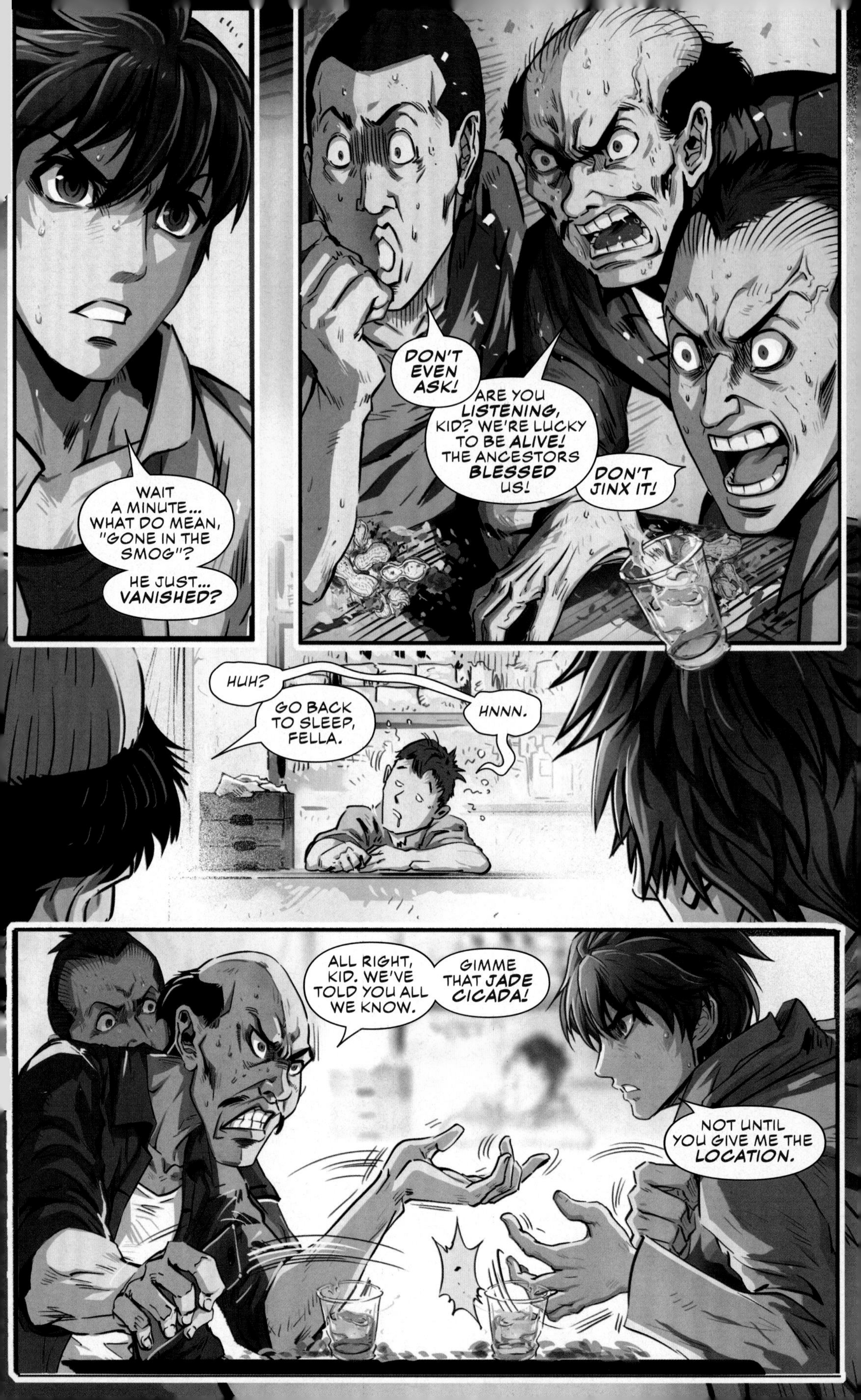
WAIT A MINUTE... WHAT DO MEAN, "GONE IN THE SMOG"?
HE JUST... VANISHED?
DON'T EVEN ASK!
ARE YOU LISTENING, KID? WE'RE LUCKY TO BE ALIVE! THE ANCESTORS BLESSED US!
DON'T JINX IT!
HUH?
GO BACK TO SLEEP, FELLA.
HNNN.
ALL RIGHT, KID. WE'VE TOLD YOU ALL WE KNOW.
GIMME THAT JADE CICADA!
NOT UNTIL YOU GIVE ME THE LOCATION.

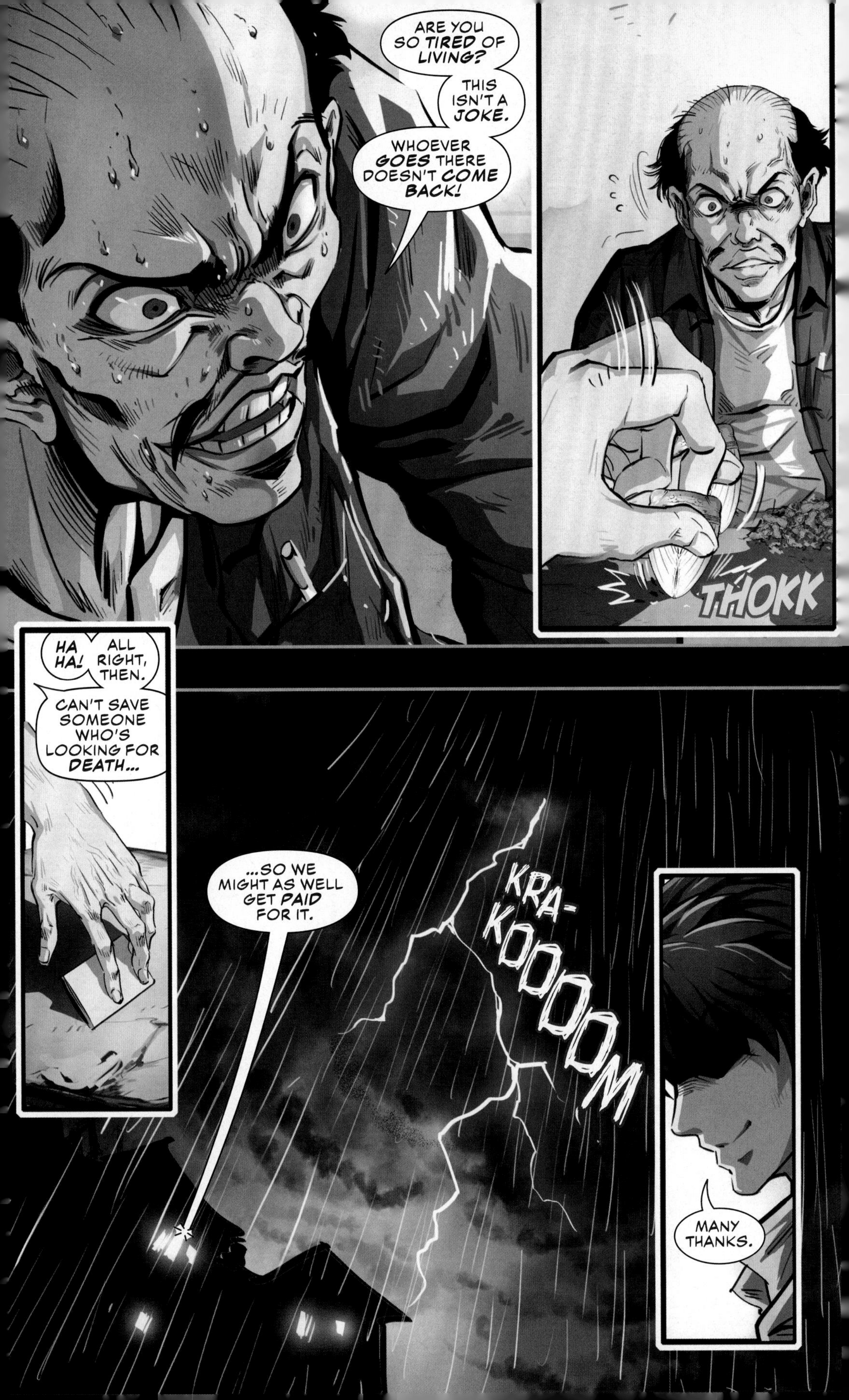
ARE YOU SO TIRED OF LIVING?
THIS ISN'T A JOKE.
WHOEVER GOES THERE DOESN'T COME BACK!
THOKK
HA HA!
ALL RIGHT, THEN.
CAN'T SAVE SOMEONE WHO'S LOOKING FOR DEATH...
...SO WE MIGHT AS WELL GET PAID FOR IT.
KRA-KOOOOM
MANY THANKS.

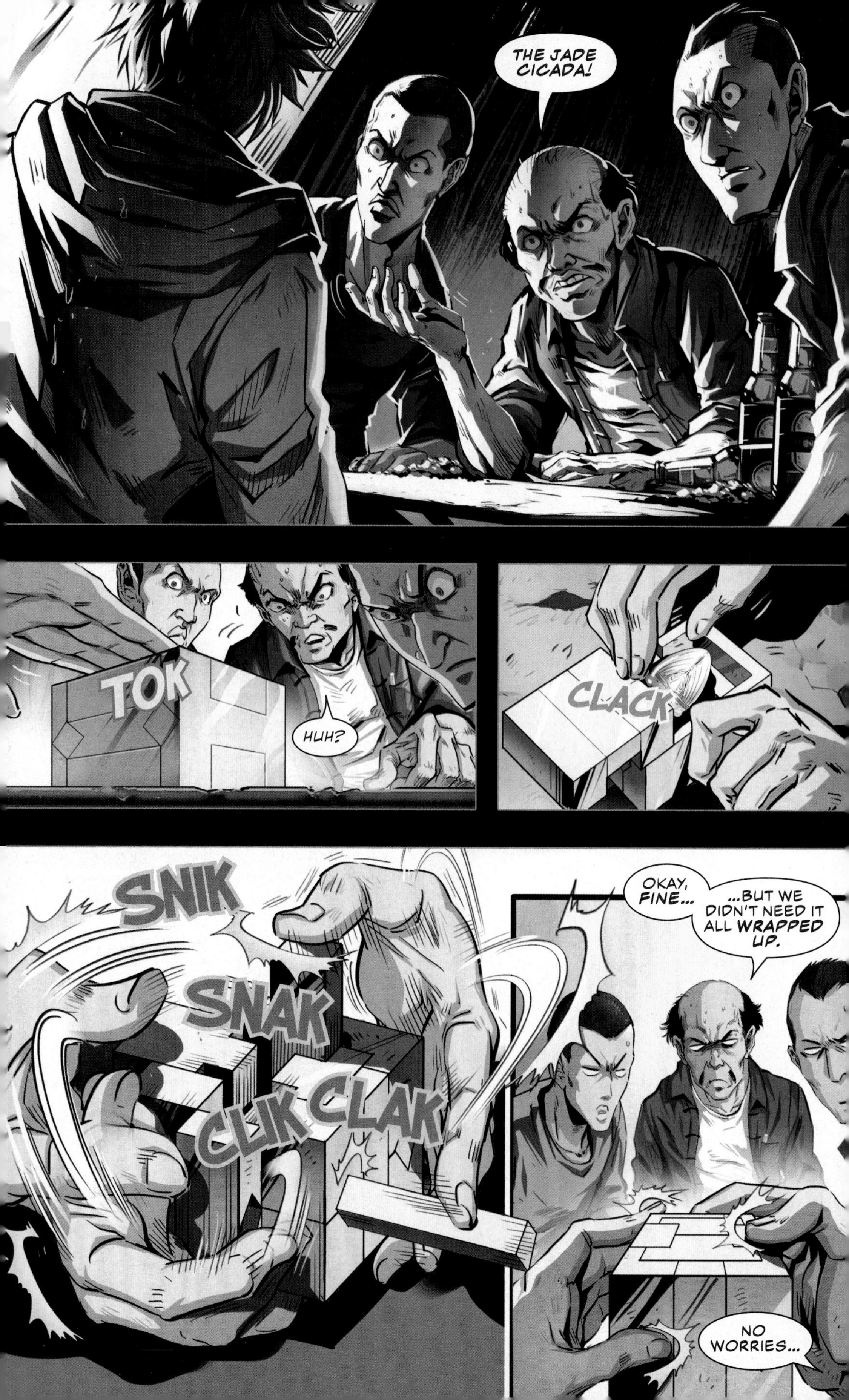
THE JADE CICADA!
TOK
HUH?
CLACK
SNIK
SNAK
CLIK CLAK
OKAY, FINE...
...BUT WE DIDN'T NEED IT ALL WRAPPED UP.
NO WORRIES...

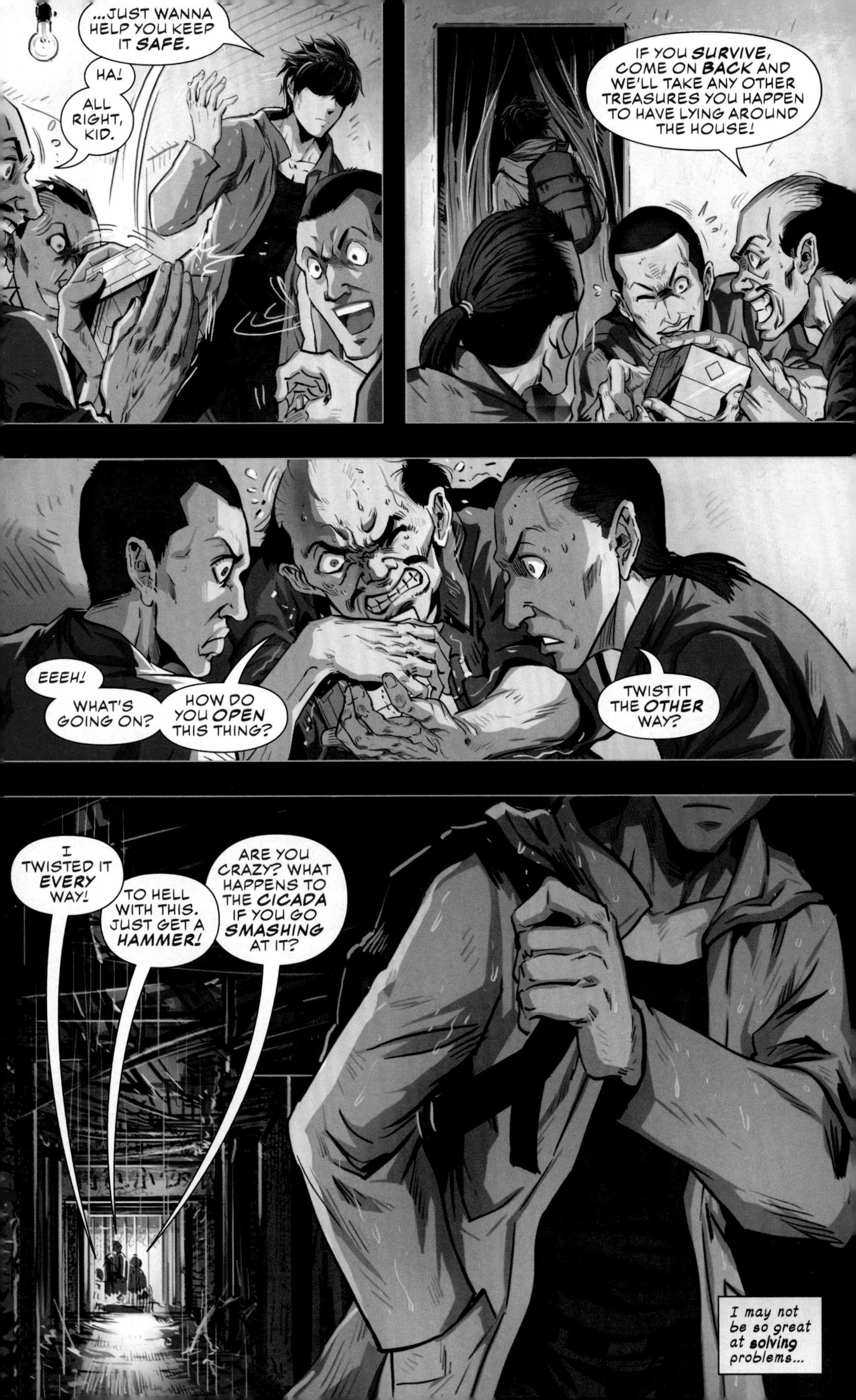
...JUST WANNA HELP YOU KEEP IT SAFE.
HA!
ALL RIGHT, KID.
IF YOU SURVIVE, COME ON BACK AND WE'LL TAKE ANY OTHER TREASURES YOU HAPPEN TO HAVE LYING AROUND THE HOUSE!
EEEH!
WHAT'S GOING ON?
HOW DO YOU OPEN THIS THING?
TWIST IT THE OTHER WAY?
I TWISTED IT EVERY WAY!
TO HELL WITH THIS. JUST GET A HAMMER!
ARE YOU CRAZY? WHAT HAPPENS TO THE CICADA IF YOU GO SMASHING AT IT?
I may not be so great at solving problems...

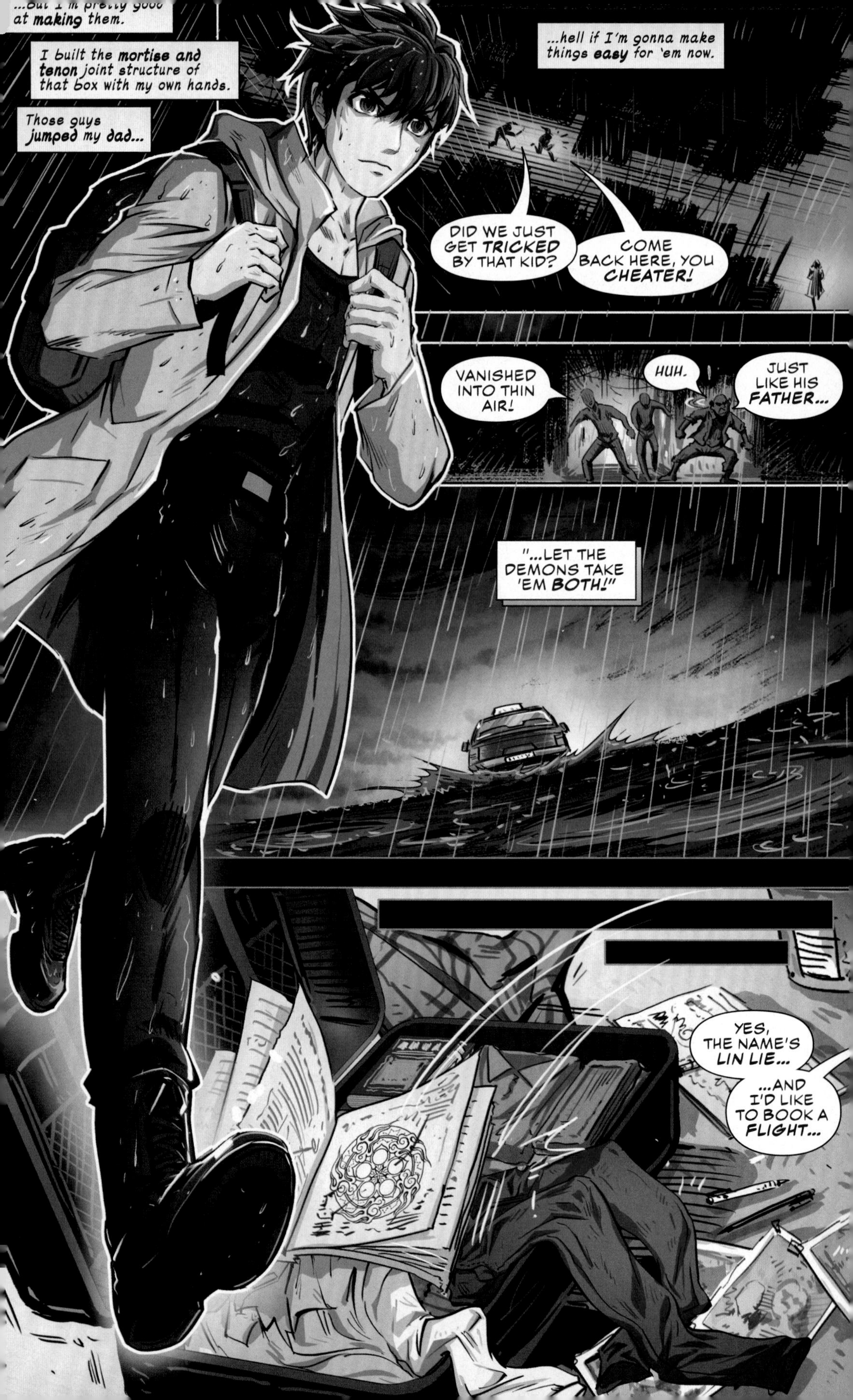

...But I'm pretty good at making them.
I built the mortise and tenon joint structure of that box with my own hands.
Those guys jumped my dad...
...hell if I'm gonna make things easy for 'em now.
DID WE JUST GET TRICKED BY THAT KID?
COME BACK HERE, YOU CHEATER!
VANISHED INTO THIN AIR!
HUH.
JUST LIKE HIS FATHER...
"...LET THE DEMONS TAKE 'EM BOTH!"
[redacted]
[redacted]
YES, THE NAME'S LIN LIE...
...AND I'D LIKE TO BOOK A FLIGHT...

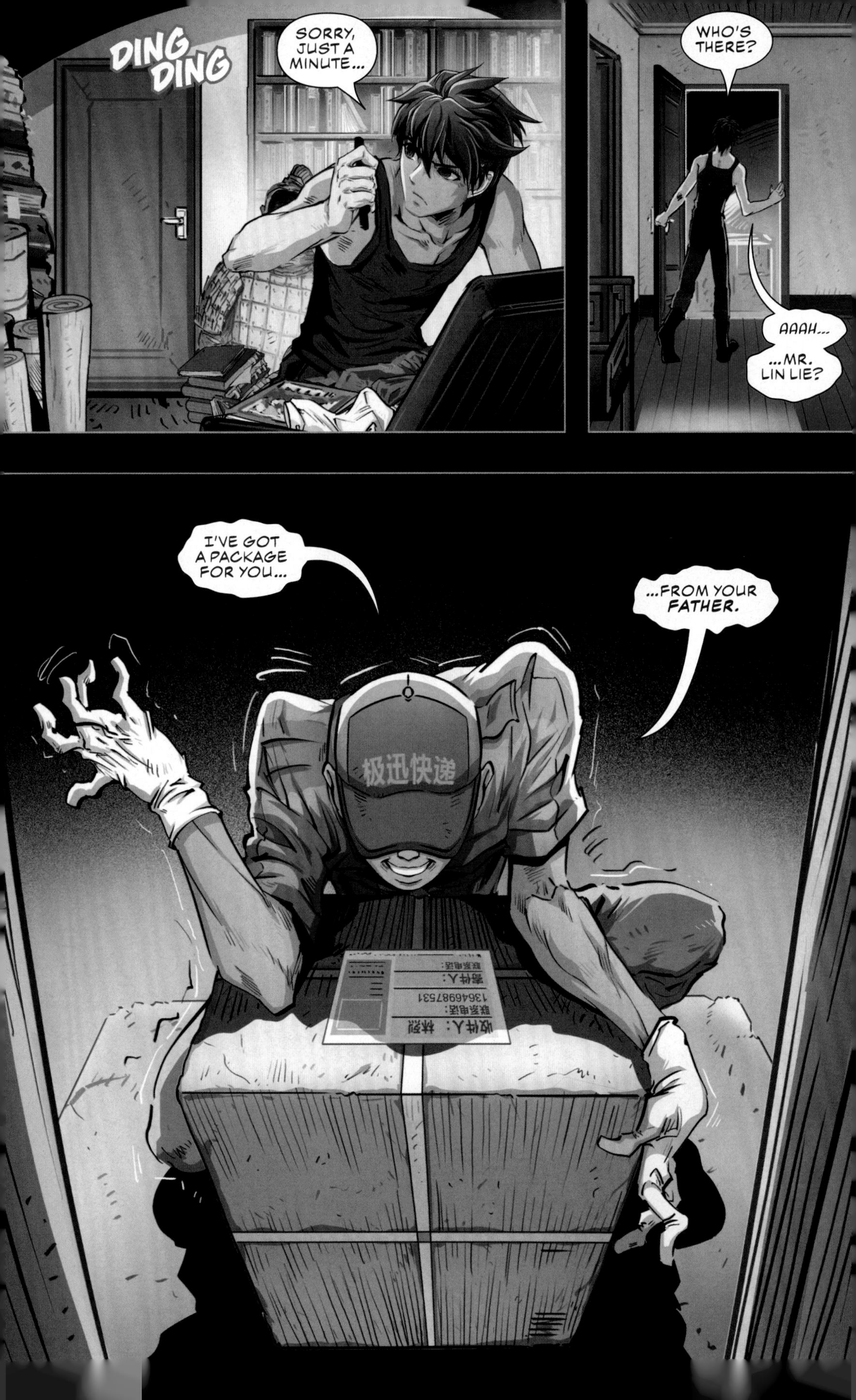

DING DING
SORRY, JUST A MINUTE...
WHO'S THERE?
AAAH...
...MR. LIN LIE?
I'VE GOT A PACKAGE FOR YOU...
...FROM YOUR FATHER.
极迅快递
收件人：林烈
联系电话：13646987531
寄件人：
联系电话：

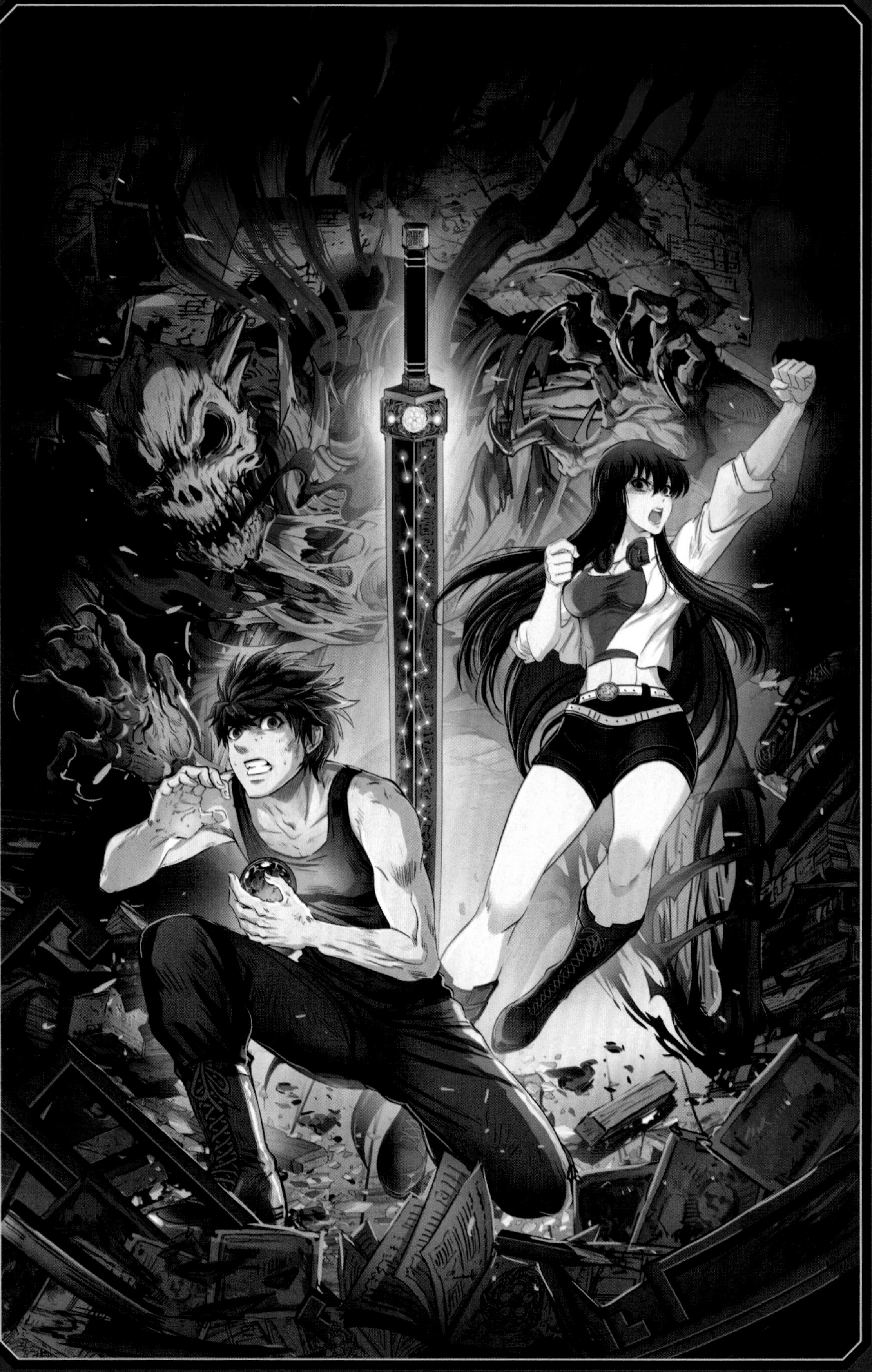

TWO BOXES WITHIN BOXES

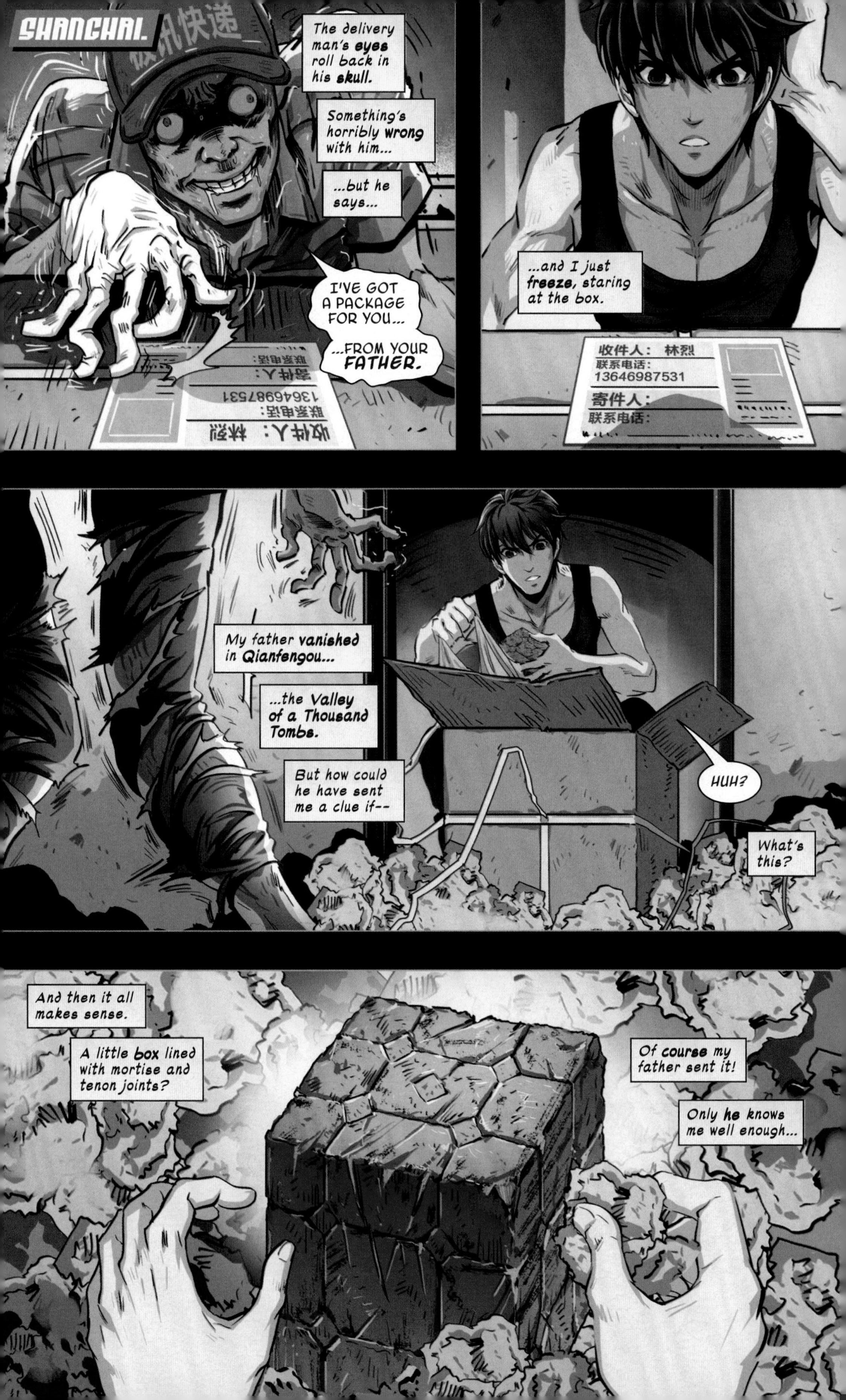
SHANGHAI.
The delivery man's eyes roll back in his skull.
Something's horribly wrong with him...
...but he says...
I'VE GOT A PACKAGE FOR YOU...
...FROM YOUR FATHER.
...and I just freeze, staring at the box.
收件人： 林烈
联系电话：
13646987531
寄件人：
联系电话：
My father vanished in Qianfengou...
...the Valley of a Thousand Tombs.
But how could he have sent me a clue if--
HUH?
What's this?
And then it all makes sense.
A little box lined with mortise and tenon joints?
Of course my father sent it!
Only he knows me well enough...

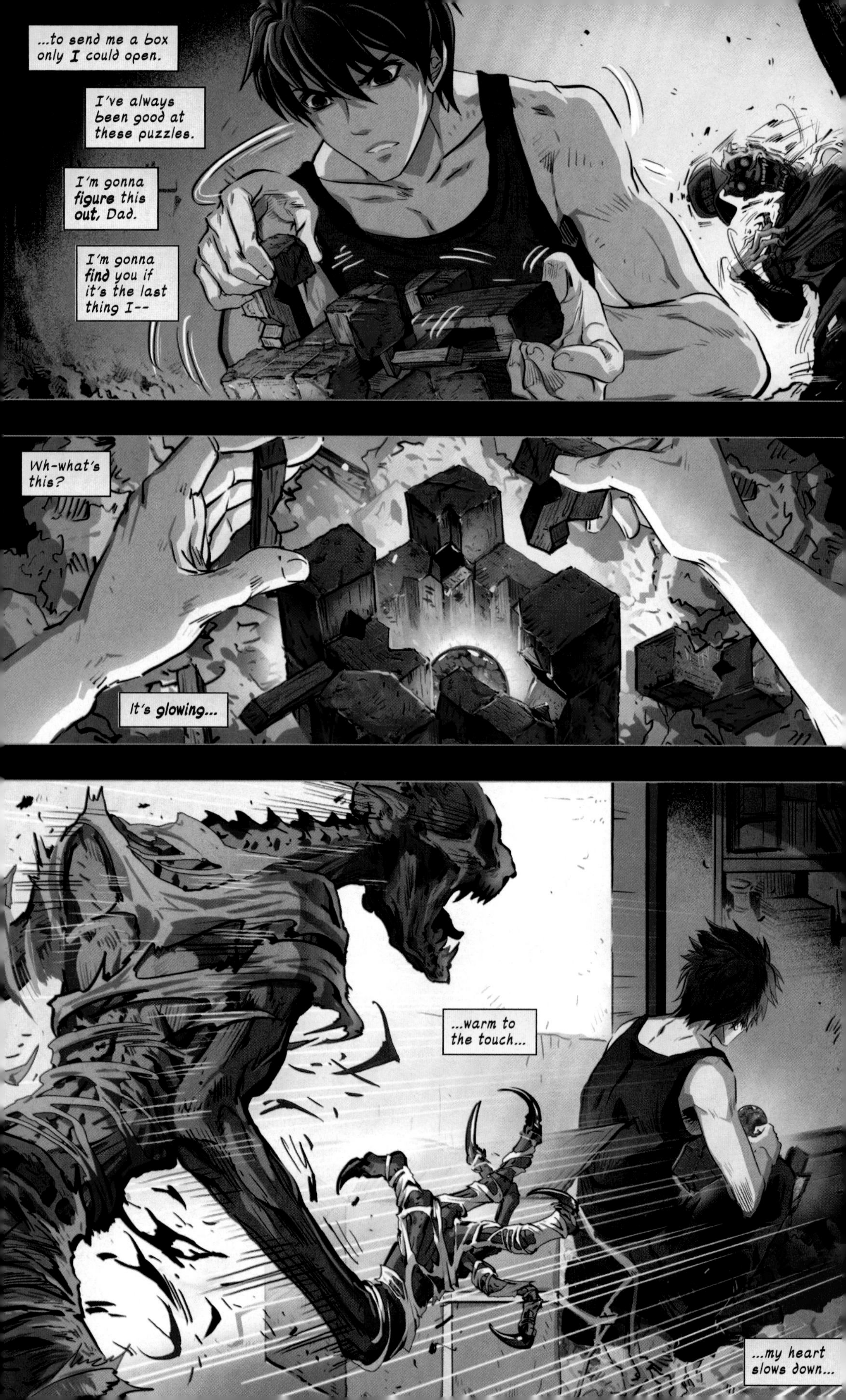
...to send me a box only I could open.
I've always been good at these puzzles.
I'm gonna figure this out, Dad.
I'm gonna find you if it's the last thing I--
Wh-what's this?
It's glowing...
...warm to the touch...
...my heart slows down...

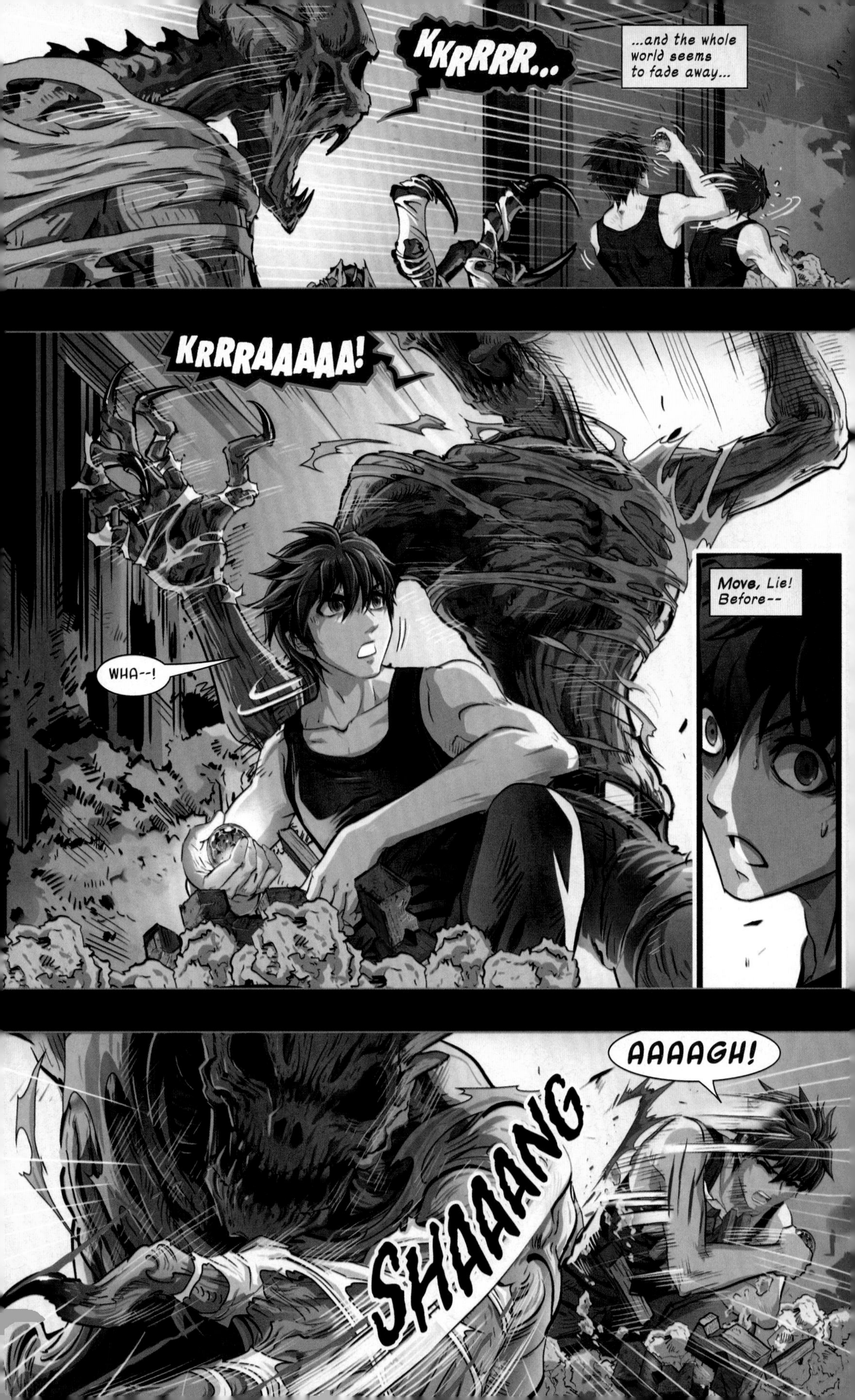
KKRRRRR...
...and the whole world seems to fade away...
KRRRAAAAA!
WHA--!
Move, Lie! Before--
AAAAGH!
SHAAANG

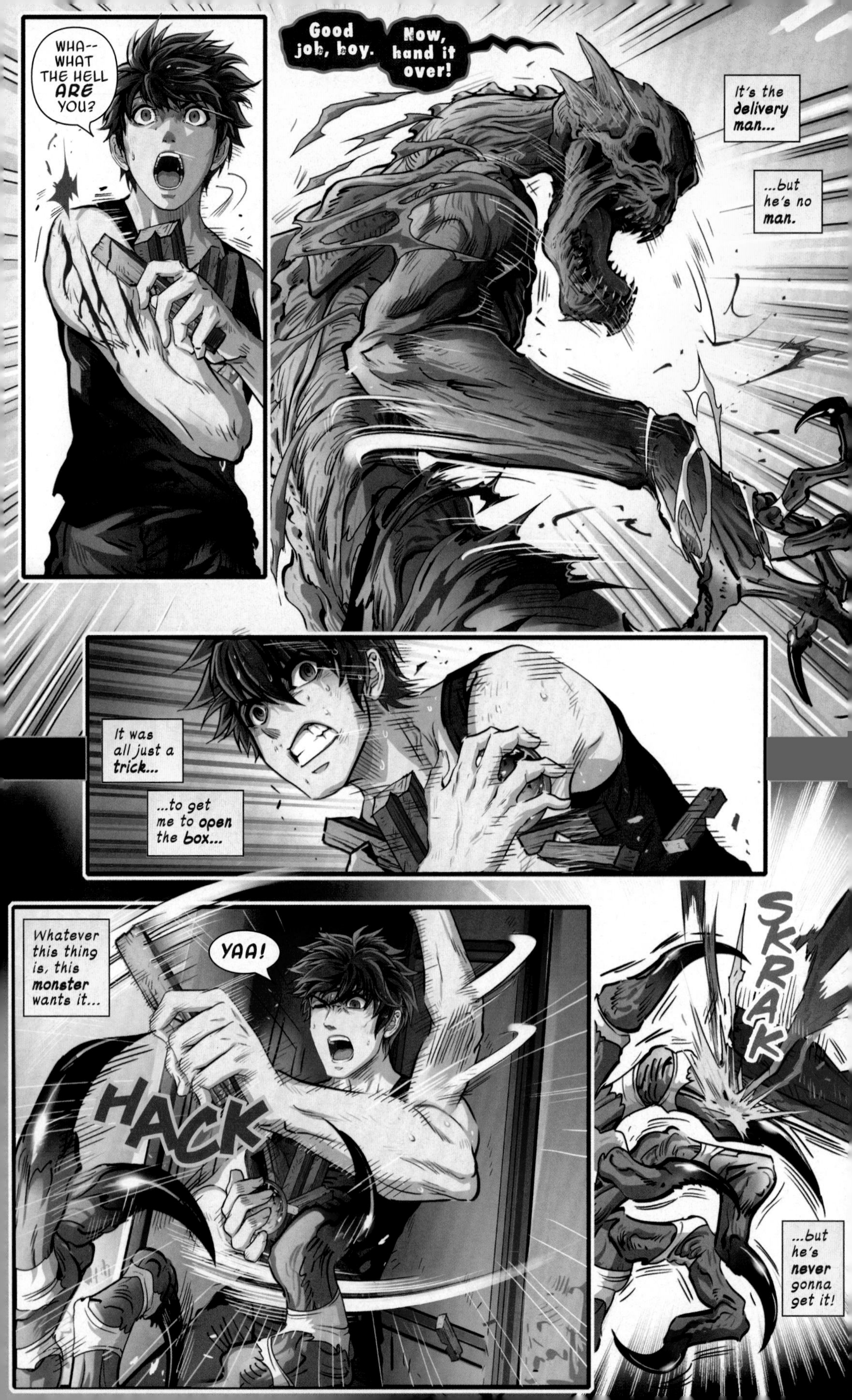
WHA-- WHAT THE HELL ARE YOU?
Good job, boy.
Now, hand it over!
It's the delivery man...
...but he's no man.
It was all just a trick...
...to get me to open the box...
Whatever this thing is, this monster wants it...
YAA!
HACK
SKRAK
...but he's never gonna get it!

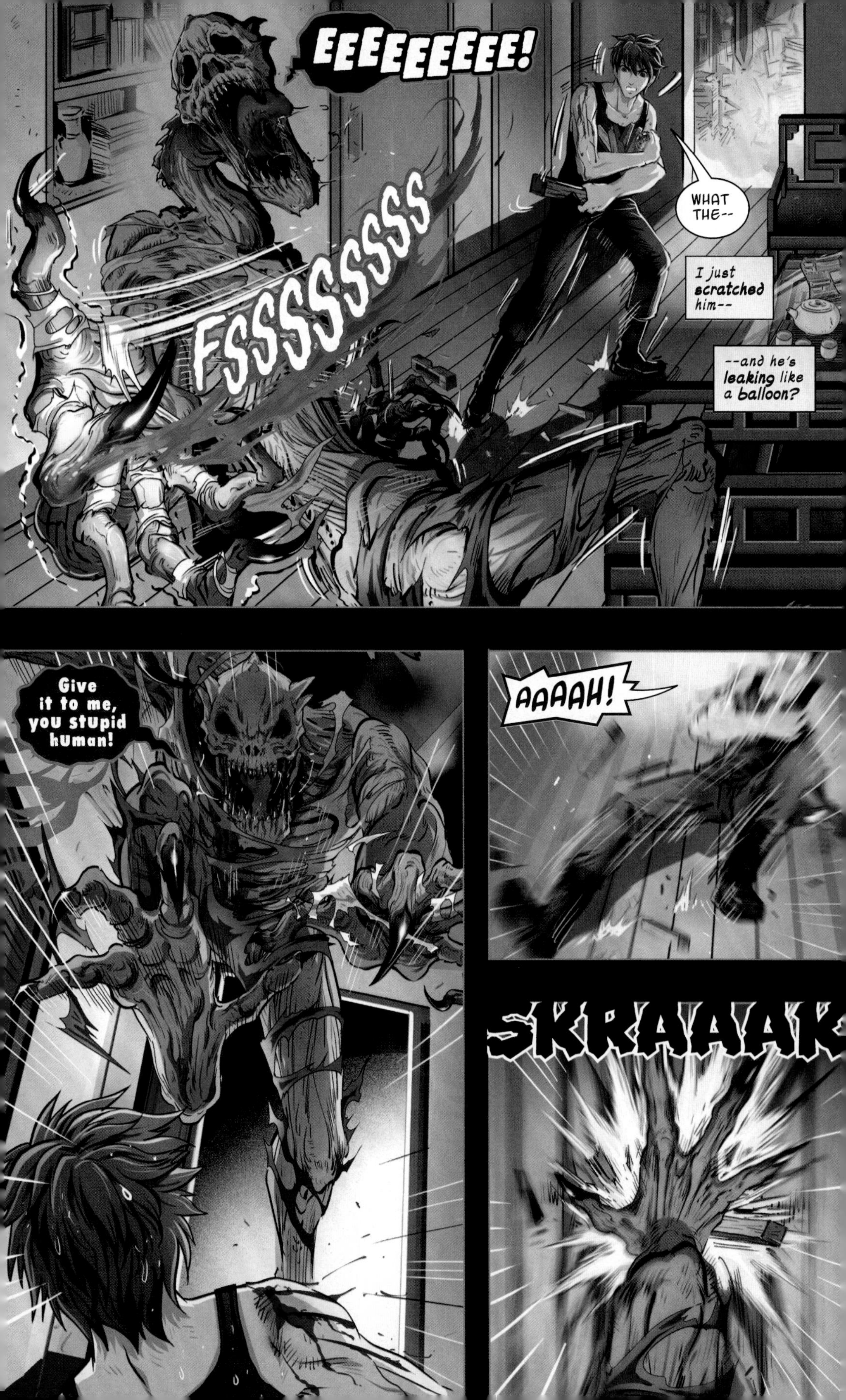
EEEEEEEEE!
FSSSSSSSS
WHAT THE--
I just scratched him--
--and he's leaking like a balloon?
Give it to me, you stupid human!
AAAAH!
SKRAAAK

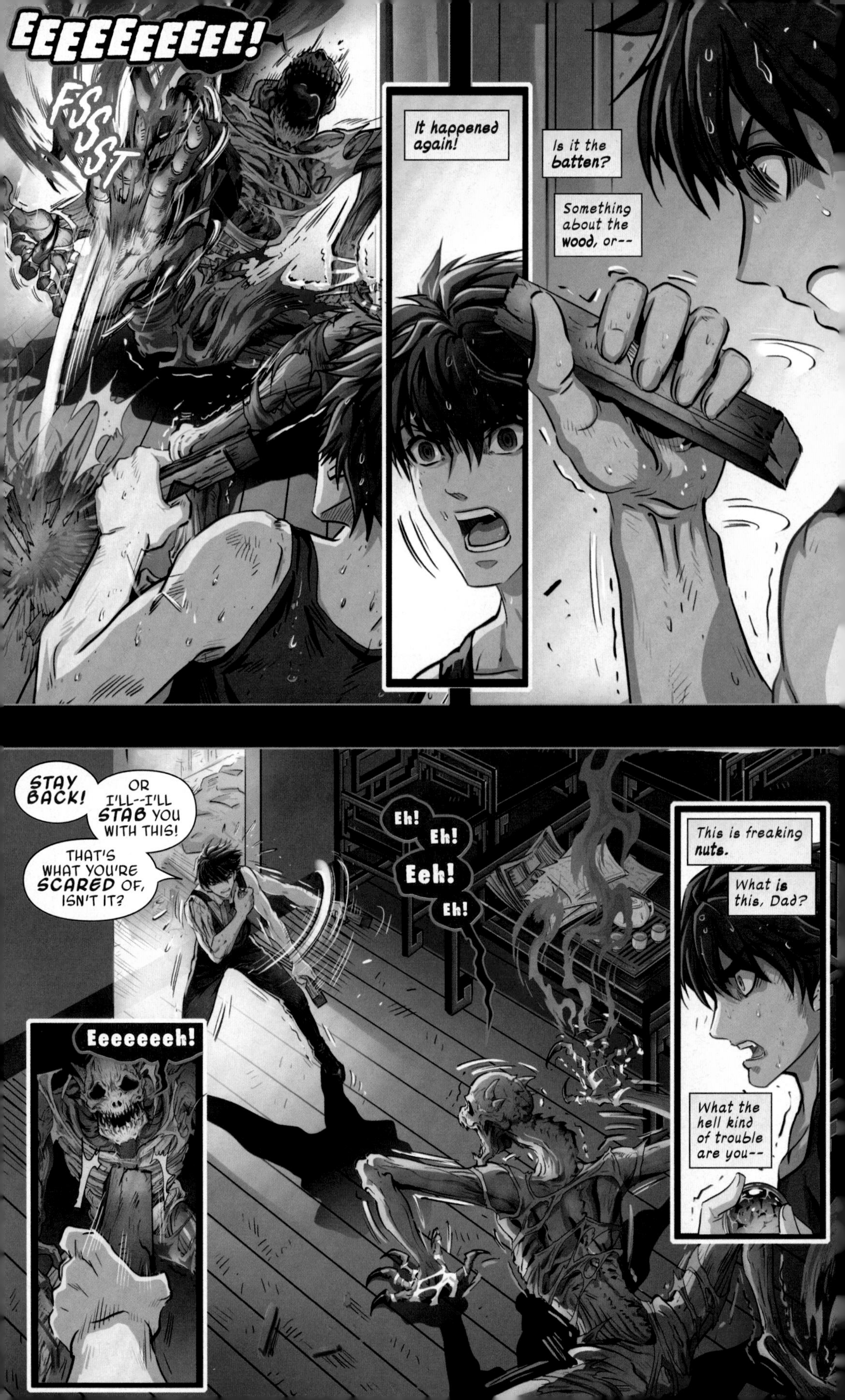
EEEEEEEEEE!
FSSST
It happened again!
Is it the batten?
Something about the wood, or--
STAY BACK!
OR I'LL--I'LL STAB YOU WITH THIS!
THAT'S WHAT YOU'RE SCARED OF, ISN'T IT?
Eh!
Eh!
Eeh!
Eh!
This is freaking nuts.
What is this, Dad?
What the hell kind of trouble are you--
Eeeeeeeh!

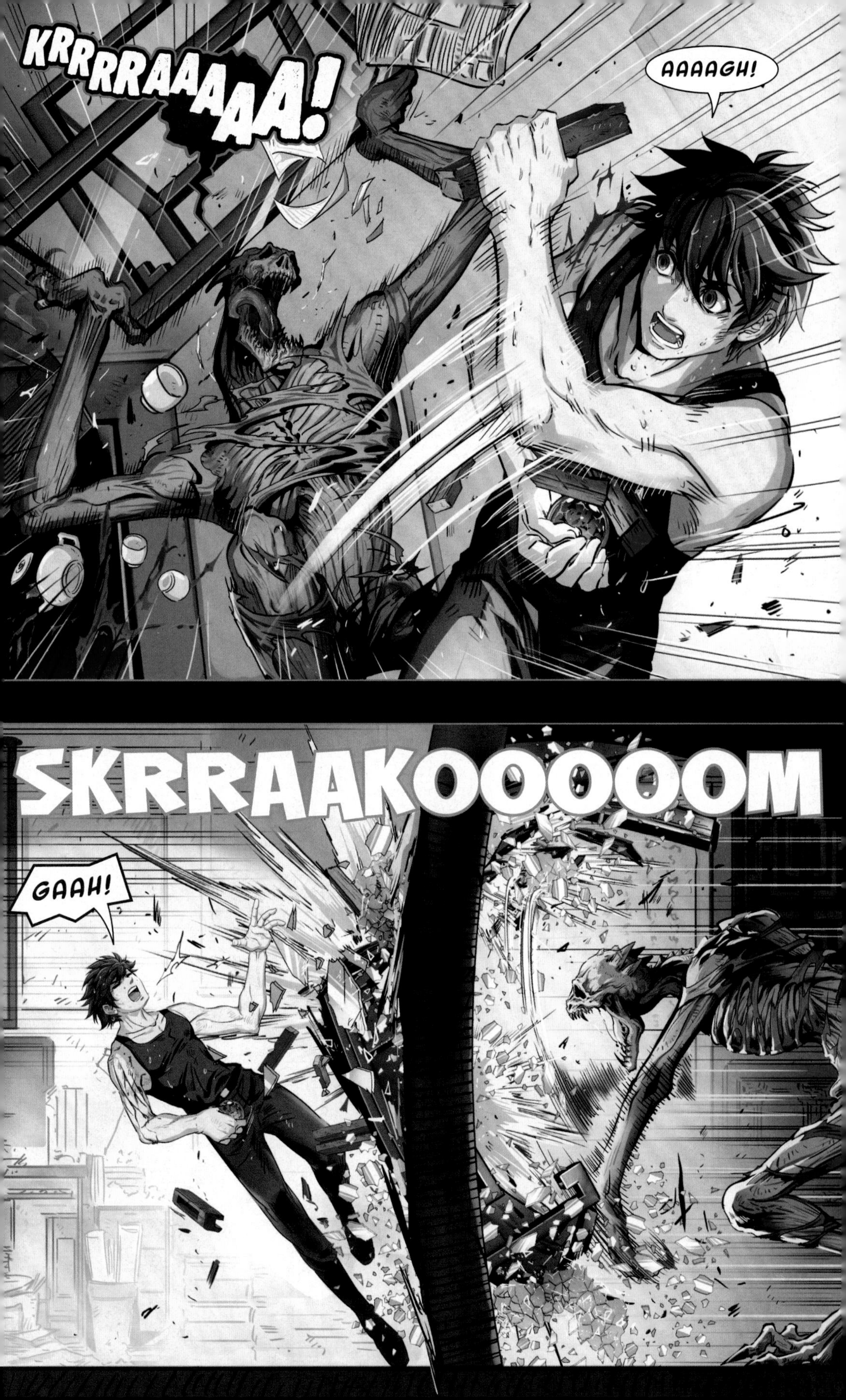
KRRRRAAAAAA!
AAAAGH!
SKRRAAKOOOOOM
GAAH!

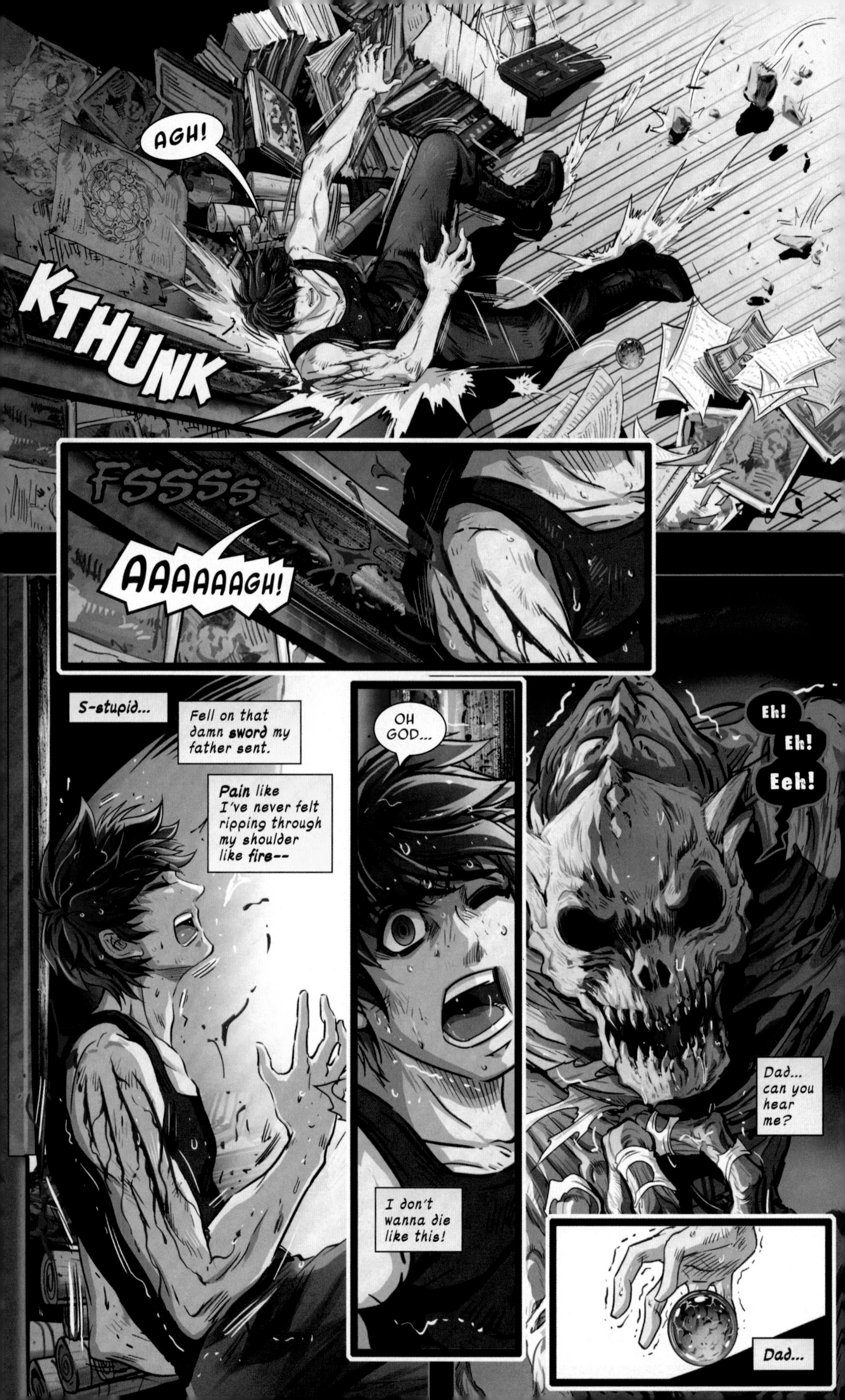
AGH!
KTHUNK
FSSSS
AAAAAAGH!
S-stupid...
Fell on that damn sword my father sent.
Pain like I've never felt ripping through my shoulder like fire--
OH GOD...
I don't wanna die like this!
Eh!
Eh!
Eeh!
Dad... can you hear me?
Dad...

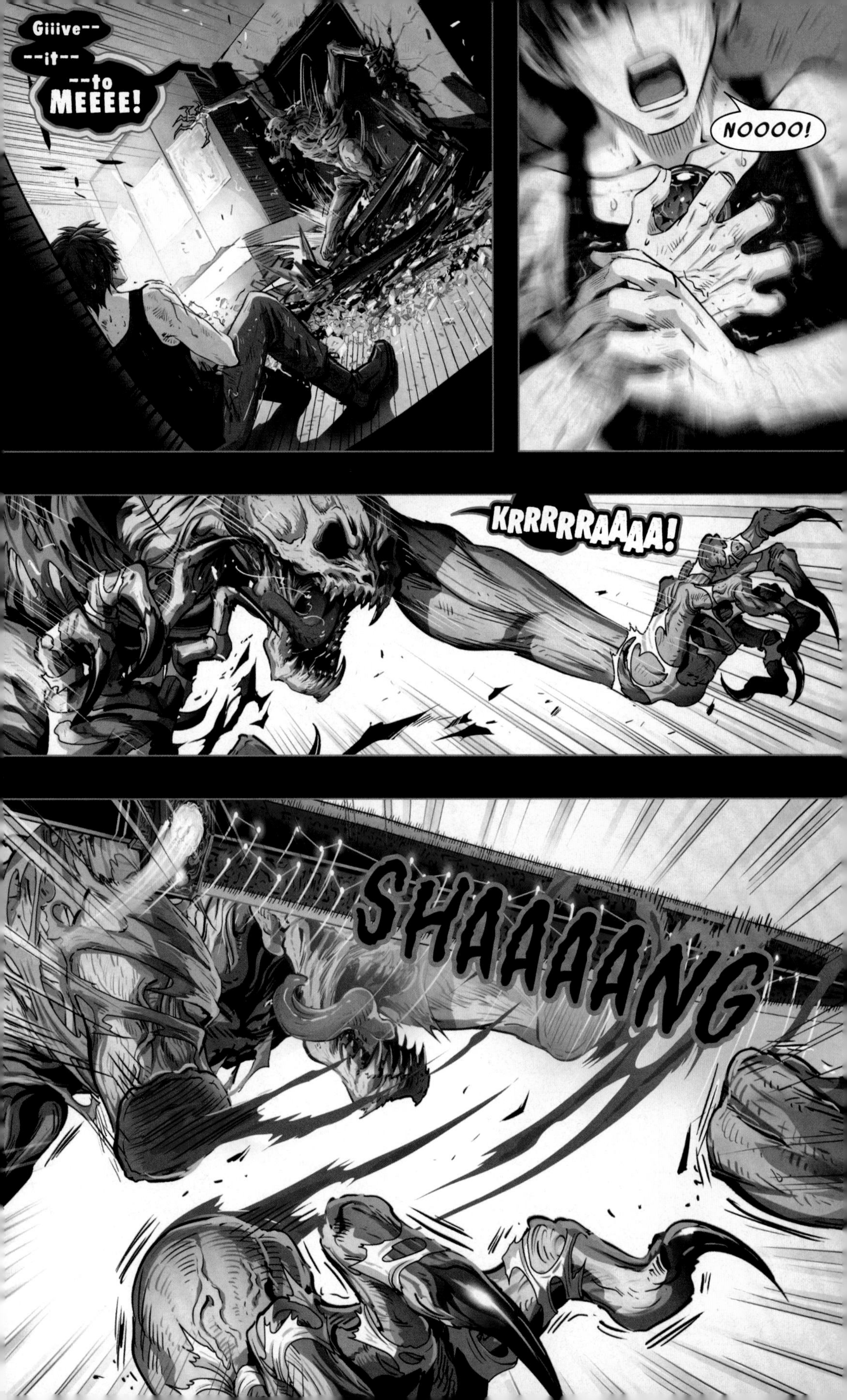
Giiive--
--it--
--to
MEEEE!
NOOOO!
KRRRRRAAAAA!
SHAAAAANG

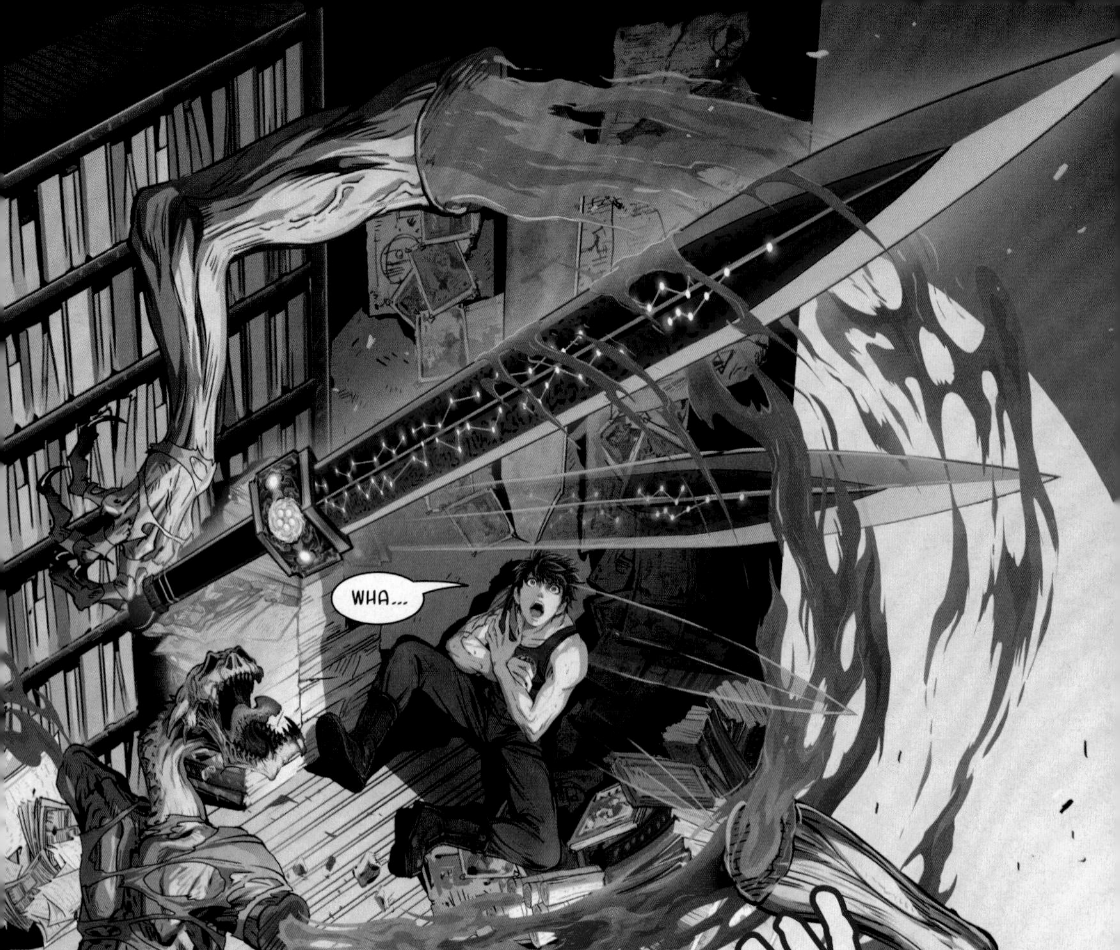
WHA...
SHAAANK

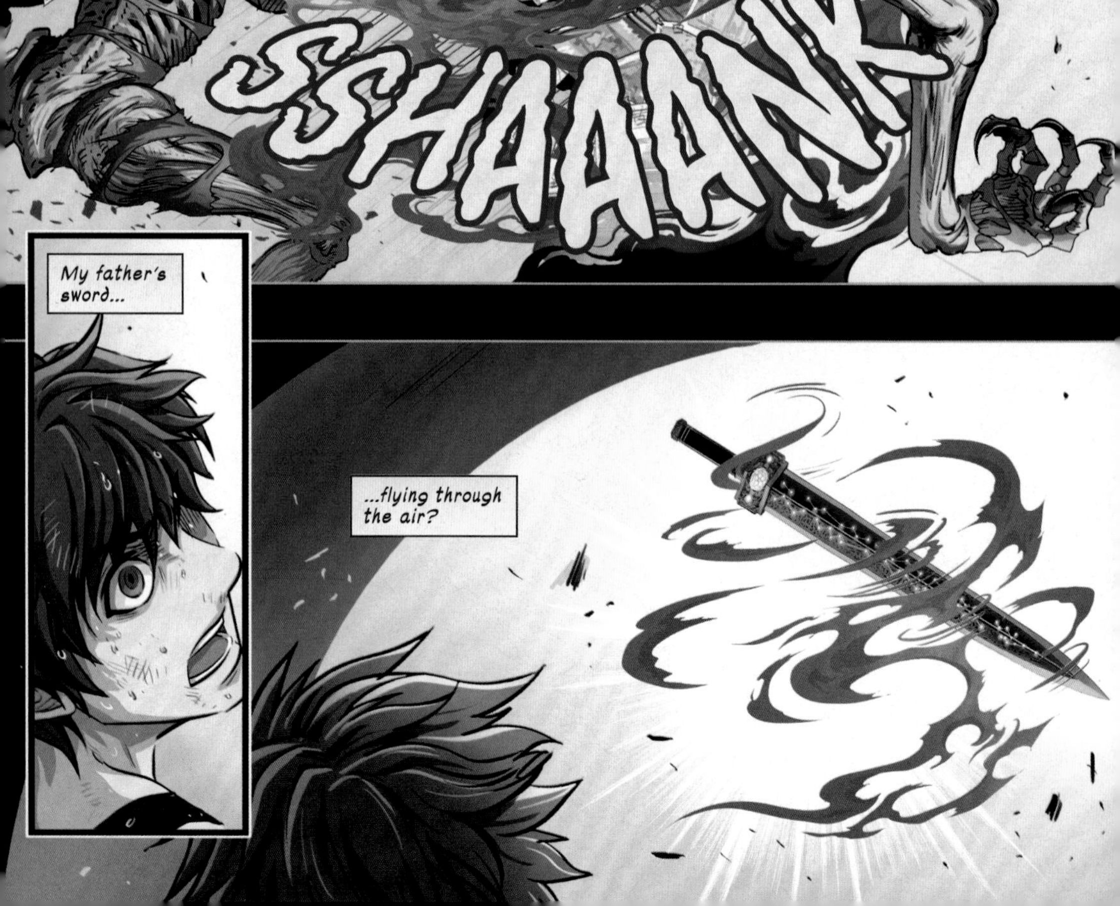
My father's sword...
...flying through the air?

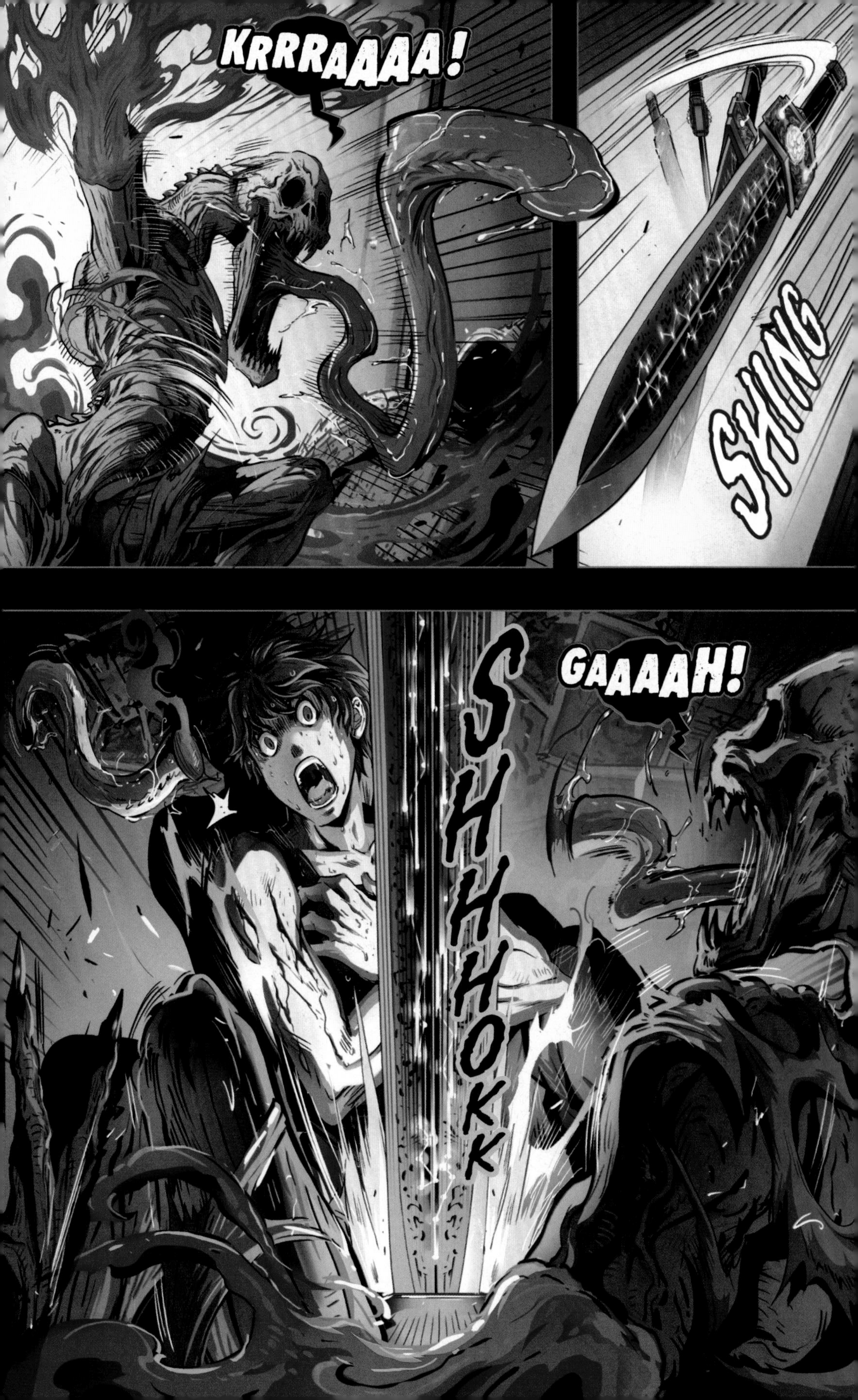
KRRRAAAA!
SHING
GAAAAH!
SHHHOKK

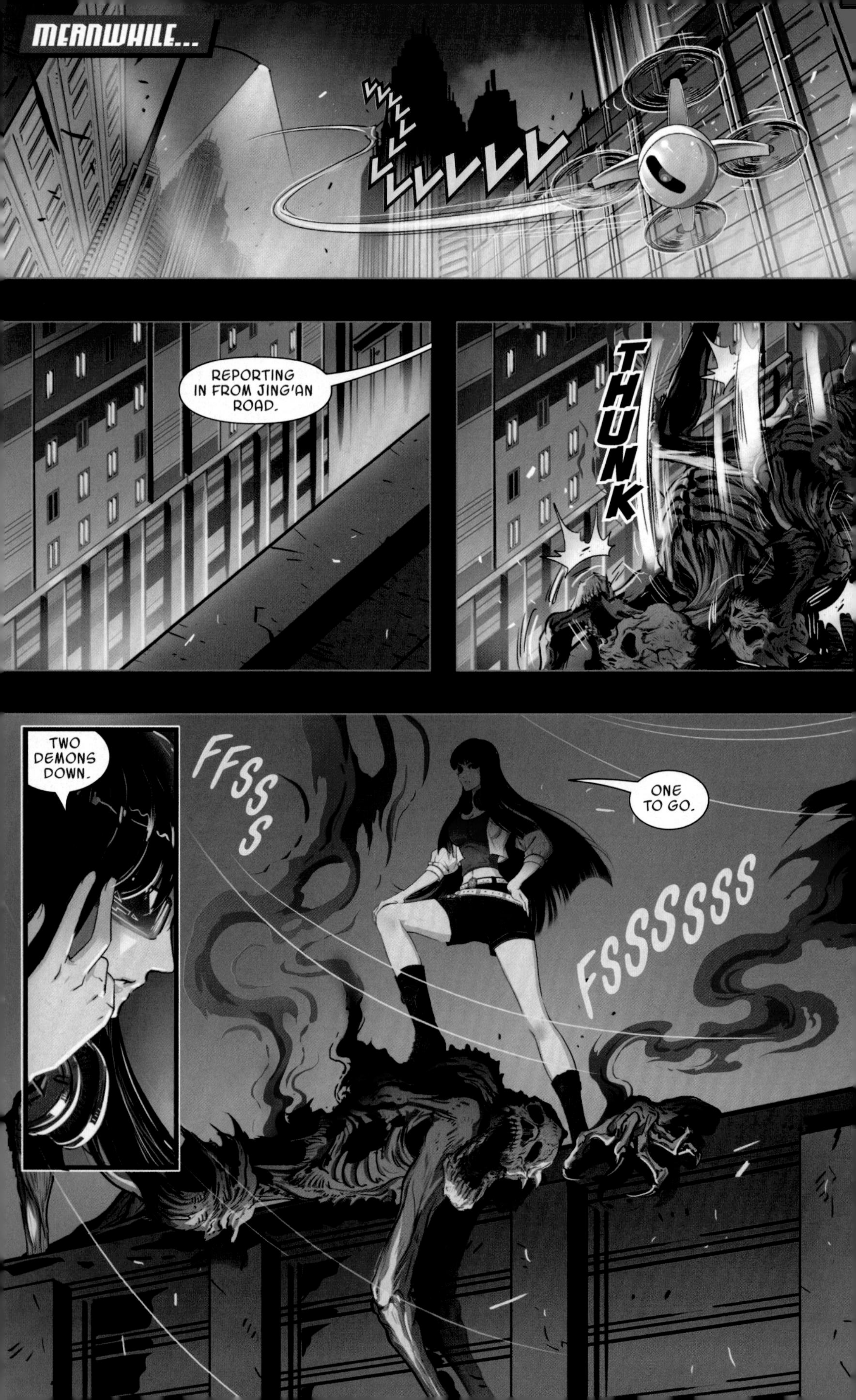
MEANWHILE...
VVVVVVLLLLL
REPORTING IN FROM JING'AN ROAD.
THUNK
TWO DEMONS DOWN.
FFSSS
ONE TO GO.
FSSSSSS

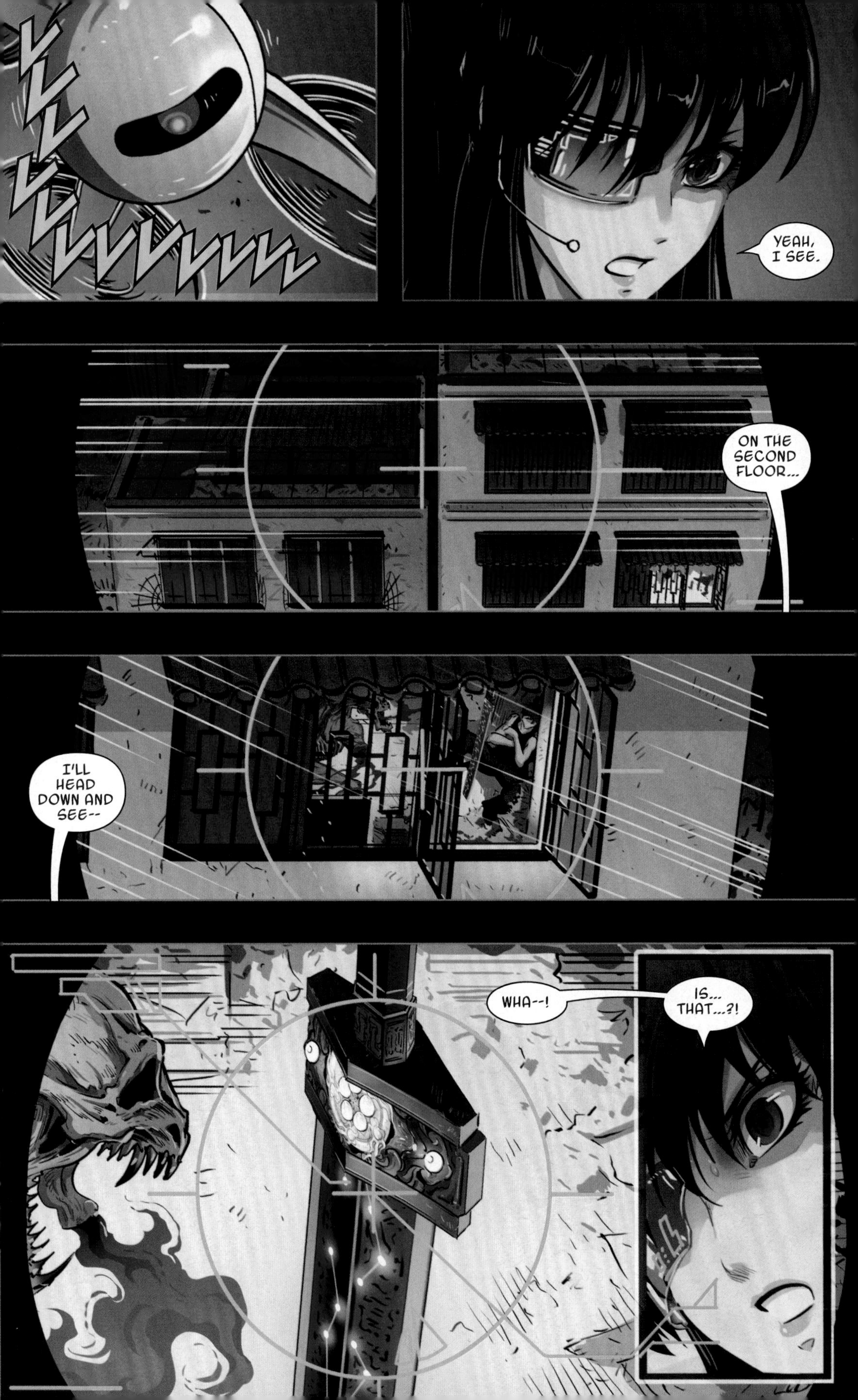
YEAH, I SEE.
ON THE SECOND FLOOR...
I'LL HEAD DOWN AND SEE--
WHA--!
IS... THAT...?!

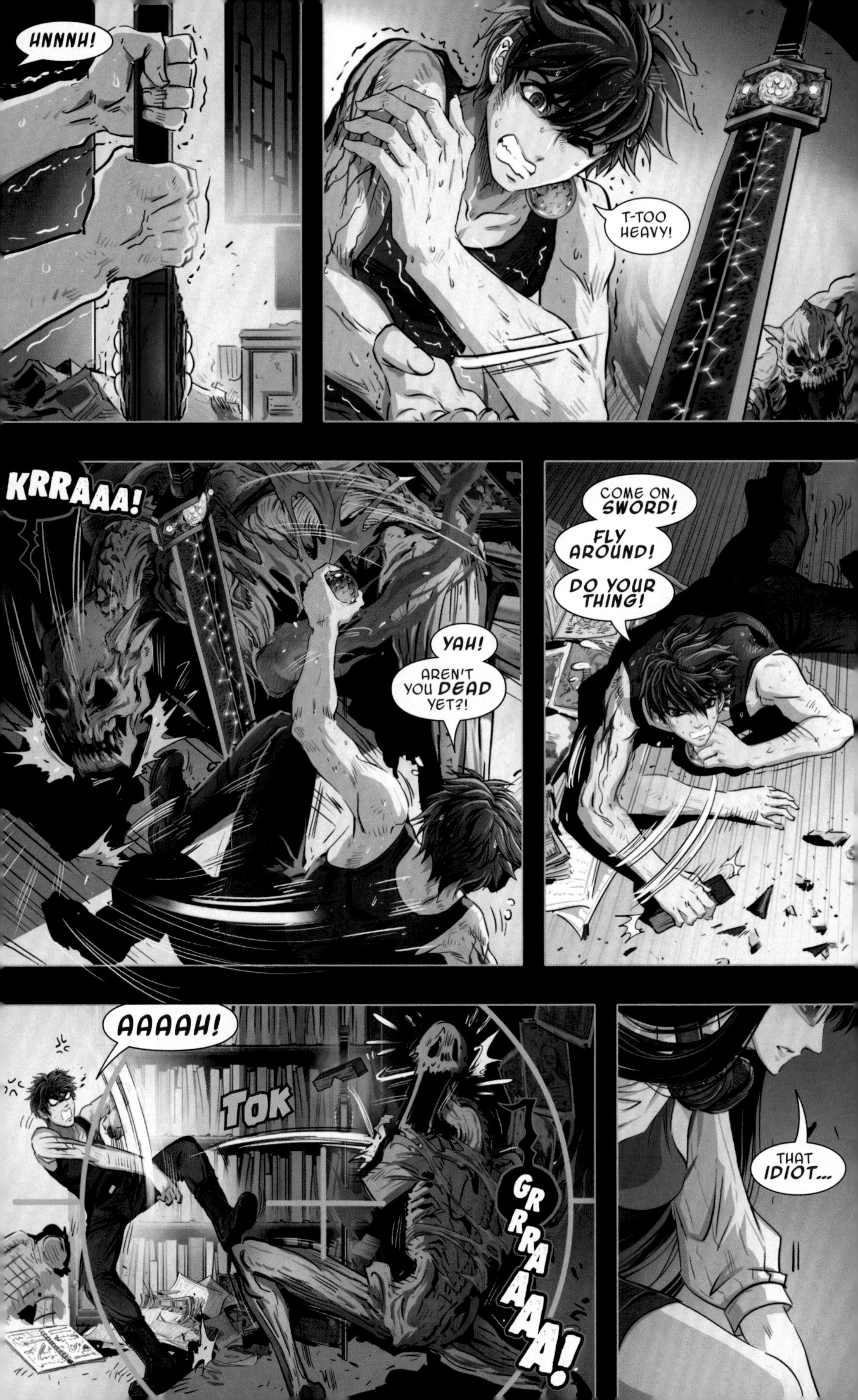
HNNNH!
T-TOO HEAVY!
KRRAAA!
YAH!
AREN'T YOU DEAD YET?!
COME ON, SWORD!
FLY AROUND!
DO YOUR THING!
AAAAH!
TOK
GRRRAAAA!
THAT IDIOT...

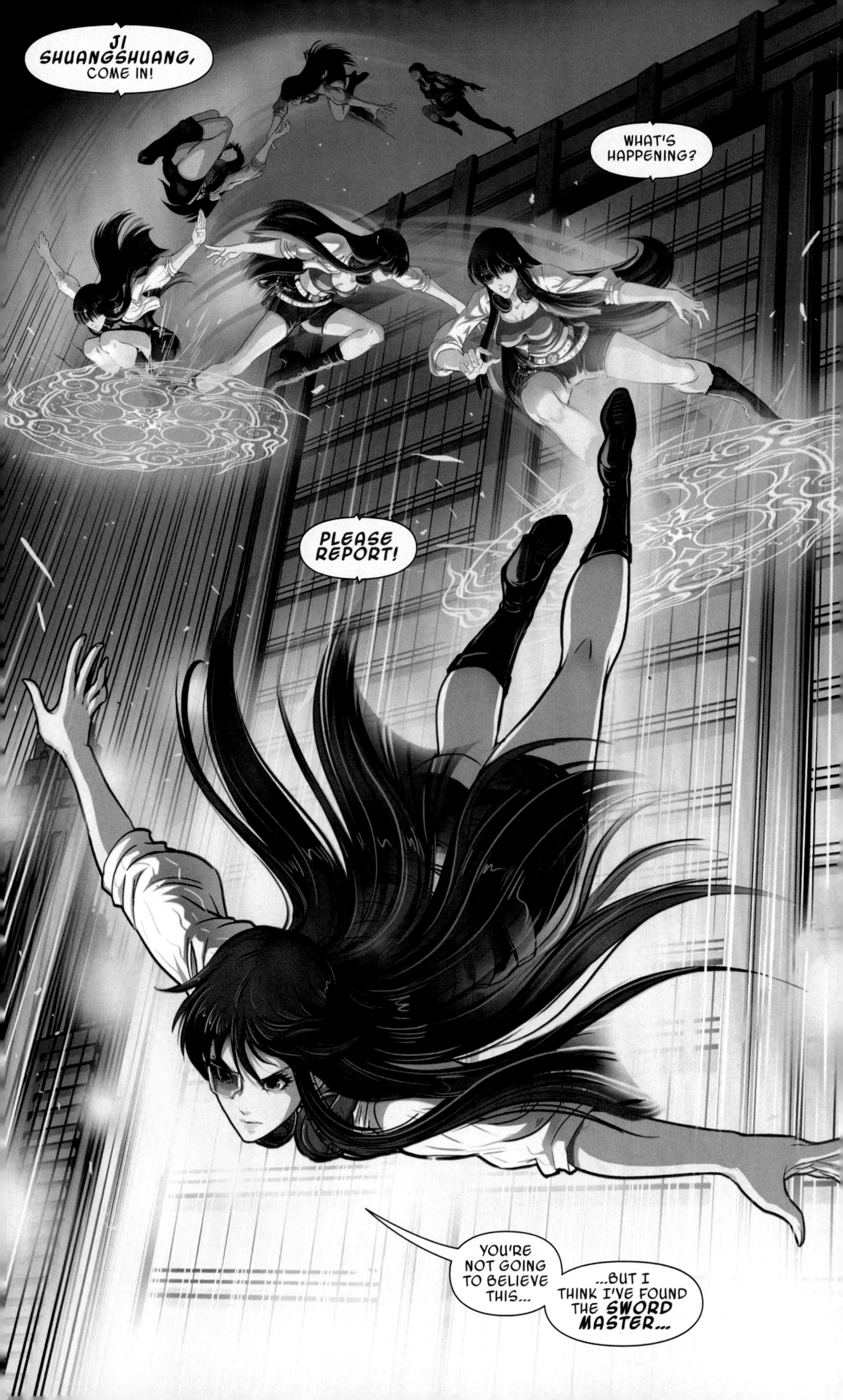
JI SHUANGSHUANG, COME IN!
WHAT'S HAPPENING?
PLEASE REPORT!
YOU'RE NOT GOING TO BELIEVE THIS...
...BUT I THINK I'VE FOUND THE SWORD MASTER...

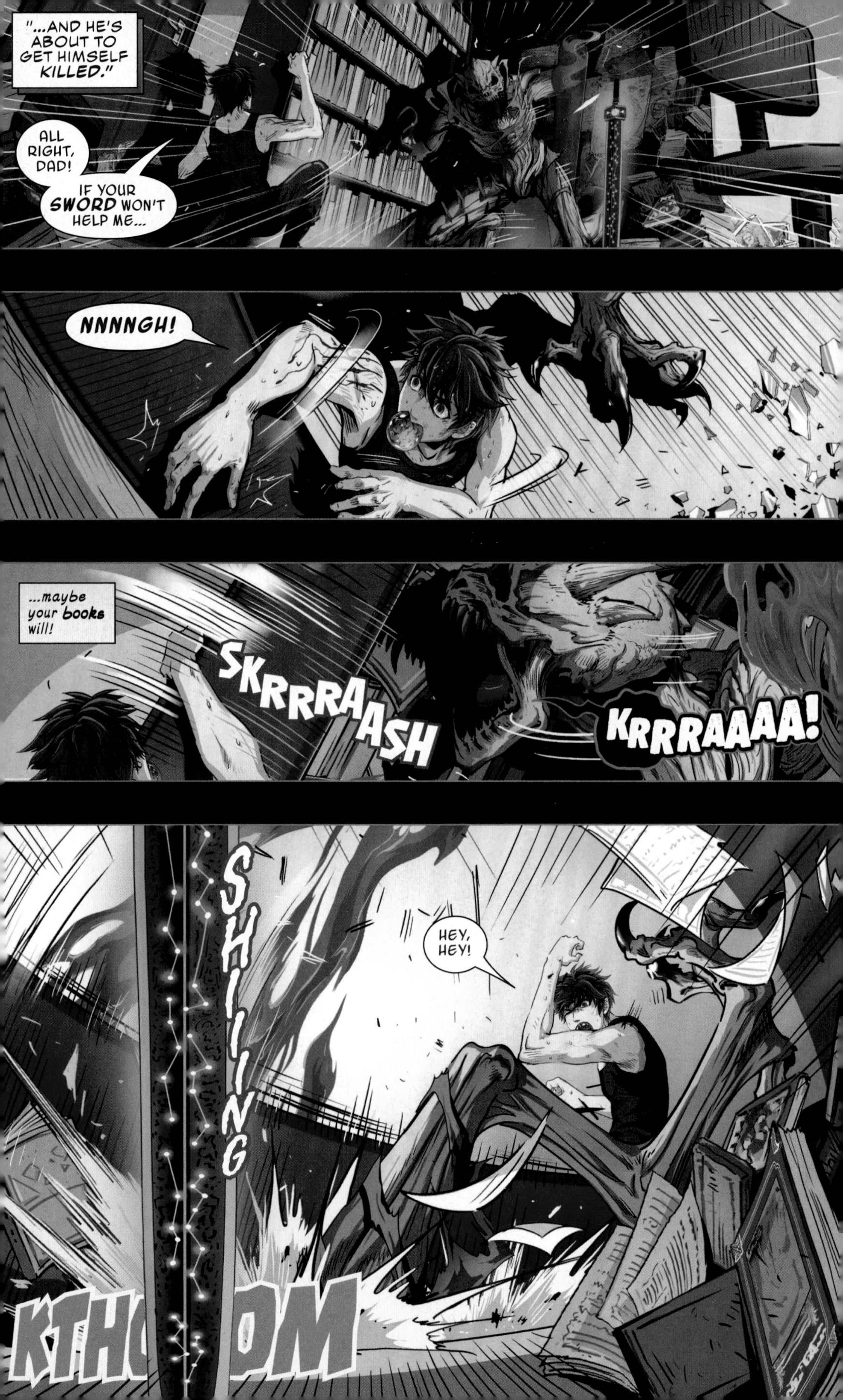
"...AND HE'S ABOUT TO GET HIMSELF KILLED."
ALL RIGHT, DAD!
IF YOUR SWORD WON'T HELP ME...
NNNNGH!
...maybe your books will!
SKRRRAASH
KRRRAAAA!
SHIIING
HEY, HEY!

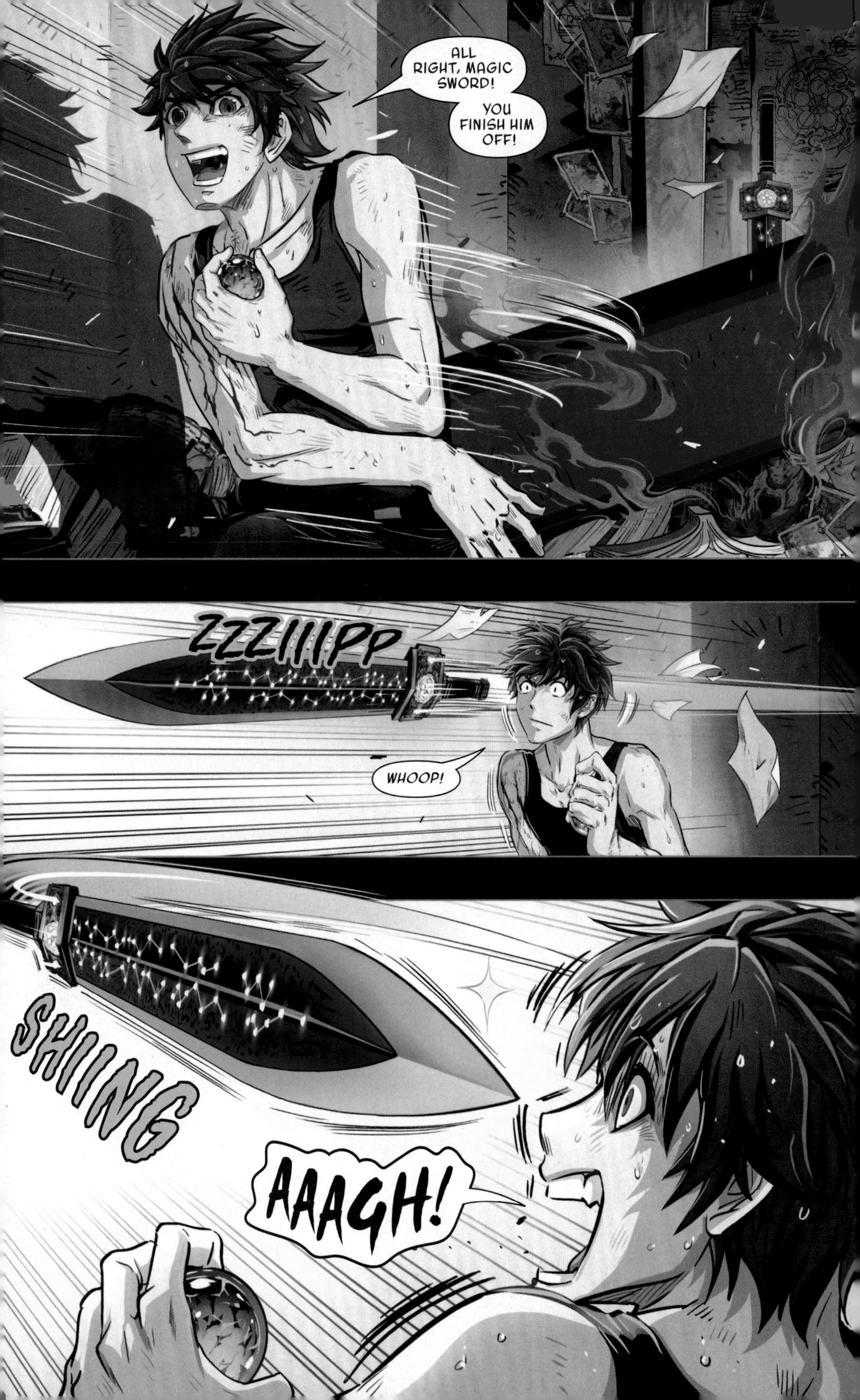
ALL RIGHT, MAGIC SWORD!
YOU FINISH HIM OFF!
ZZZIIIPP
WHOOP!
SHING
AAAGH!

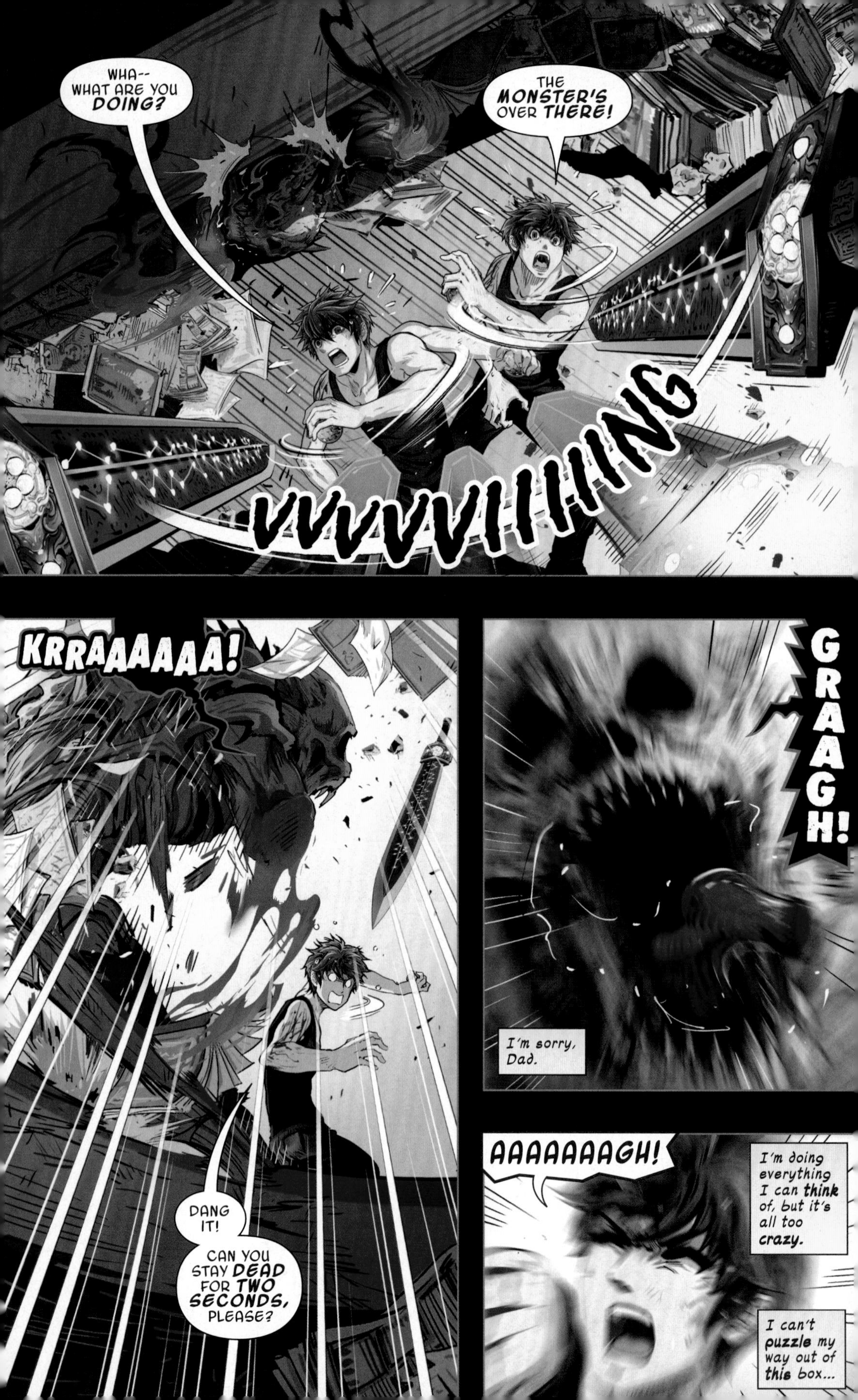

WHA-- WHAT ARE YOU DOING?
THE MONSTER'S OVER THERE!
VVVVVIIIIING
KRRAAAAAAA!
DANG IT!
CAN YOU STAY DEAD FOR TWO SECONDS, PLEASE?
GRAAGH!
I'm sorry, Dad.
AAAAAAAGH!
I'm doing everything I can think of, but it's all too crazy.
I can't puzzle my way out of this box...

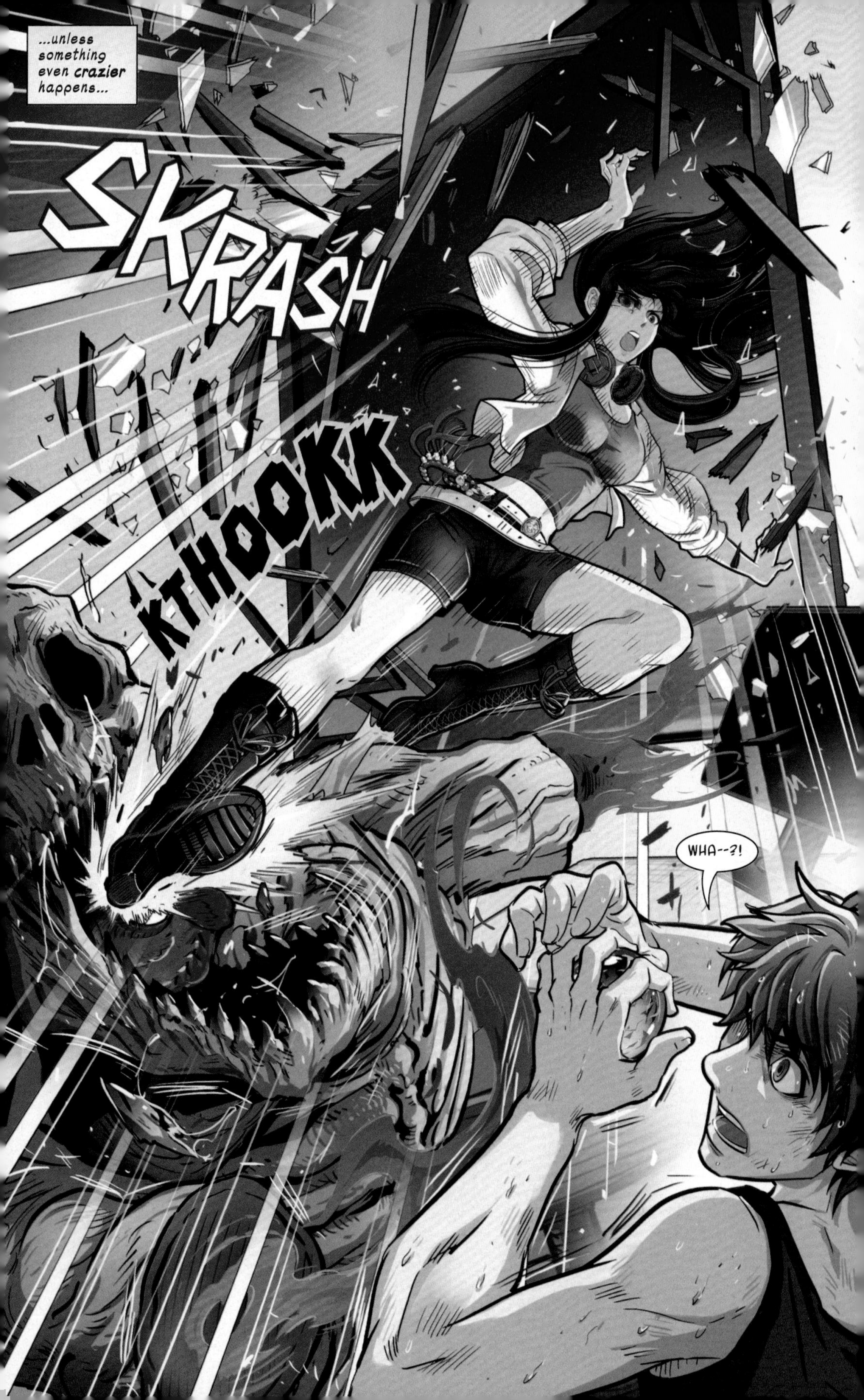
...unless something even crazier happens...
SKRASH
KTHOOKK
WHA--?!

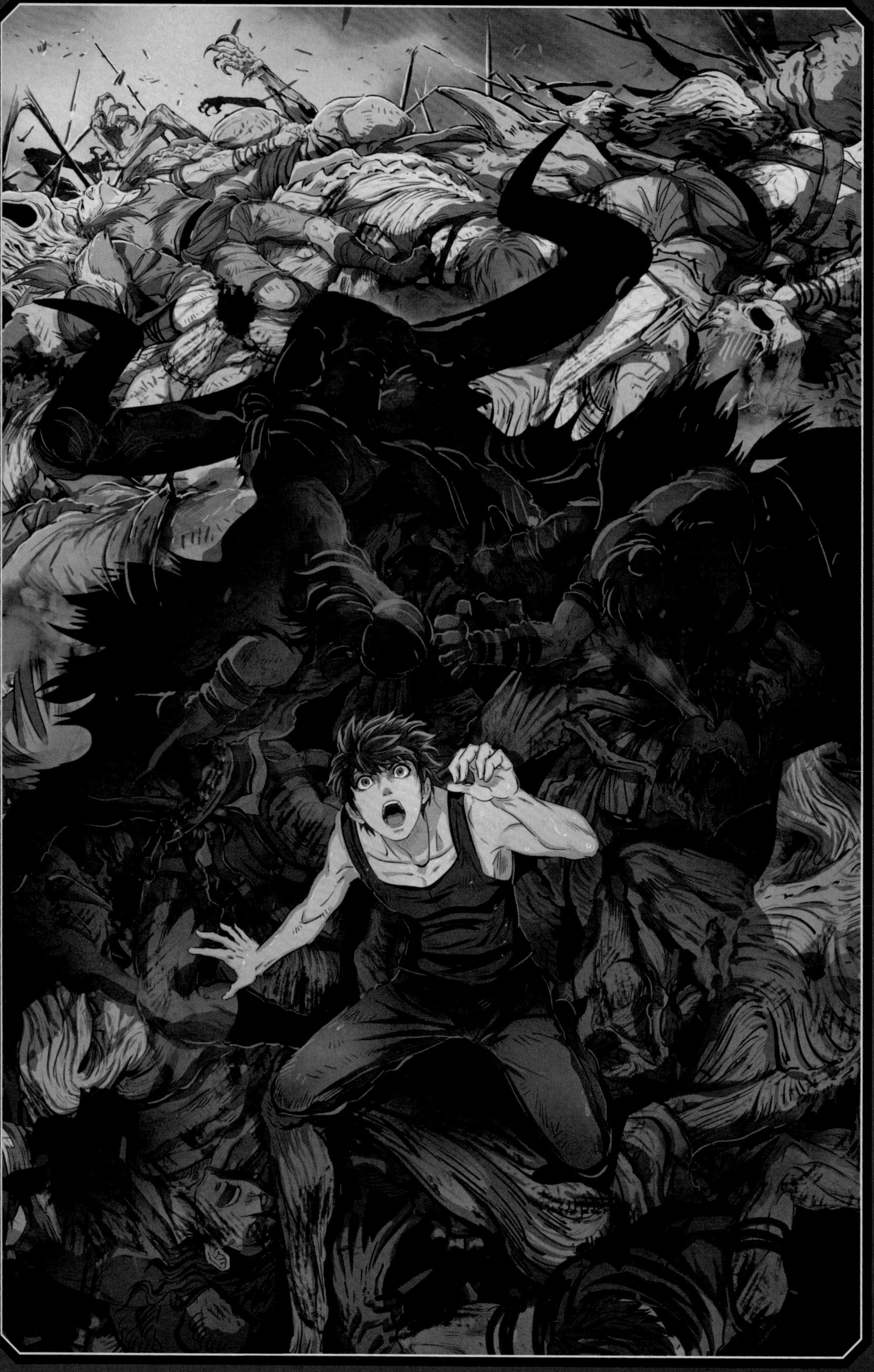

THREE THE ANCIENT WAR

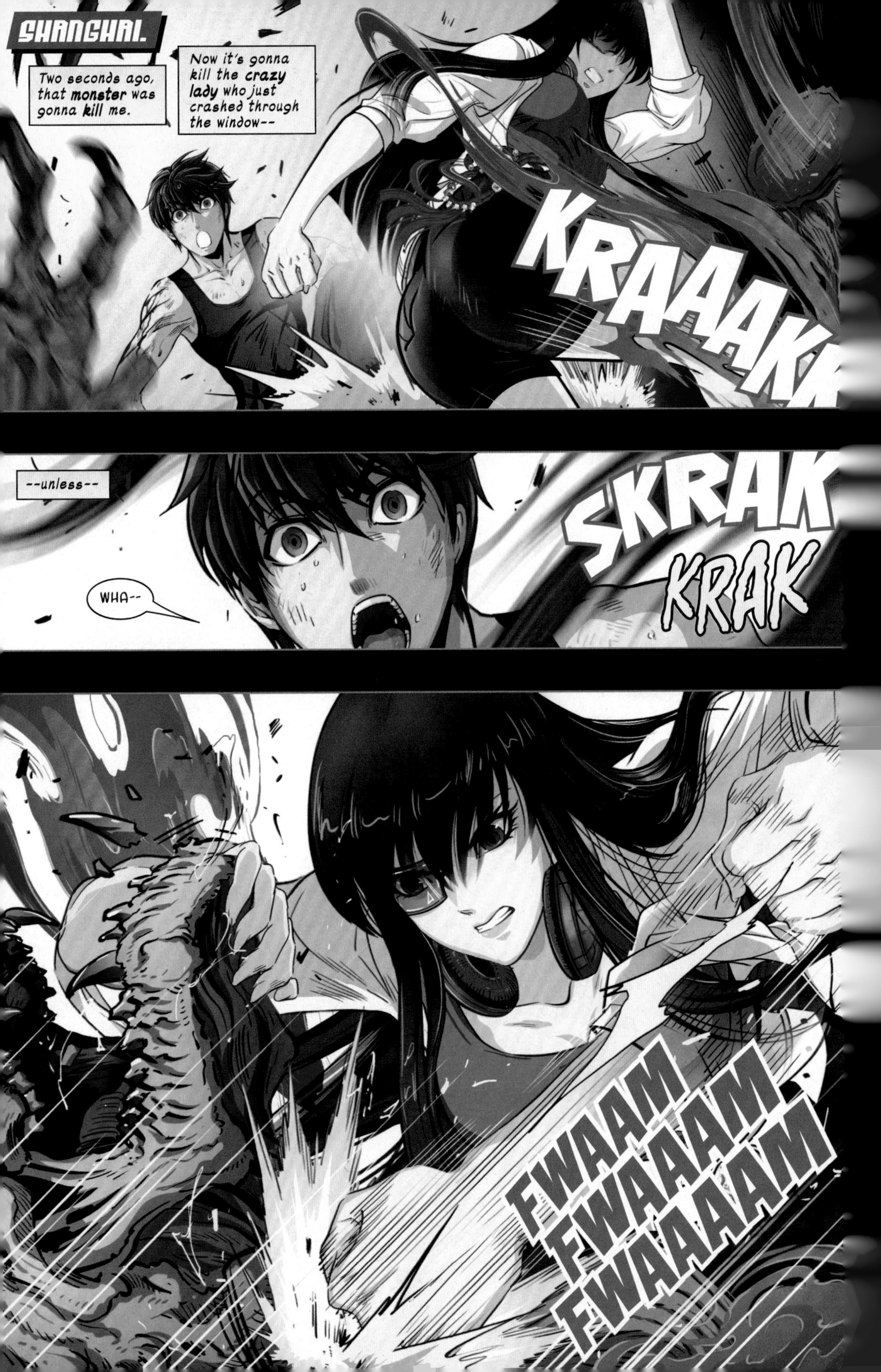
SHANGHAI.
Two seconds ago, that **monster** was gonna **kill** me.
Now it's gonna kill the **crazy lady** who just crashed through the window--
KRAAAAKK
--unless--
SKRAK
KRAK
WHA--
FWAAM
FWAAAM
FWAAAAM

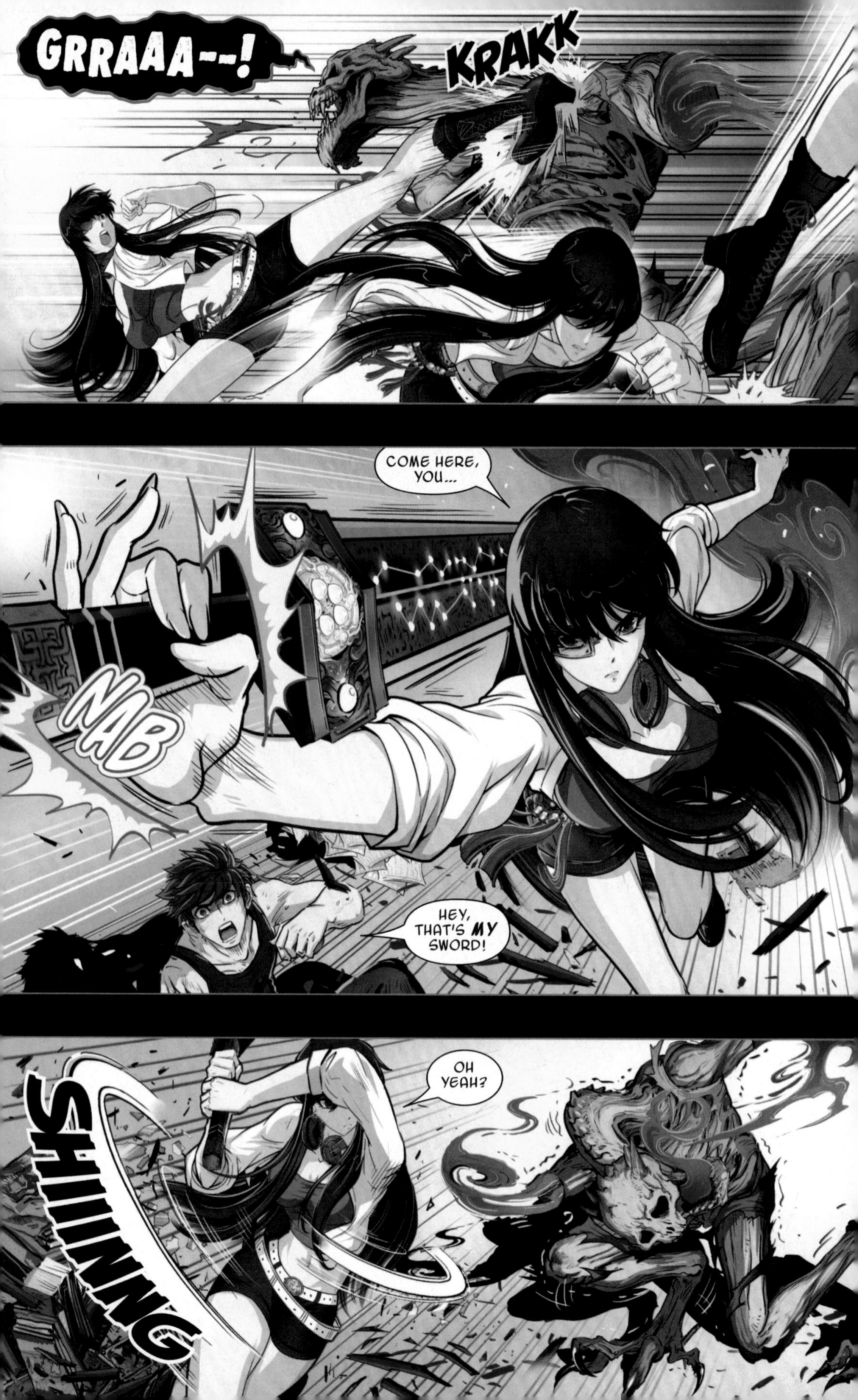
GRRAAA--!
KRAKK
COME HERE, YOU...
NAB
HEY, THAT'S MY SWORD!
OH YEAH?
SHIIINNG

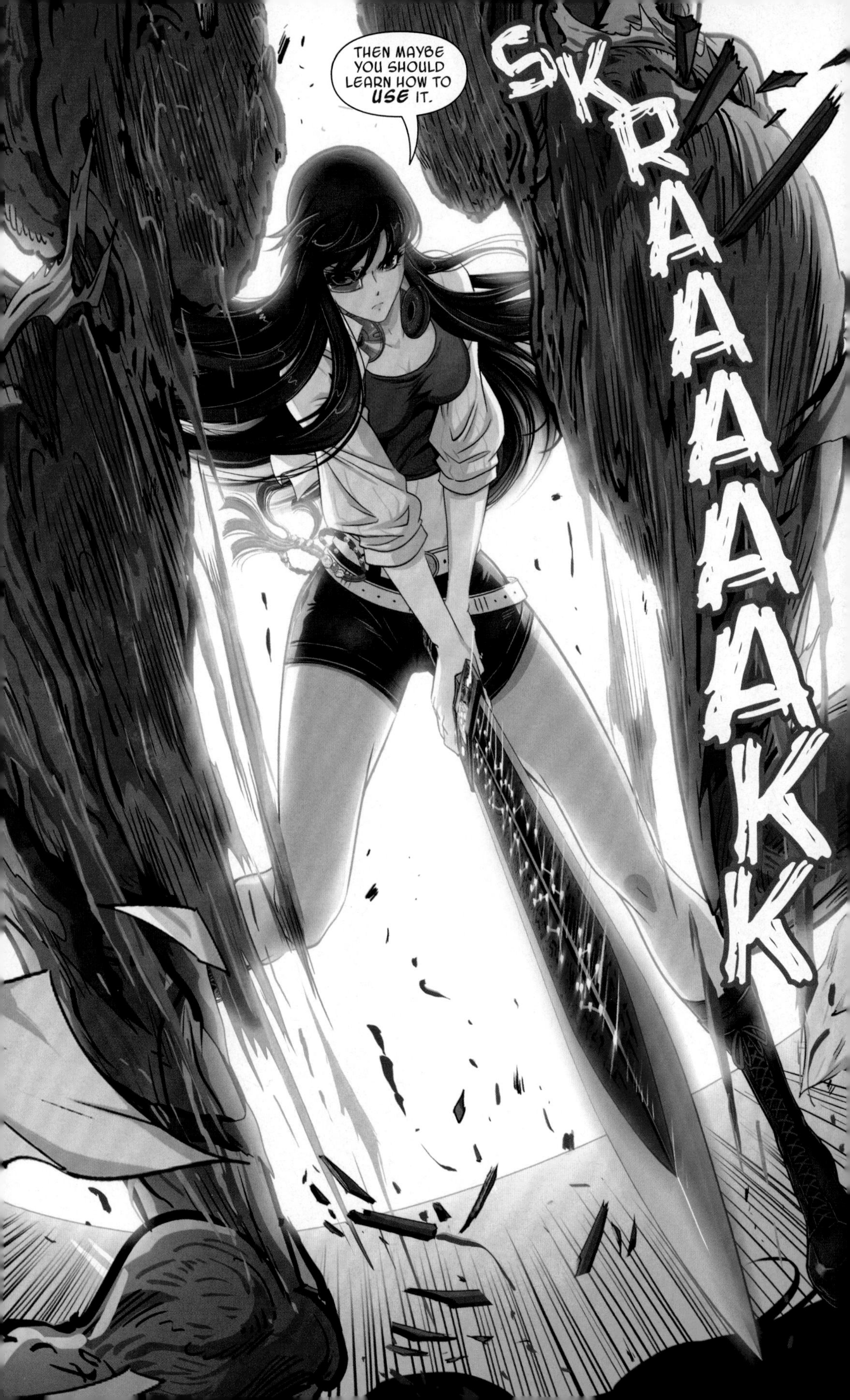
THEN MAYBE YOU SHOULD LEARN HOW TO USE IT.
SKRAAAAAAK

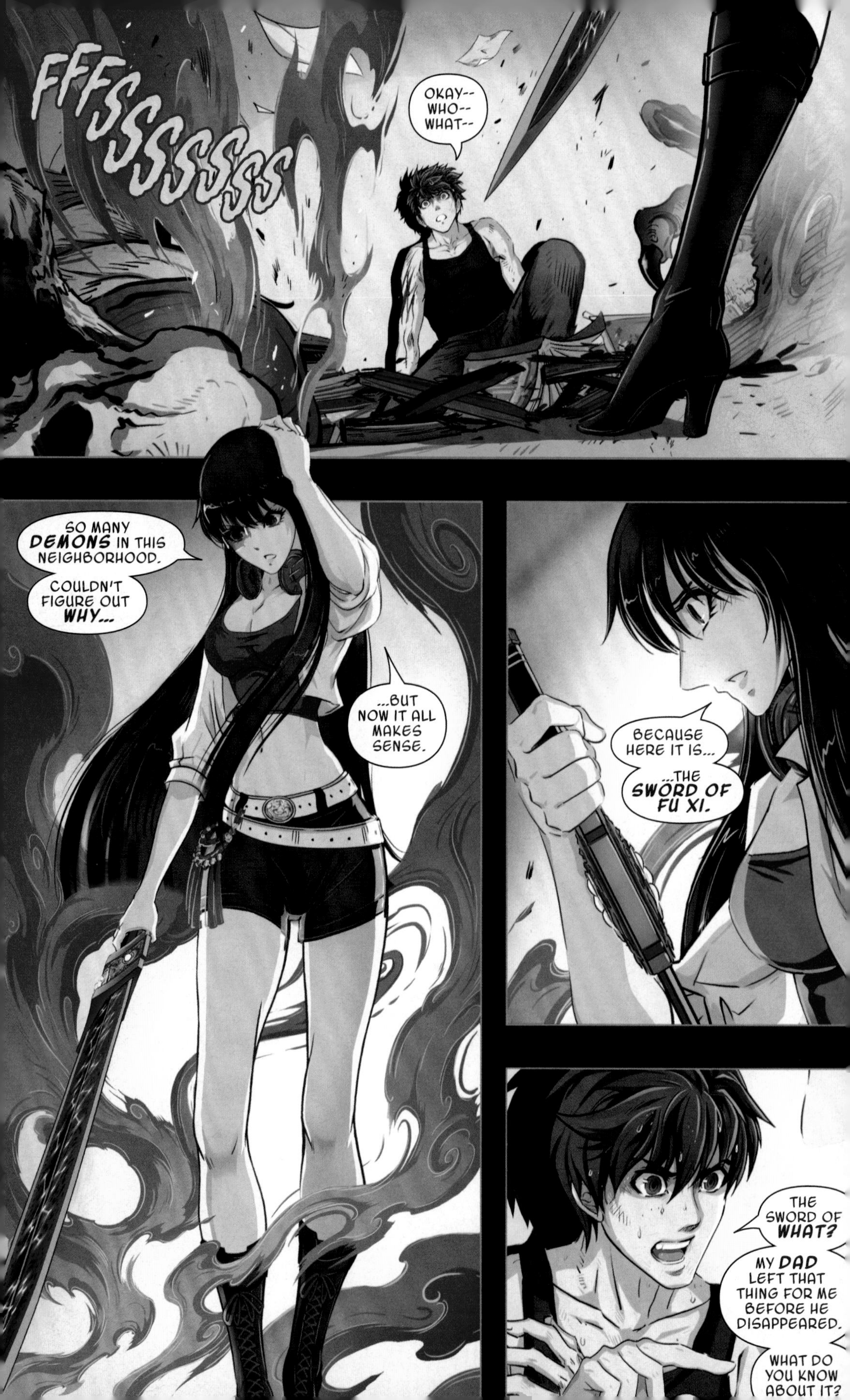
FFFSSSSSSSS
OKAY--
WHO--
WHAT--
SO MANY DEMONS IN THIS NEIGHBORHOOD.
COULDN'T FIGURE OUT WHY...
...BUT NOW IT ALL MAKES SENSE.
BECAUSE HERE IT IS...
...THE SWORD OF FU XI.
THE SWORD OF WHAT?
MY DAD LEFT THAT THING FOR ME BEFORE HE DISAPPEARED.
WHAT DO YOU KNOW ABOUT IT?

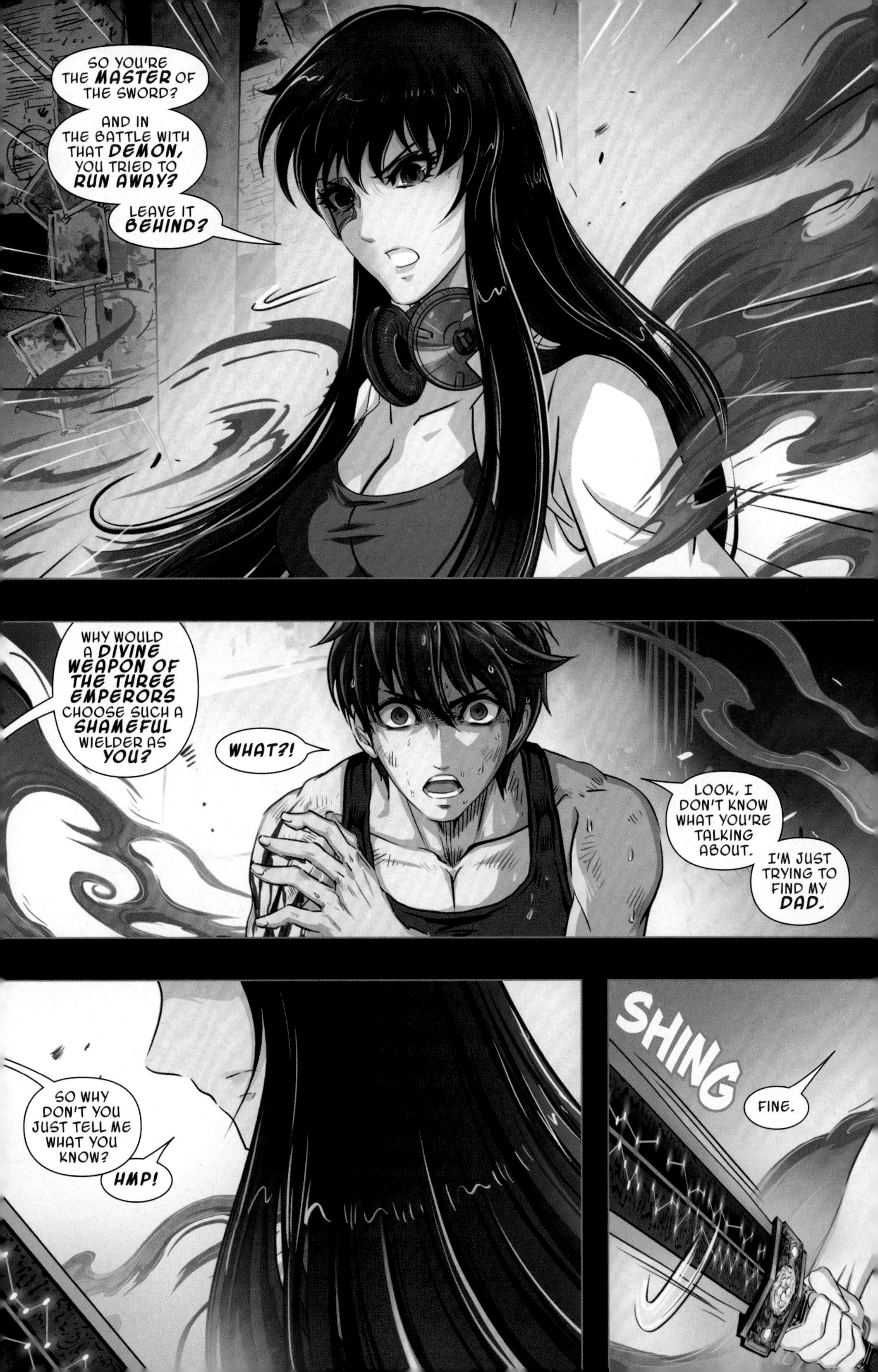
SO YOU'RE THE MASTER OF THE SWORD?
AND IN THE BATTLE WITH THAT DEMON, YOU TRIED TO RUN AWAY?
LEAVE IT BEHIND?
WHY WOULD A DIVINE WEAPON OF THE THREE EMPERORS CHOOSE SUCH A SHAMEFUL WIELDER AS YOU?
WHAT?!
LOOK, I DON'T KNOW WHAT YOU'RE TALKING ABOUT.
I'M JUST TRYING TO FIND MY DAD.
SO WHY DON'T YOU JUST TELL ME WHAT YOU KNOW?
HMP!
SHING
FINE.

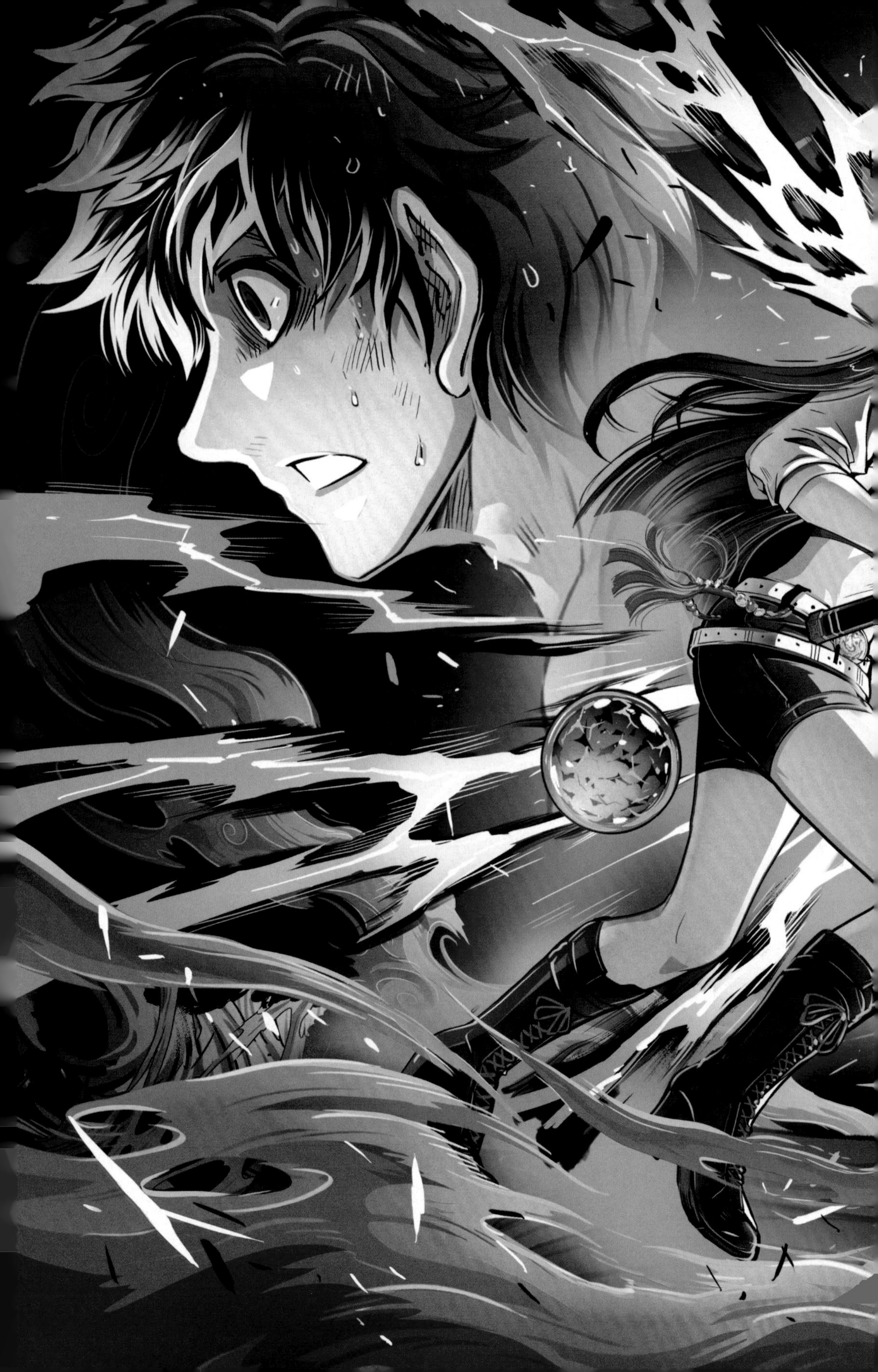

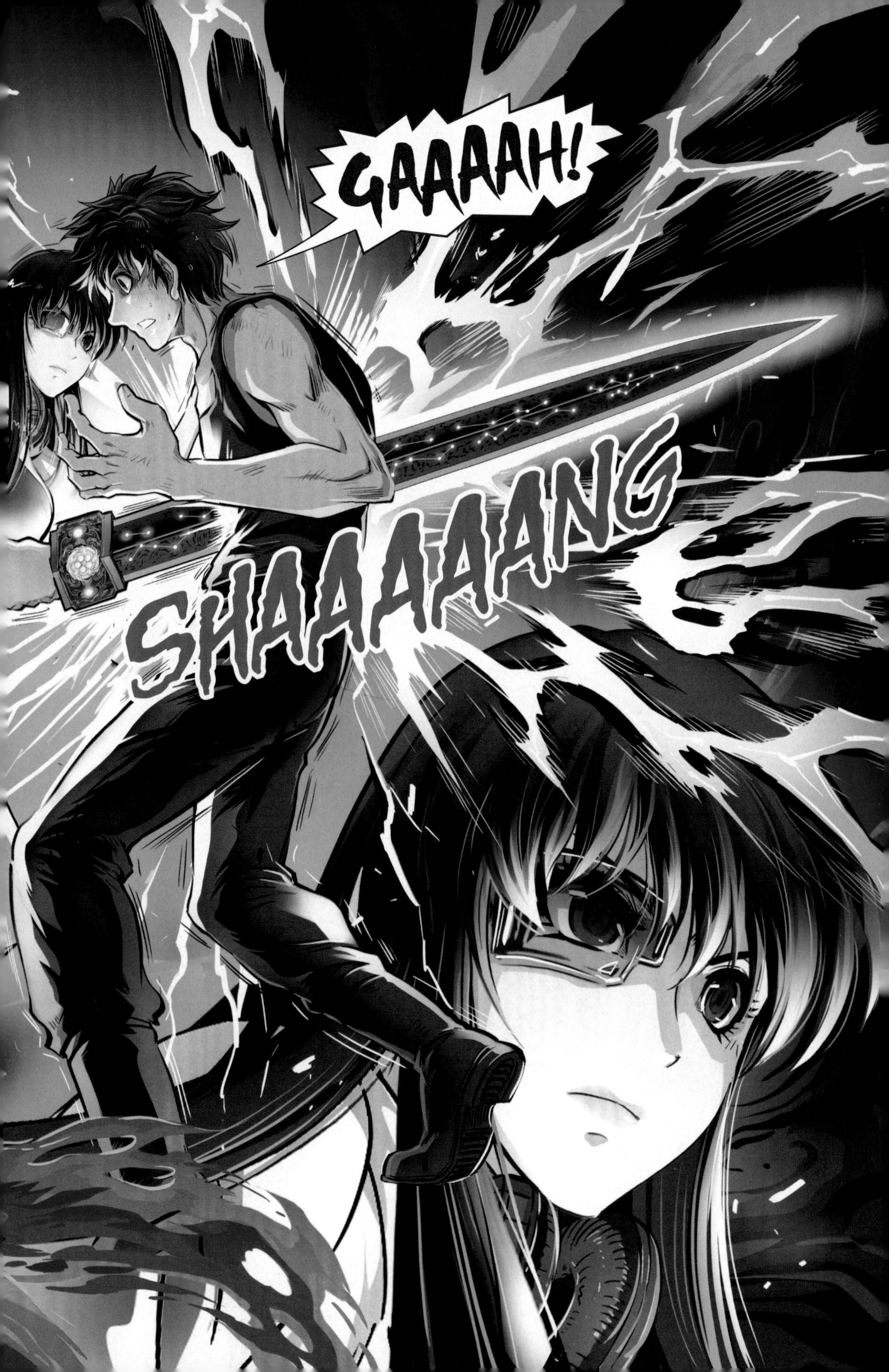
GAAAAH!
SHAAAAANG

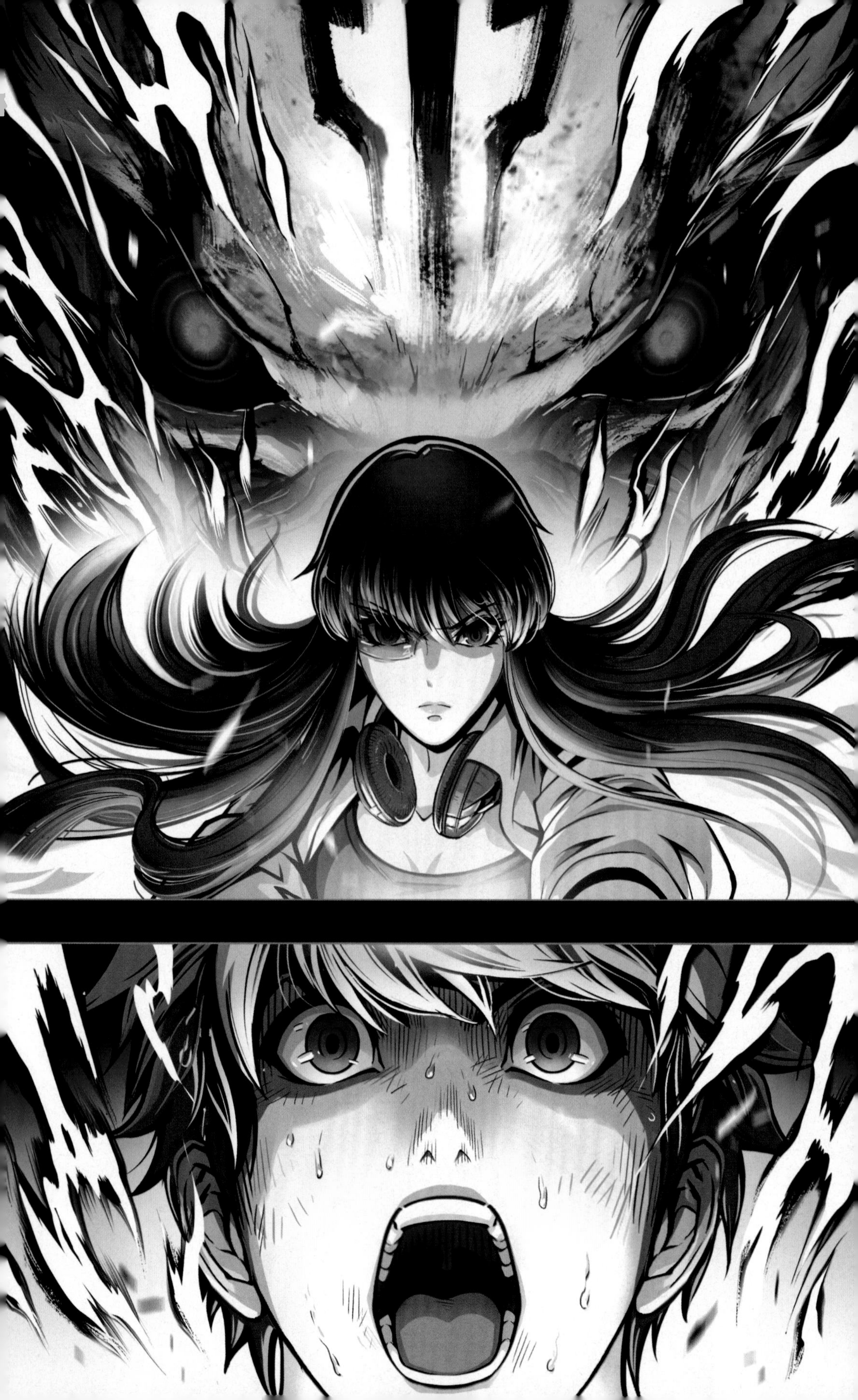

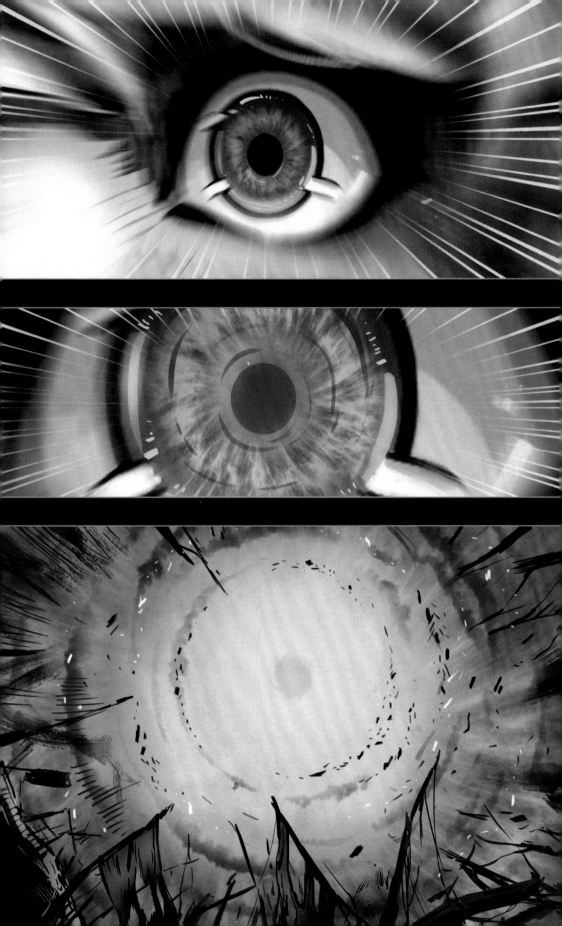

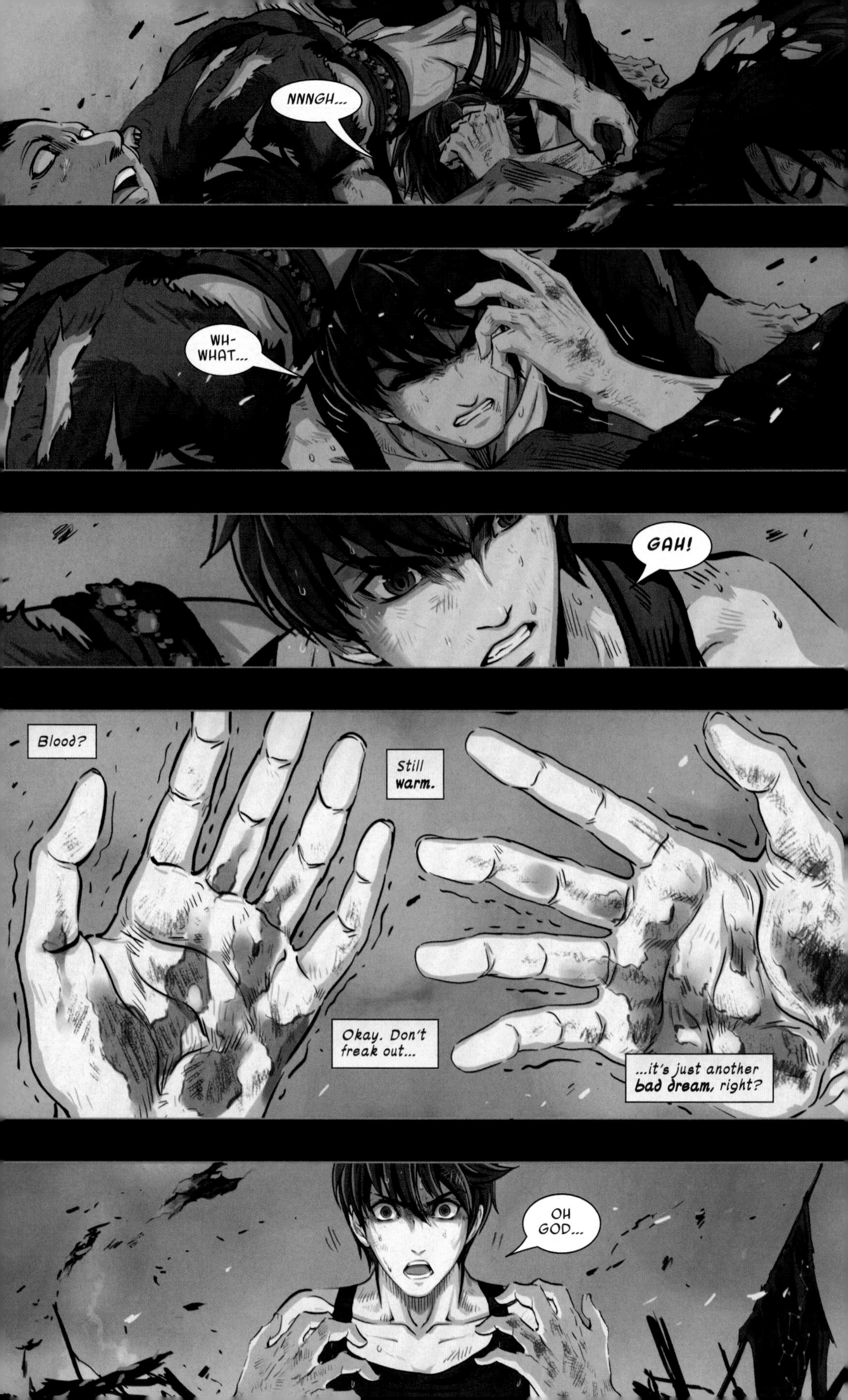
NNNGH...
WH-
WHAT...
GAH!
Blood?
Still
warm.
Okay. Don't
freak out...
...it's just another
bad dream, right?
OH
GOD...

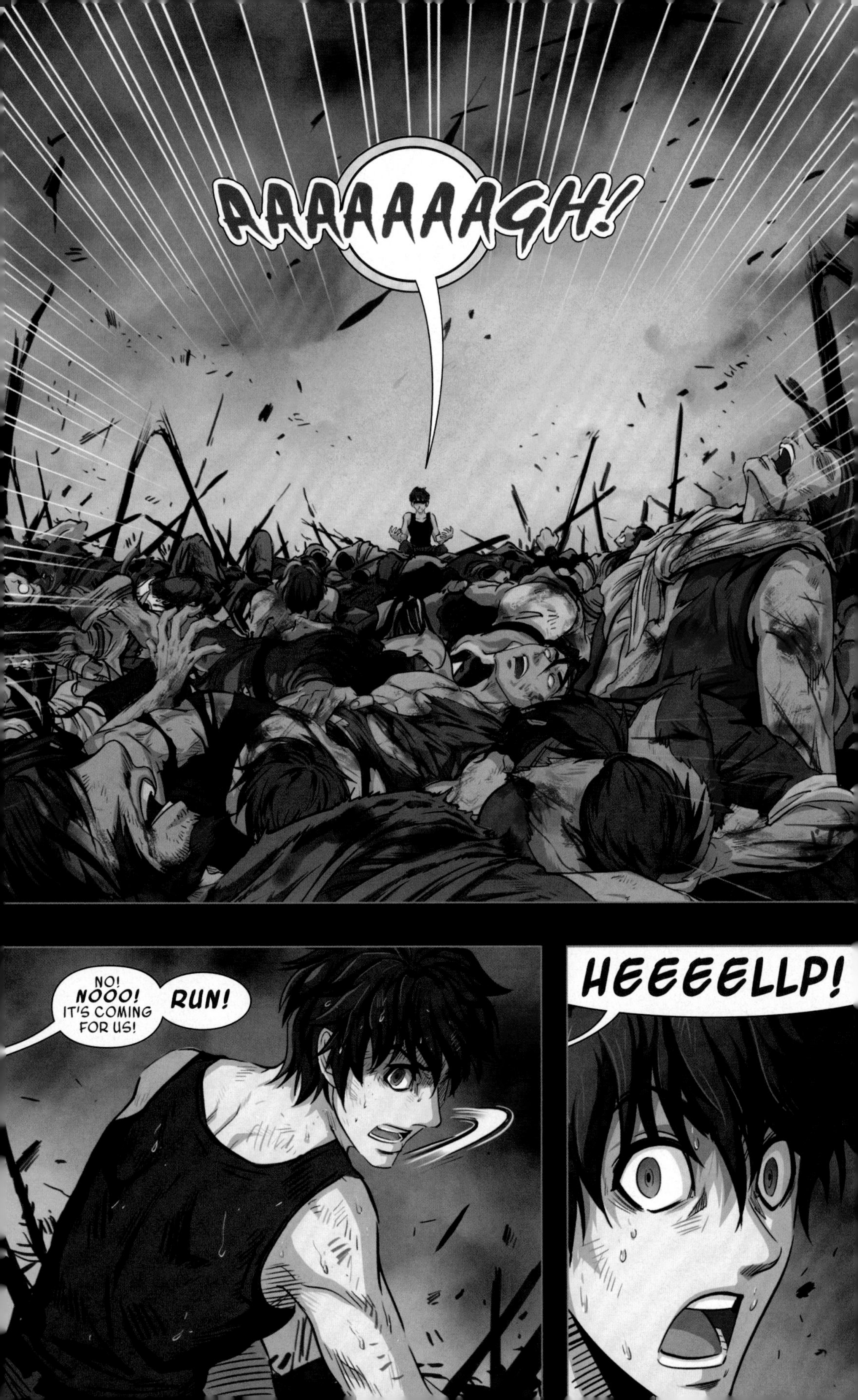
AAAAAAAAGH!
NO! NOOO! IT'S COMING FOR US!
RUN!
HEEEEELLP!

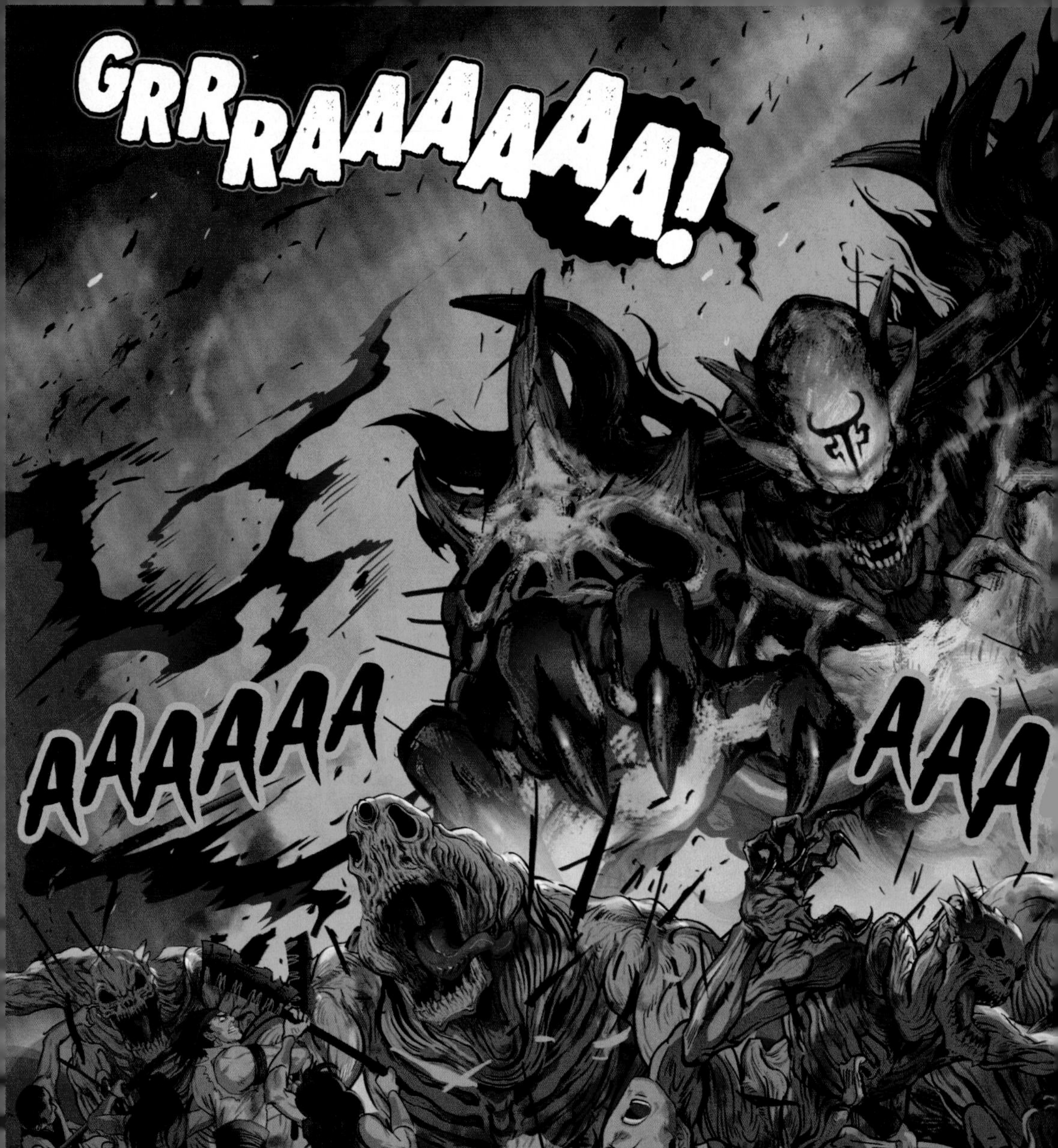
GRRRAAAAAAA!
AAAAAA
AAA
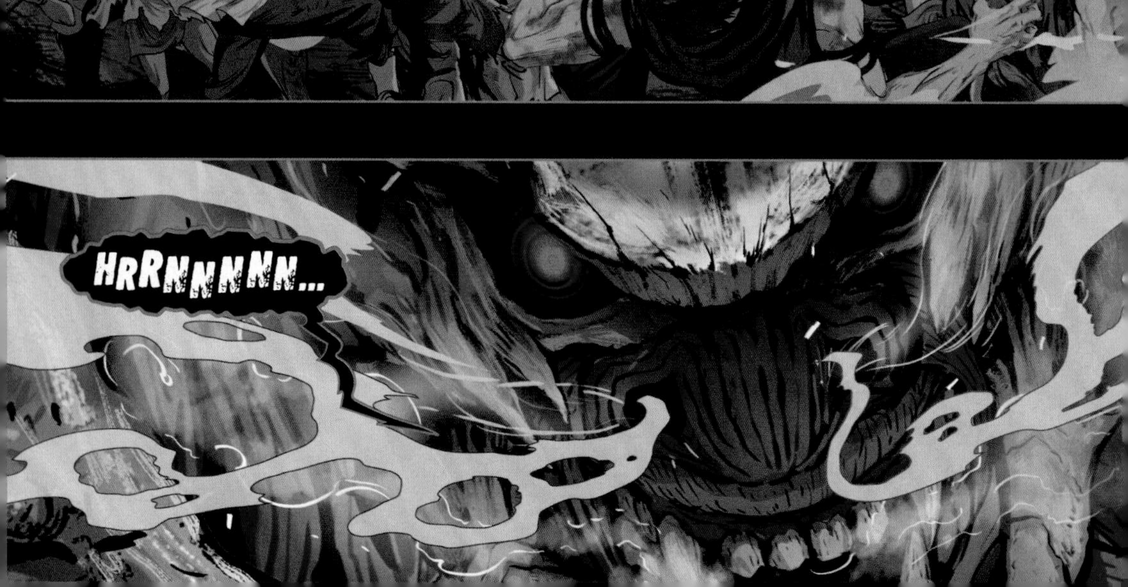
HRRNNNNN...

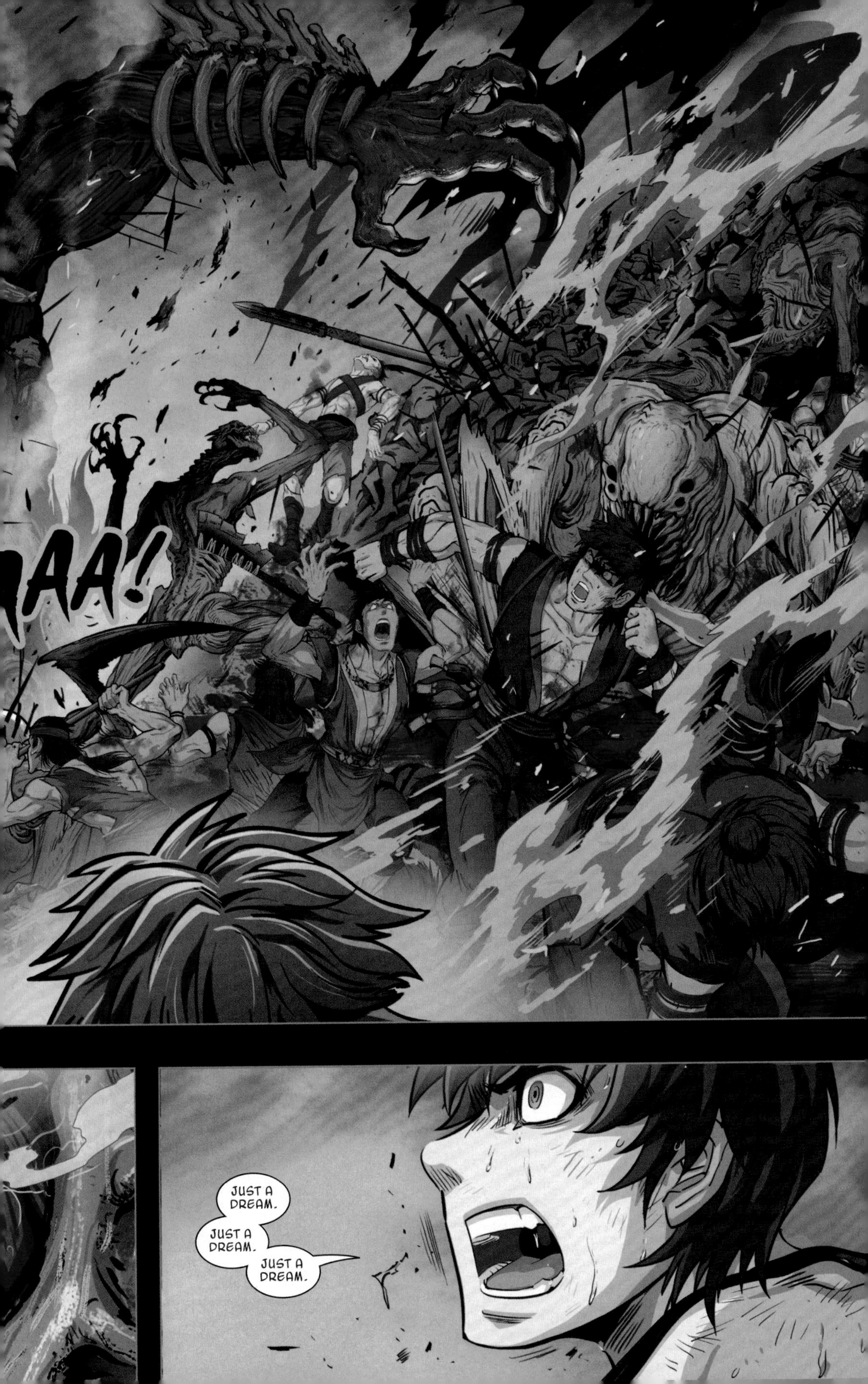

AA!
JUST A DREAM.
JUST A DREAM.
JUST A DREAM.

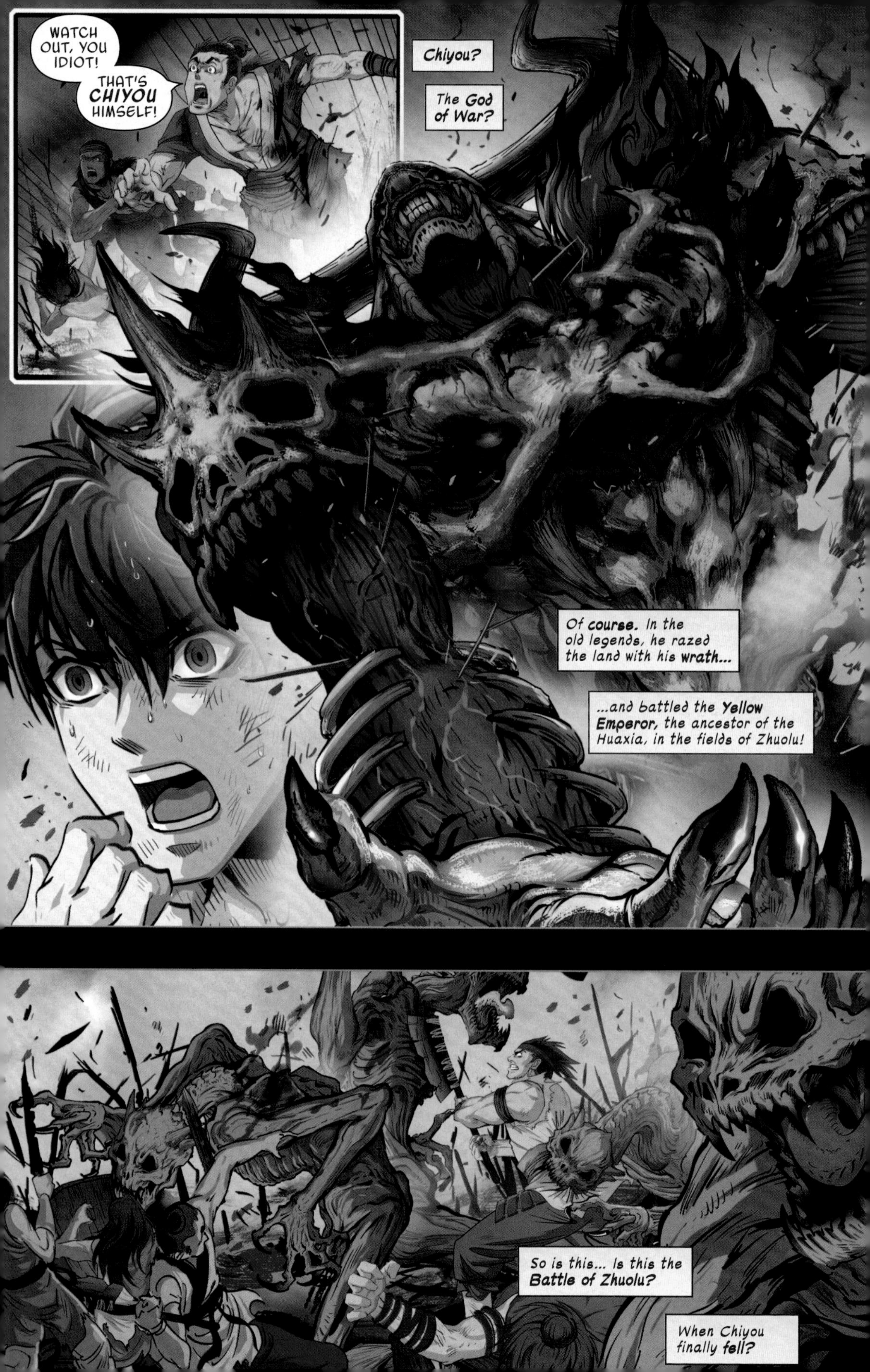
WATCH OUT, YOU IDIOT!
THAT'S CHIYOU HIMSELF!
Chiyou?
The God of War?
Of course. In the old legends, he razed the land with his wrath...
...and battled the Yellow Emperor, the ancestor of the Huaxia, in the fields of Zhuolu!
So is this... Is this the Battle of Zhuolu?
When Chiyou finally fell?

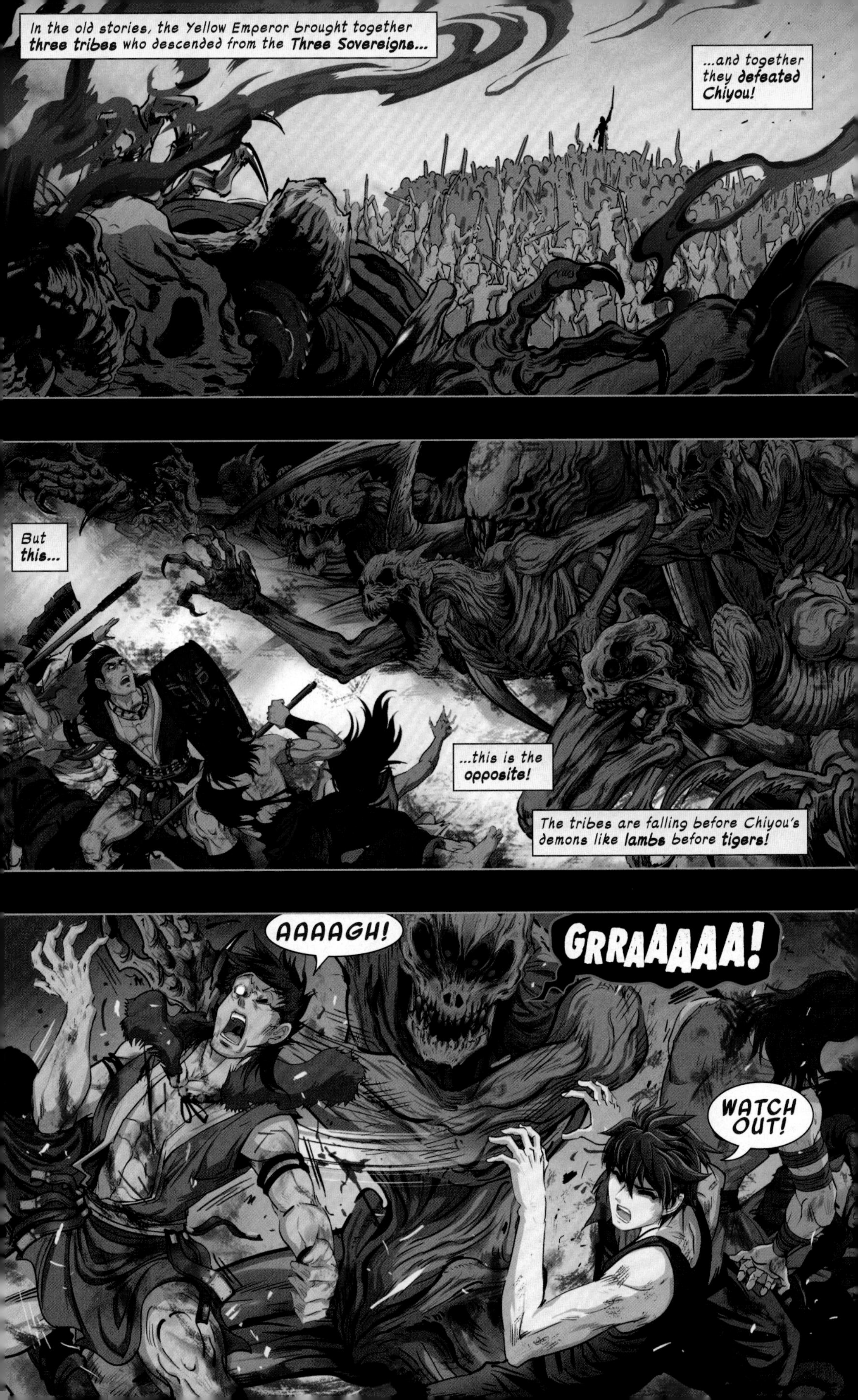
In the old stories, the Yellow Emperor brought together three tribes who descended from the Three Sovereigns...
...and together they defeated Chiyou!
But this...
...this is the opposite!
The tribes are falling before Chiyou's demons like lambs before tigers!
AAAAGH!
GRRAAAAA!
WATCH OUT!

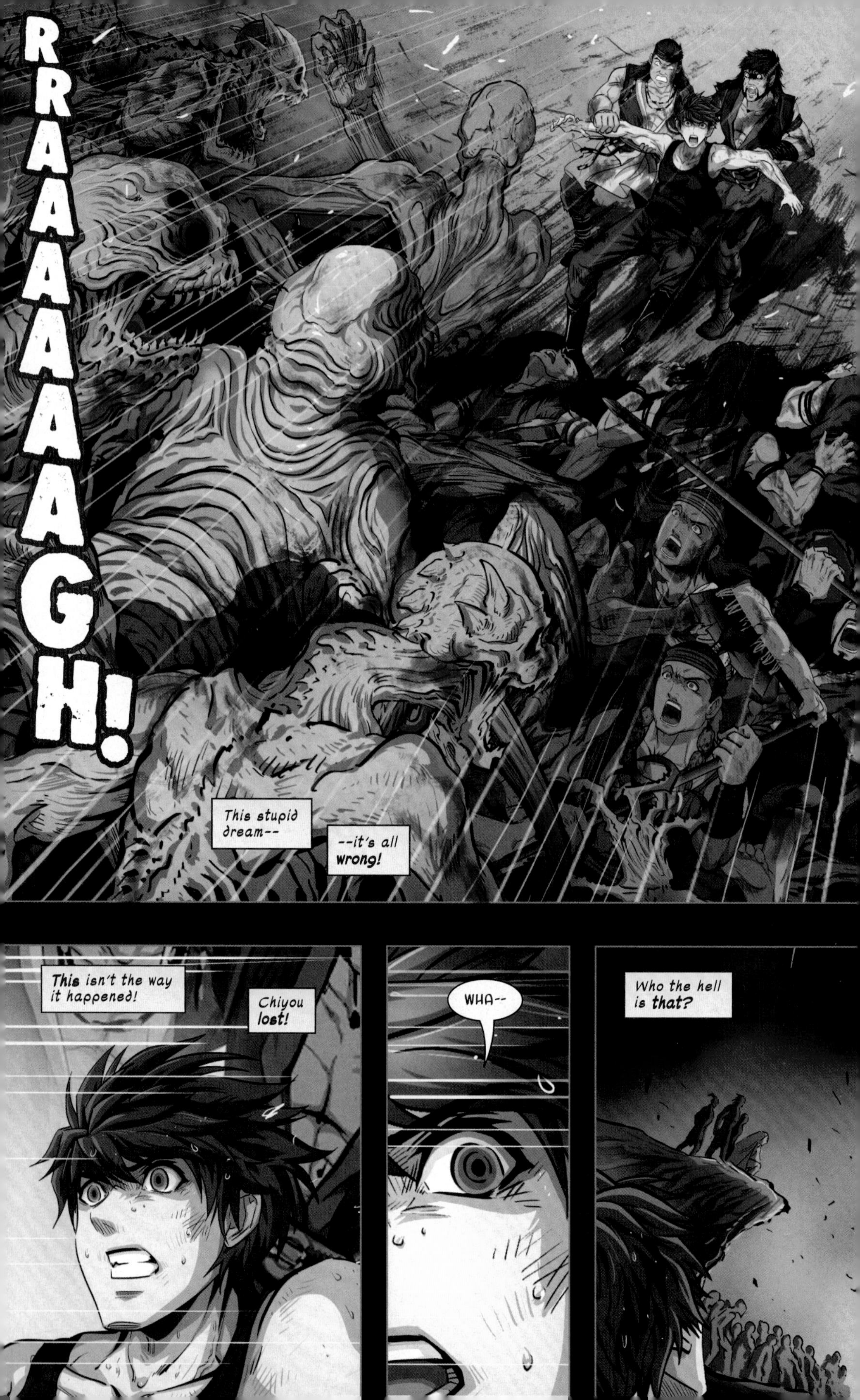
RRAAAAAAAGH!
This stupid dream--
--it's all wrong!
This isn't the way it happened!
Chiyou lost!
WHA--
Who the hell is that?

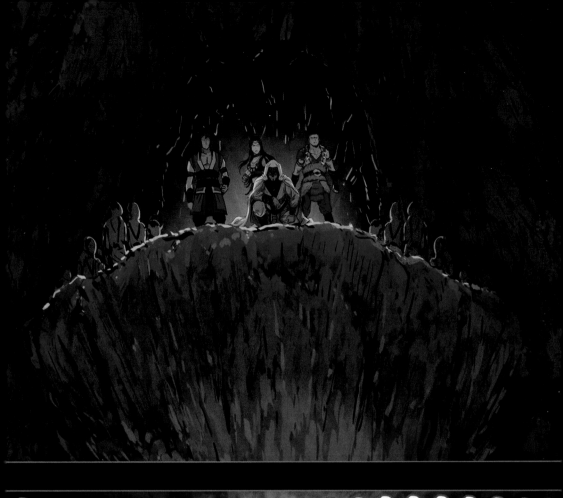

AAAAAAAAAAAAAAAAAAAAAAAA!

HE'S KILLING EVERYONE WHO STANDS IN HIS WAY.

AND SOON HE'LL REACH US.

MY LORD...

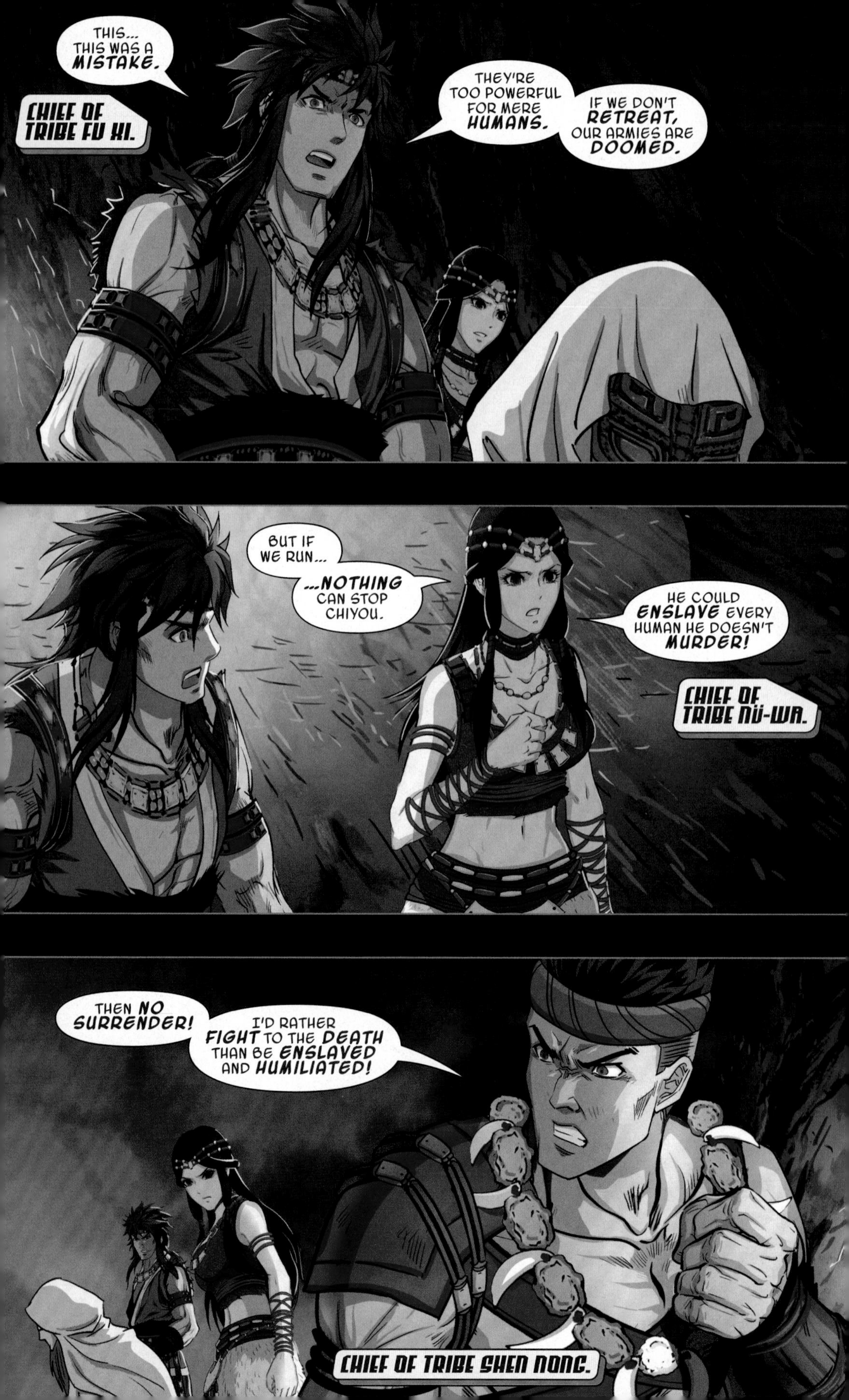
THIS... THIS WAS A MISTAKE.
CHIEF OF TRIBE FU XI.
THEY'RE TOO POWERFUL FOR MERE HUMANS.
IF WE DON'T RETREAT, OUR ARMIES ARE DOOMED.
BUT IF WE RUN...
...NOTHING CAN STOP CHIYOU.
HE COULD ENSLAVE EVERY HUMAN HE DOESN'T MURDER!
CHIEF OF TRIBE NÜ-WA.
THEN NO SURRENDER!
I'D RATHER FIGHT TO THE DEATH THAN BE ENSLAVED AND HUMILIATED!
CHIEF OF TRIBE SHEN NONG.

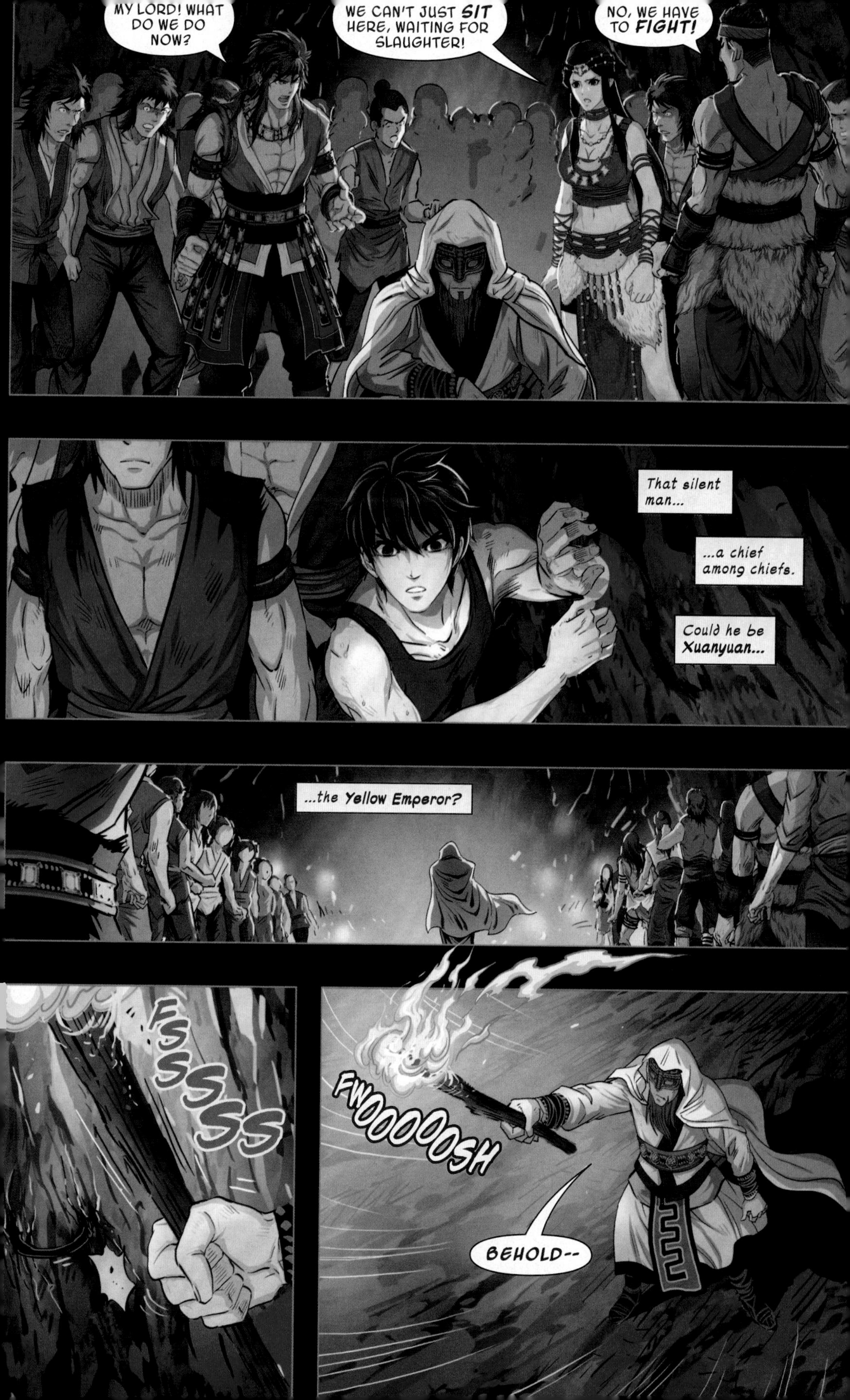
MY LORD! WHAT DO WE DO NOW?
WE CAN'T JUST SIT HERE, WAITING FOR SLAUGHTER!
NO, WE HAVE TO FIGHT!
That silent man...
...a chief among chiefs.
Could he be Xuanyuan...
...the Yellow Emperor?
FSSSSSS
FWOOOOOSH
BEHOLD--

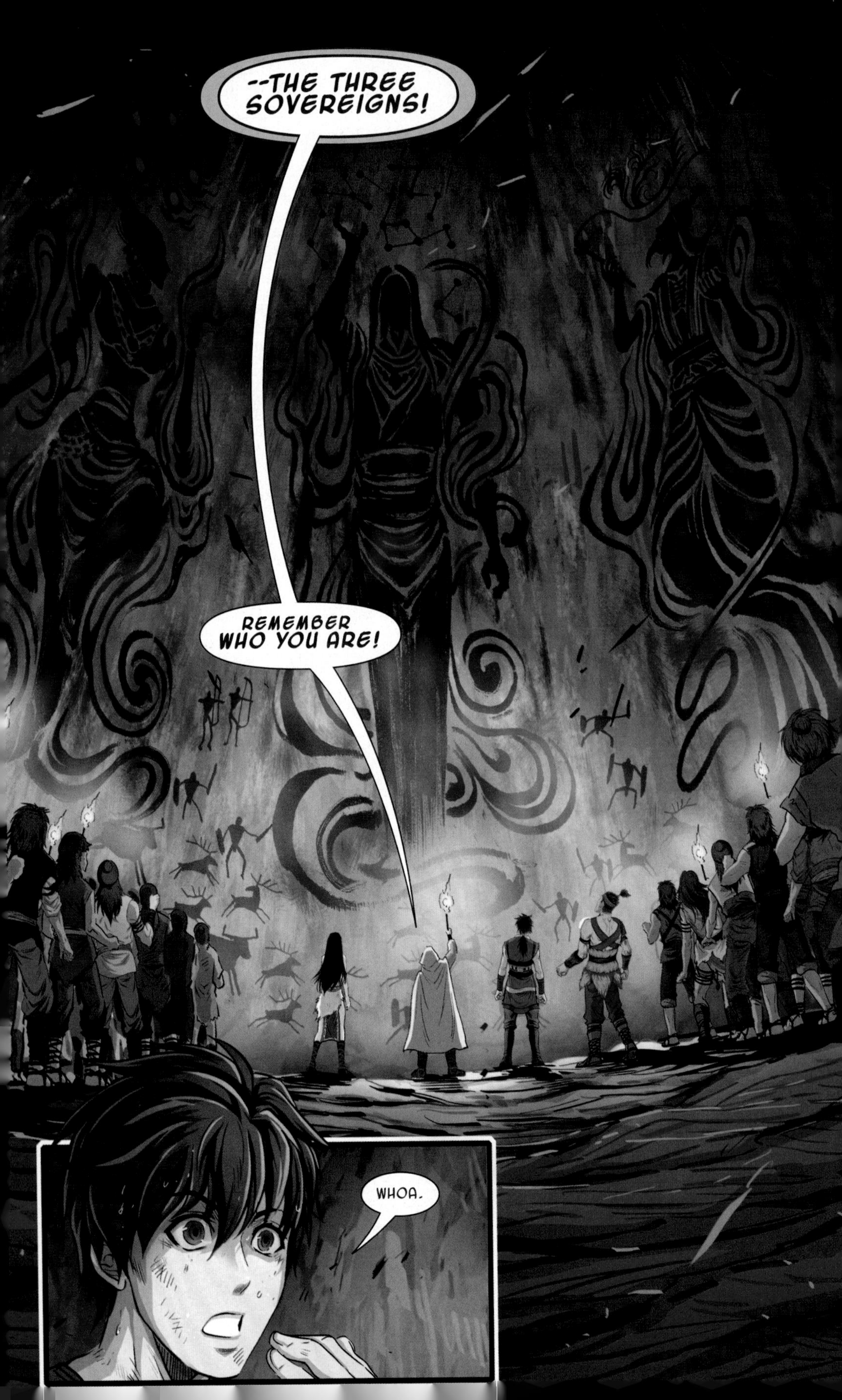
--THE THREE SOVEREIGNS!
REMEMBER WHO YOU ARE!
WHOA.

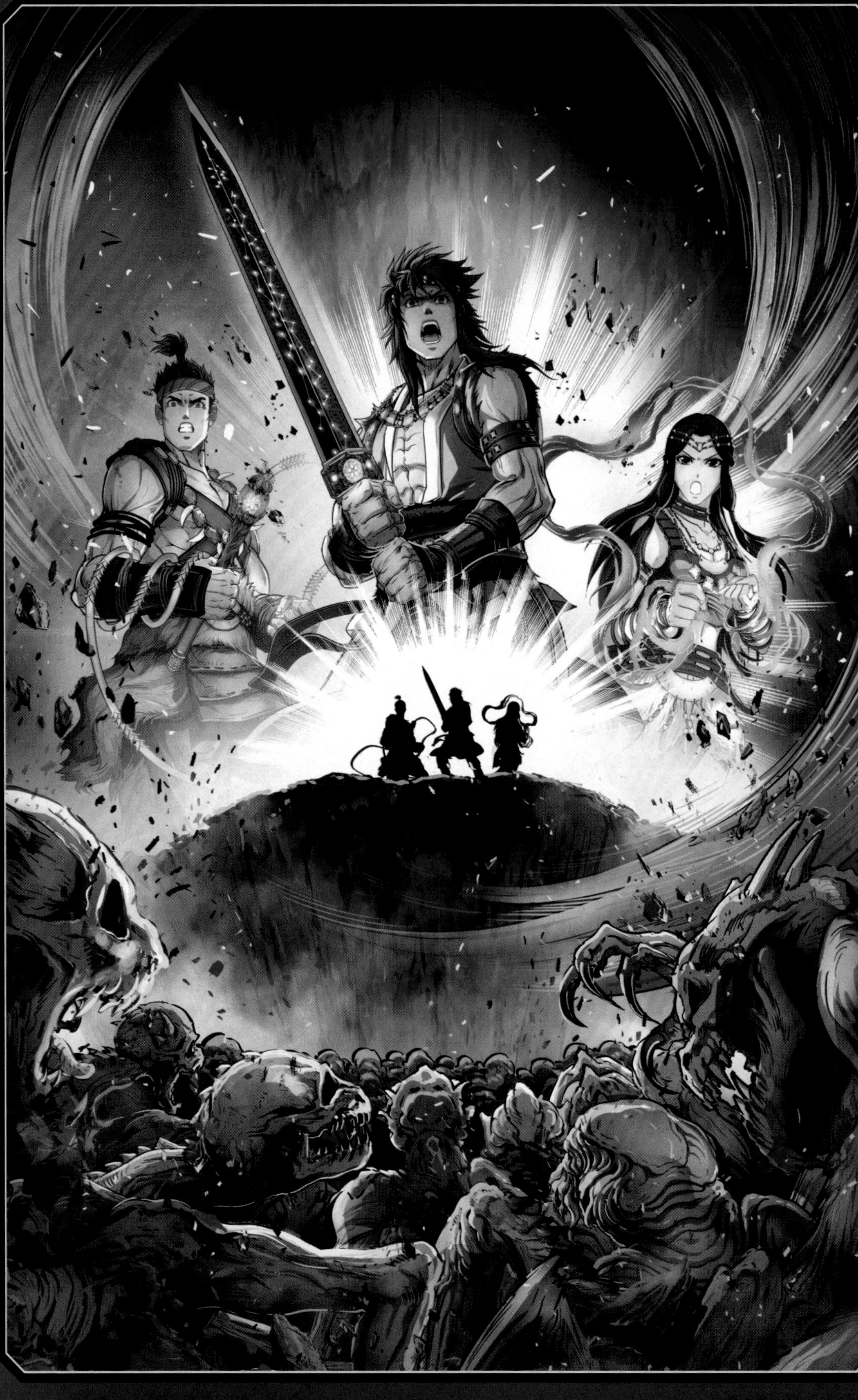

FOUR THE ARTIFACTS

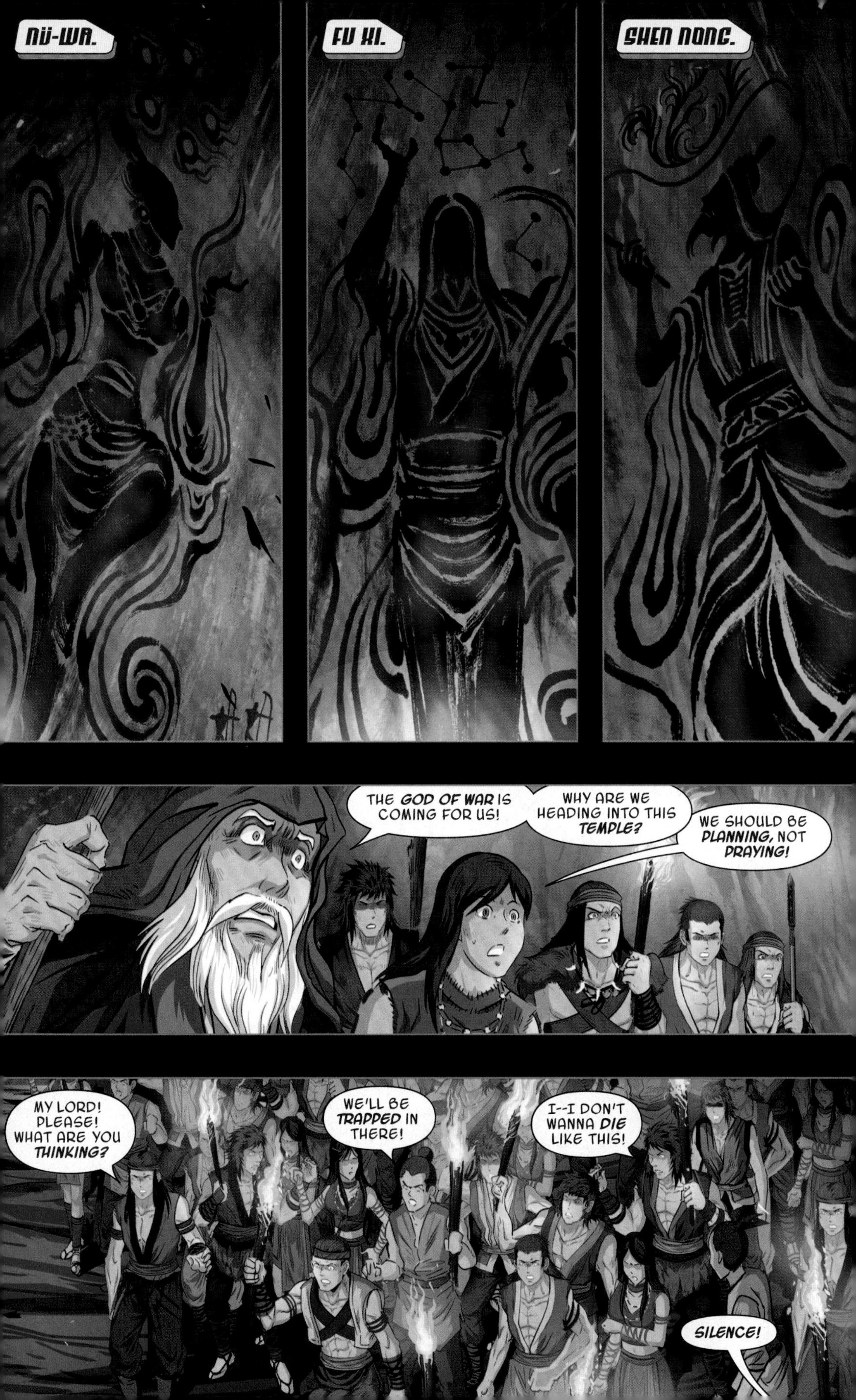
NÜ-WA.
FU XI.
SHEN NONG.
THE GOD OF WAR IS COMING FOR US!
WHY ARE WE HEADING INTO THIS TEMPLE?
WE SHOULD BE PLANNING, NOT PRAYING!
MY LORD! PLEASE! WHAT ARE YOU THINKING?
WE'LL BE TRAPPED IN THERE!
I--I DON'T WANNA DIE LIKE THIS!
SILENCE!

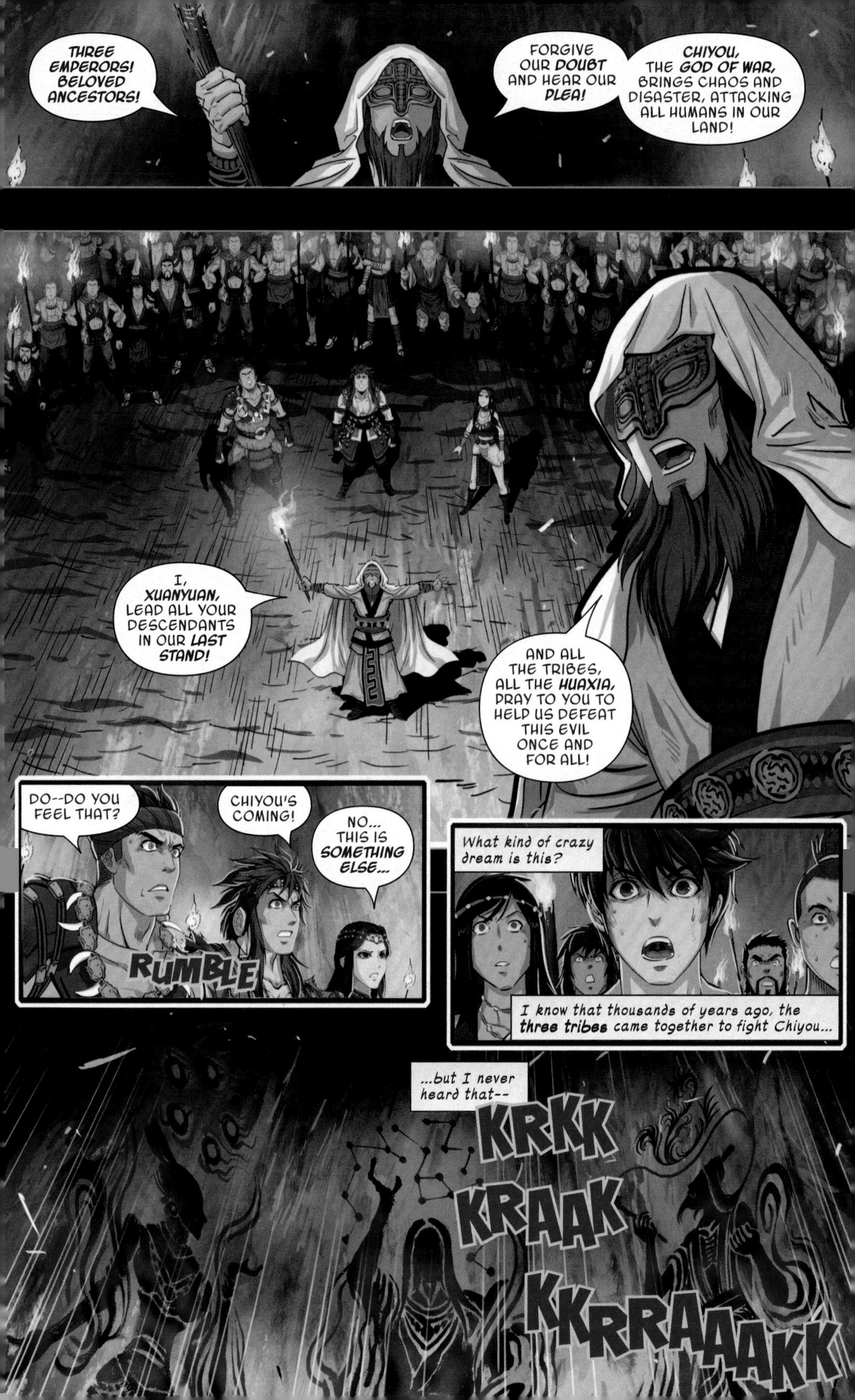
THREE EMPERORS! BELOVED ANCESTORS!
FORGIVE OUR DOUBT AND HEAR OUR PLEA!
CHIYOU, THE GOD OF WAR, BRINGS CHAOS AND DISASTER, ATTACKING ALL HUMANS IN OUR LAND!
I, XUANYUAN, LEAD ALL YOUR DESCENDANTS IN OUR LAST STAND!
AND ALL THE TRIBES, ALL THE HUAXIA, PRAY TO YOU TO HELP US DEFEAT THIS EVIL ONCE AND FOR ALL!
DO--DO YOU FEEL THAT?
CHIYOU'S COMING!
NO... THIS IS SOMETHING ELSE...
RUMBLE
What kind of crazy dream is this?
I know that thousands of years ago, the three tribes came together to fight Chiyou...
...but I never heard that--
KRKK
KRAAK
KKRRAAAKK

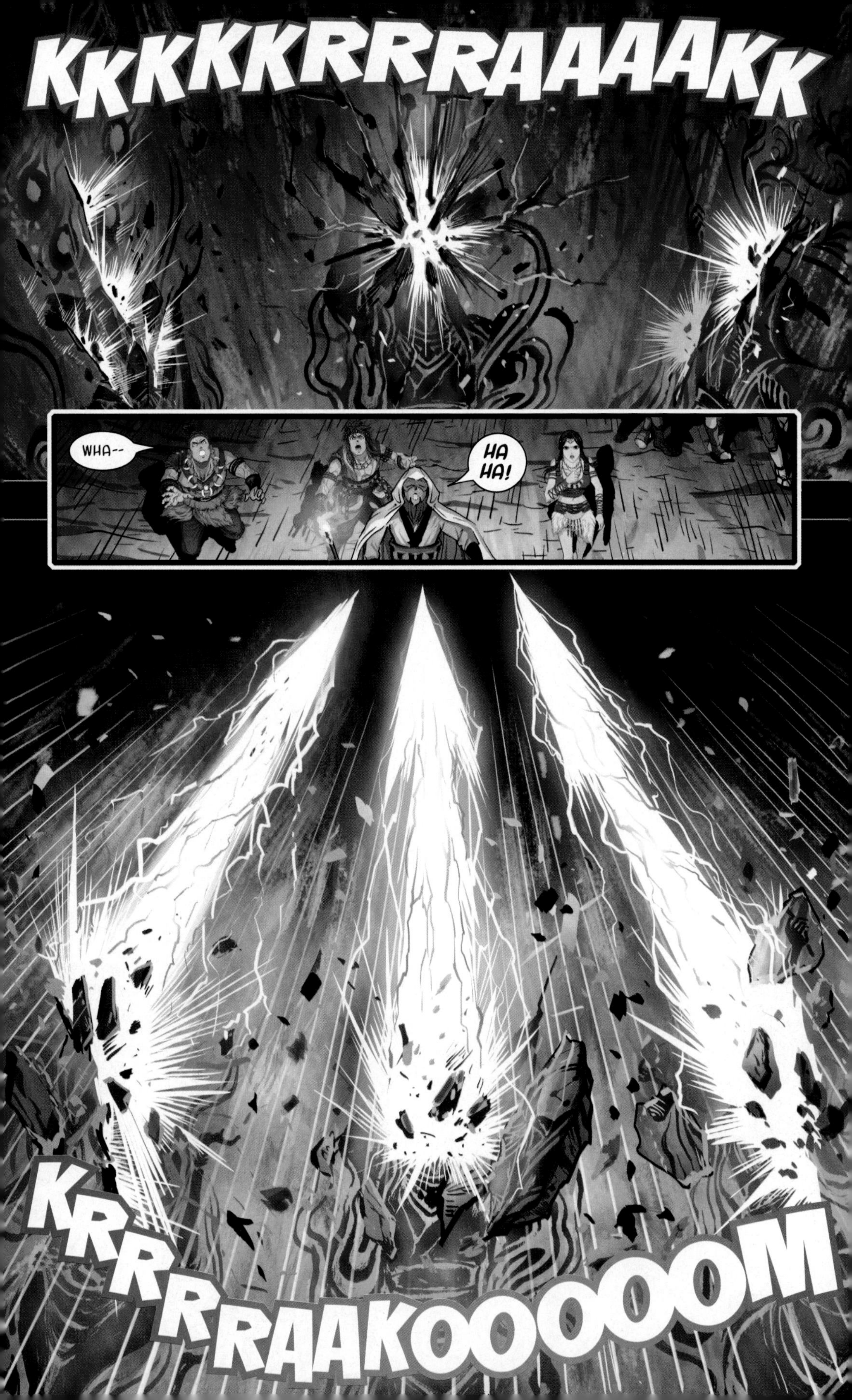
KKKKKRRRRAAAAKK
WHA--
HA HA!
KRRRRRAAKOOOOOOM

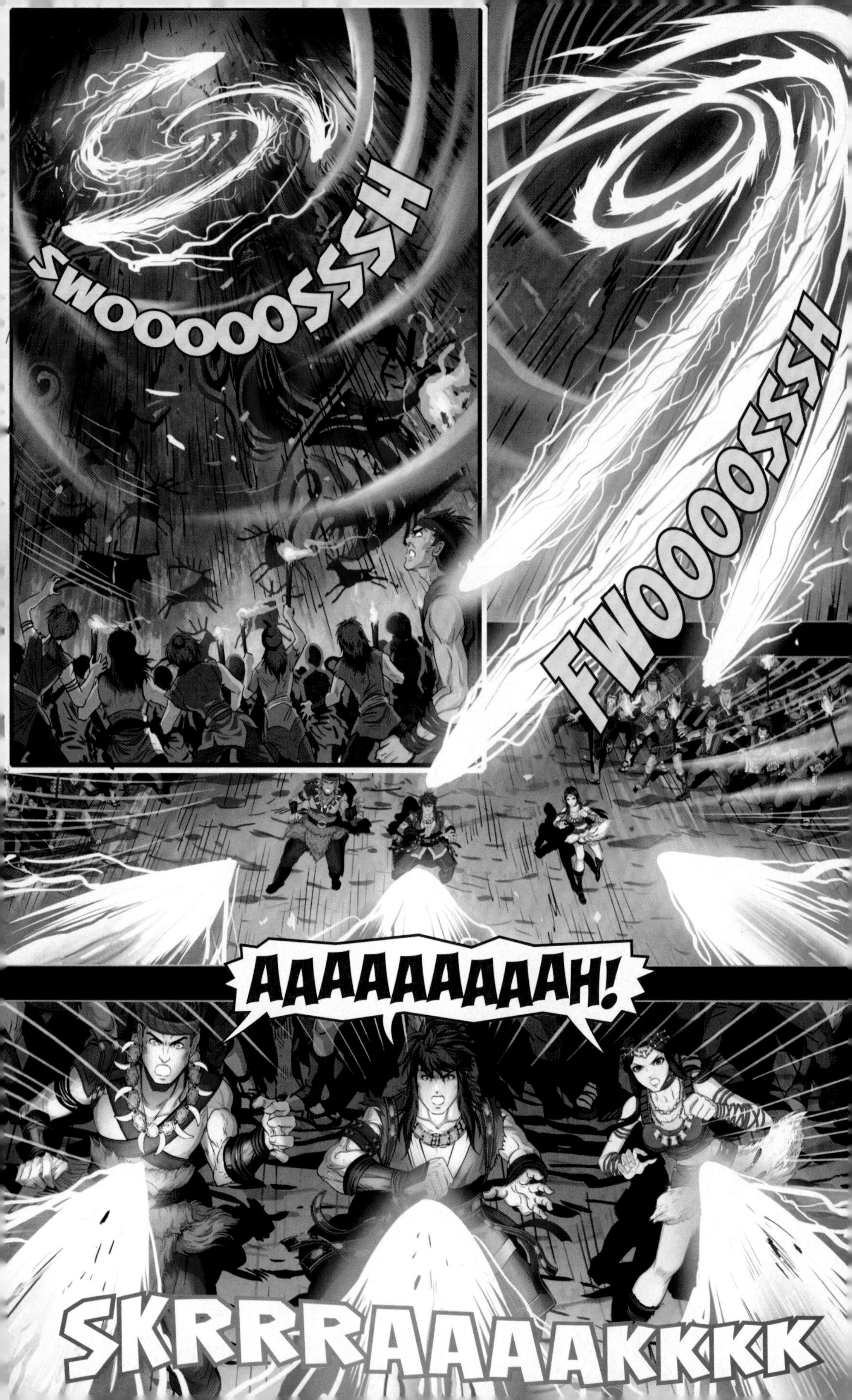
SWOOOOOSSSH
FWOOOOSSSH
AAAAAAAAAH!
SKRRRAAAAKKKK

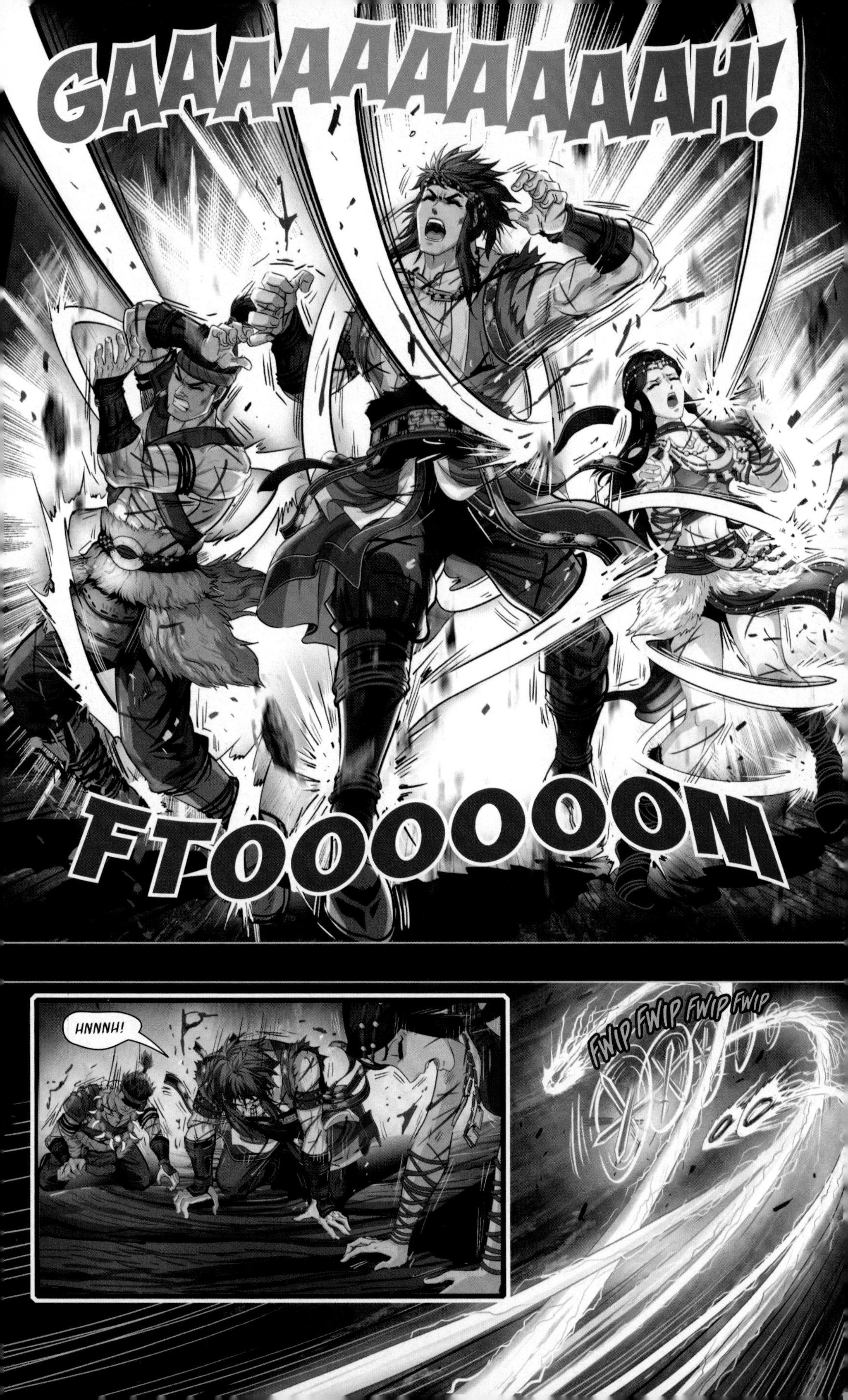
GAAAAAAAAAAH!
FTOOOOOOM
HNNNH!
FWIP FWIP FWIP FWIP

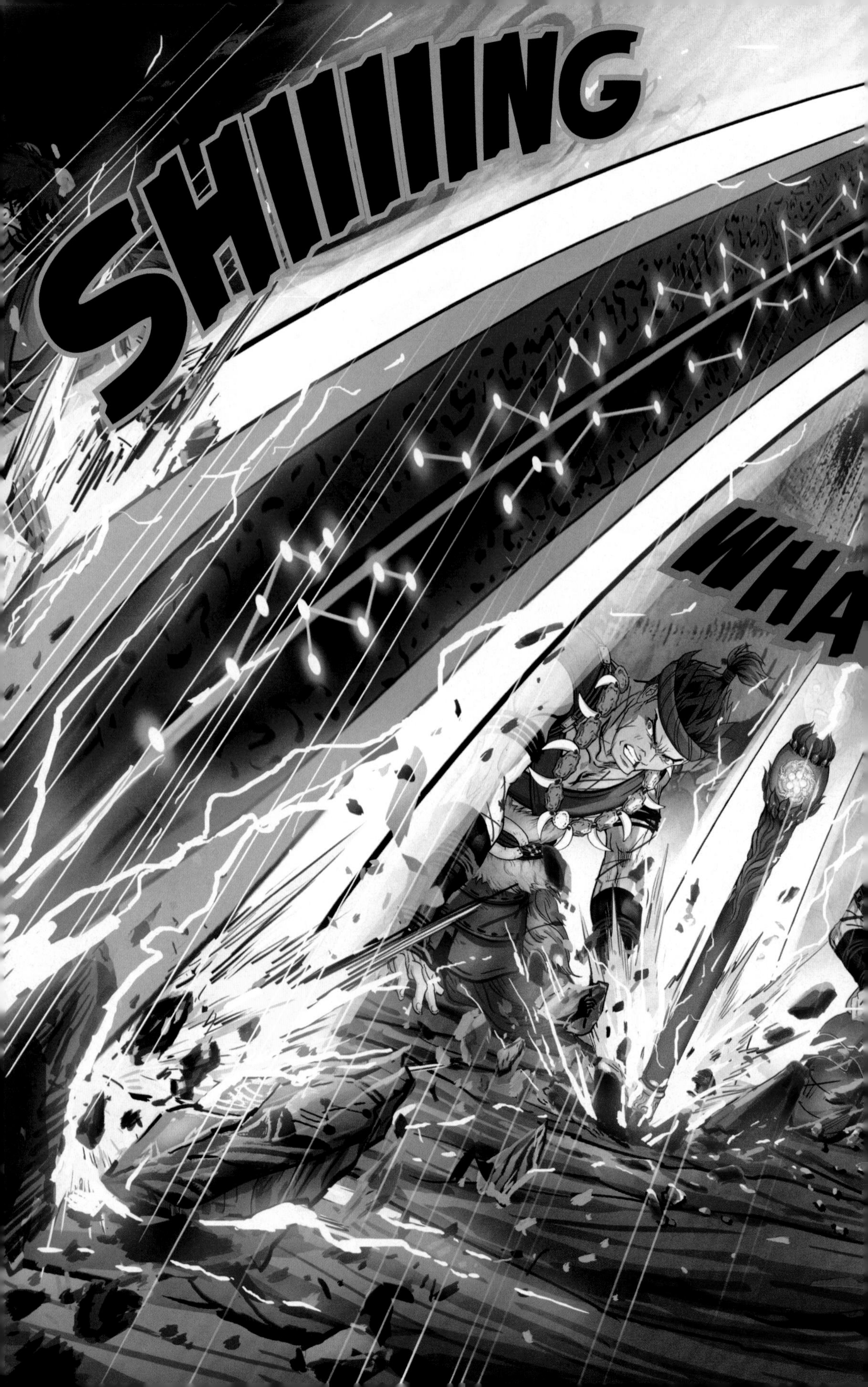
SHIIIIING
WHA

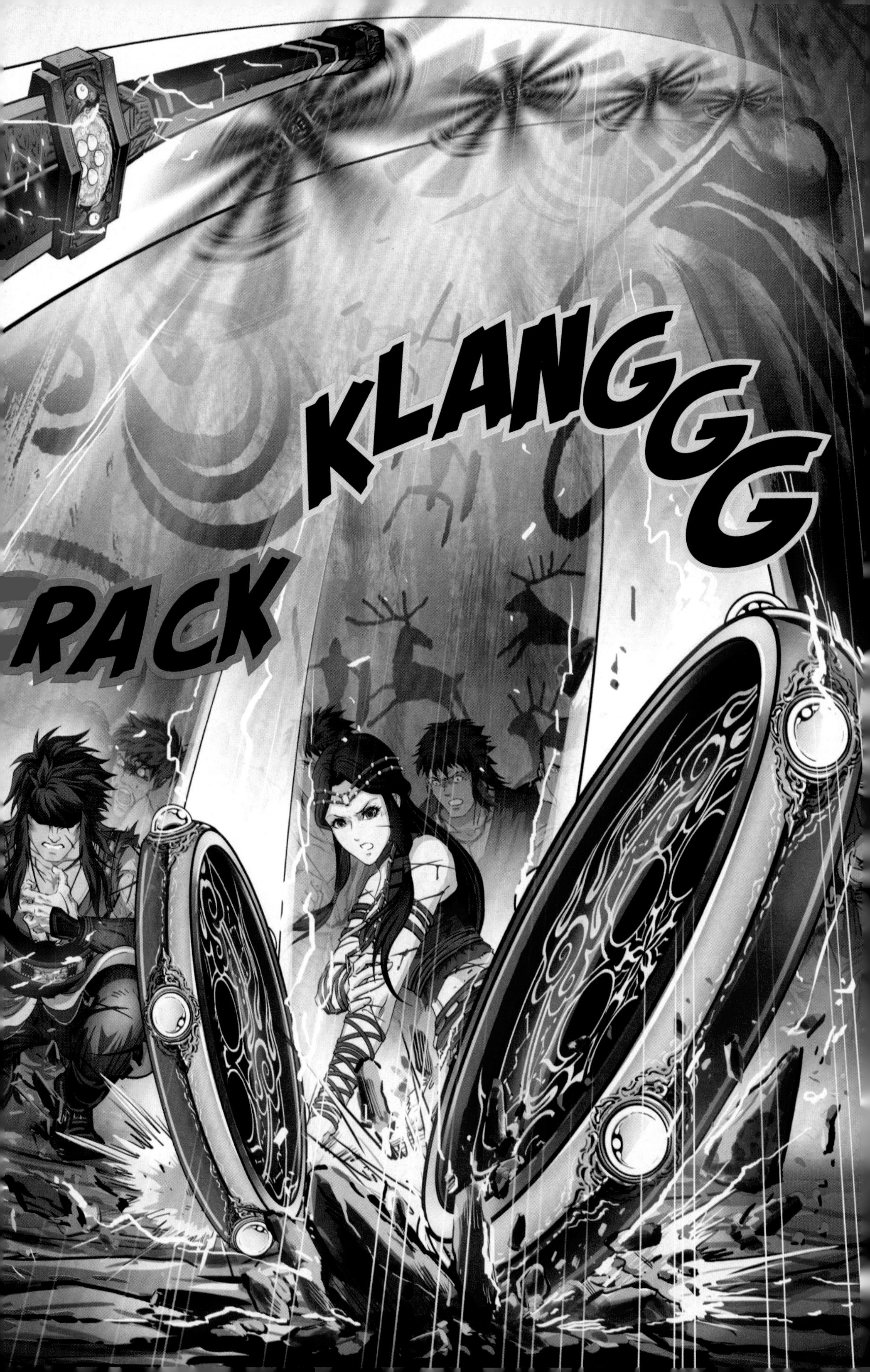
KLANGGG
RACK

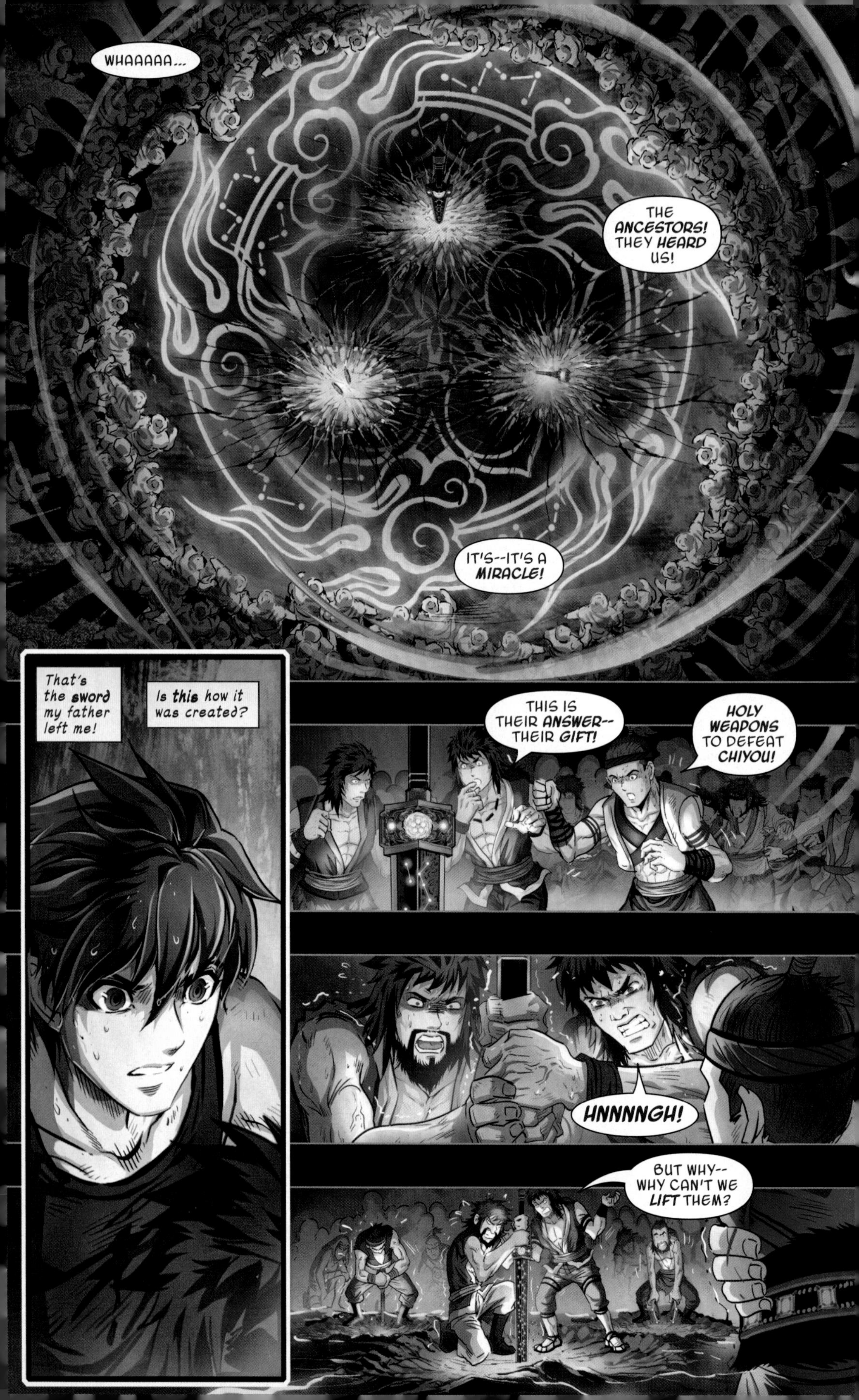
WHAAAAA...
THE ANCESTORS! THEY HEARD US!
IT'S--IT'S A MIRACLE!
That's the sword my father left me!
Is this how it was created?
THIS IS THEIR ANSWER-- THEIR GIFT!
HOLY WEAPONS TO DEFEAT CHIYOU!
HNNNNGH!
BUT WHY-- WHY CAN'T WE LIFT THEM?

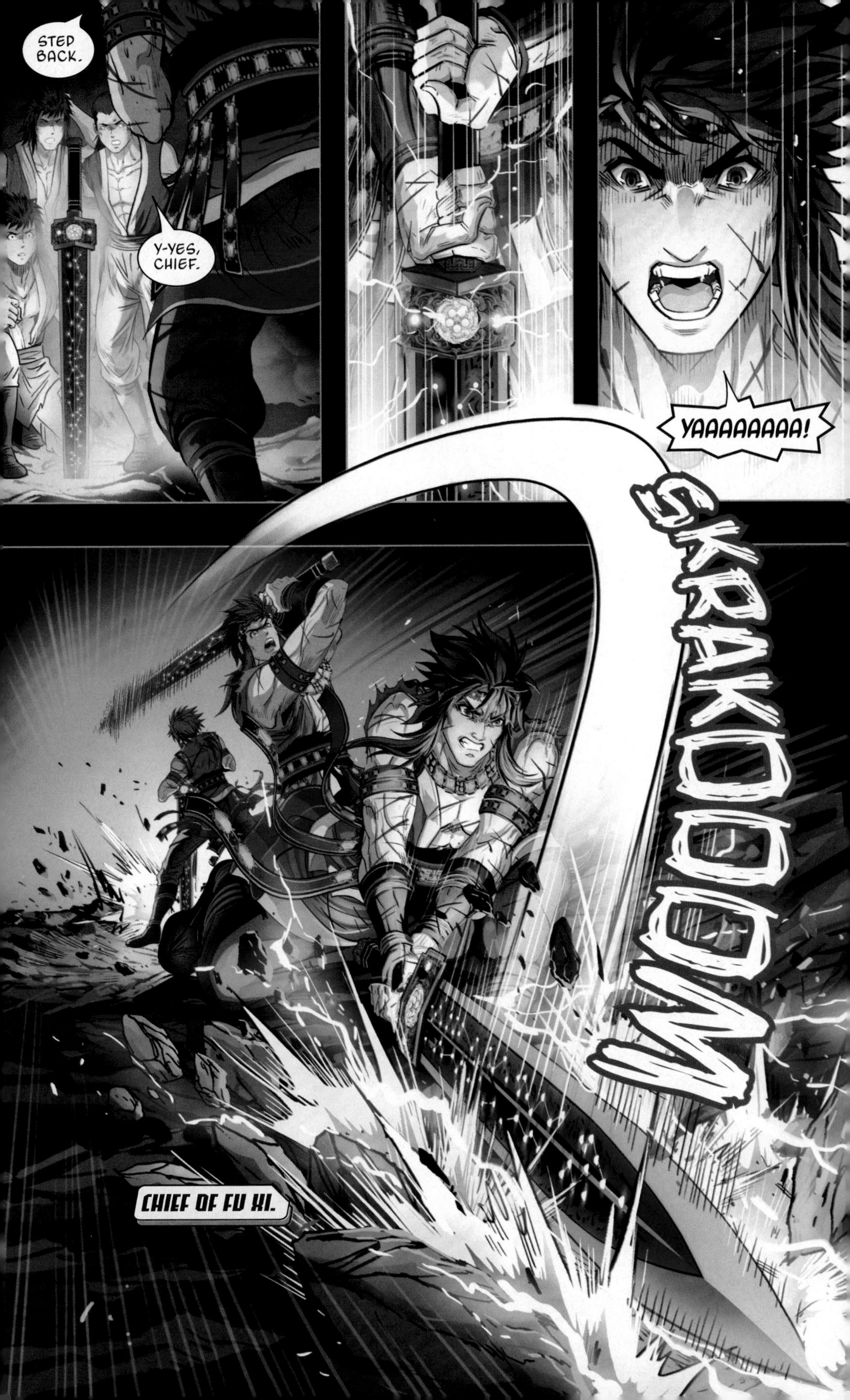
STEP BACK.
Y-YES, CHIEF.
YAAAAAAAA!
SKRAKOOOM
CHIEF OF FU XI.

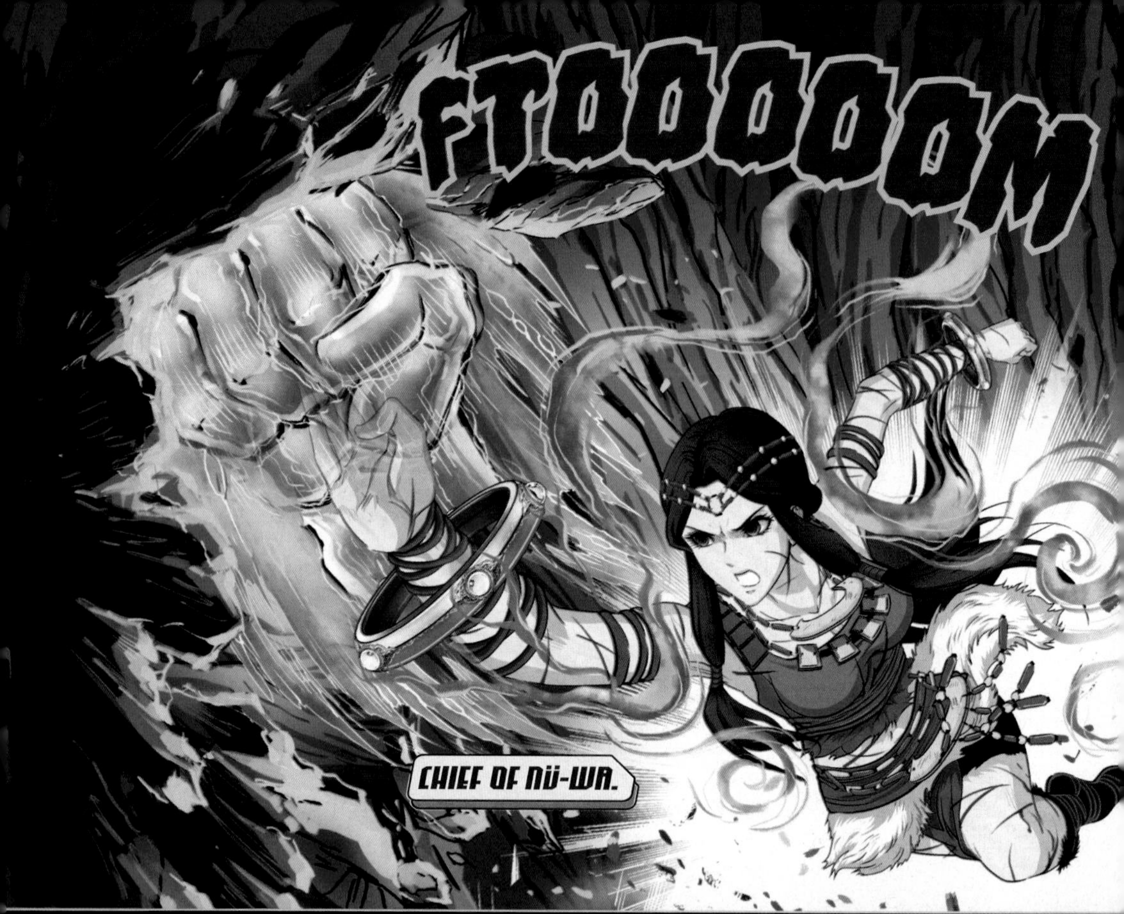
FTOOOOOM
CHIEF OF NÜ-WA.

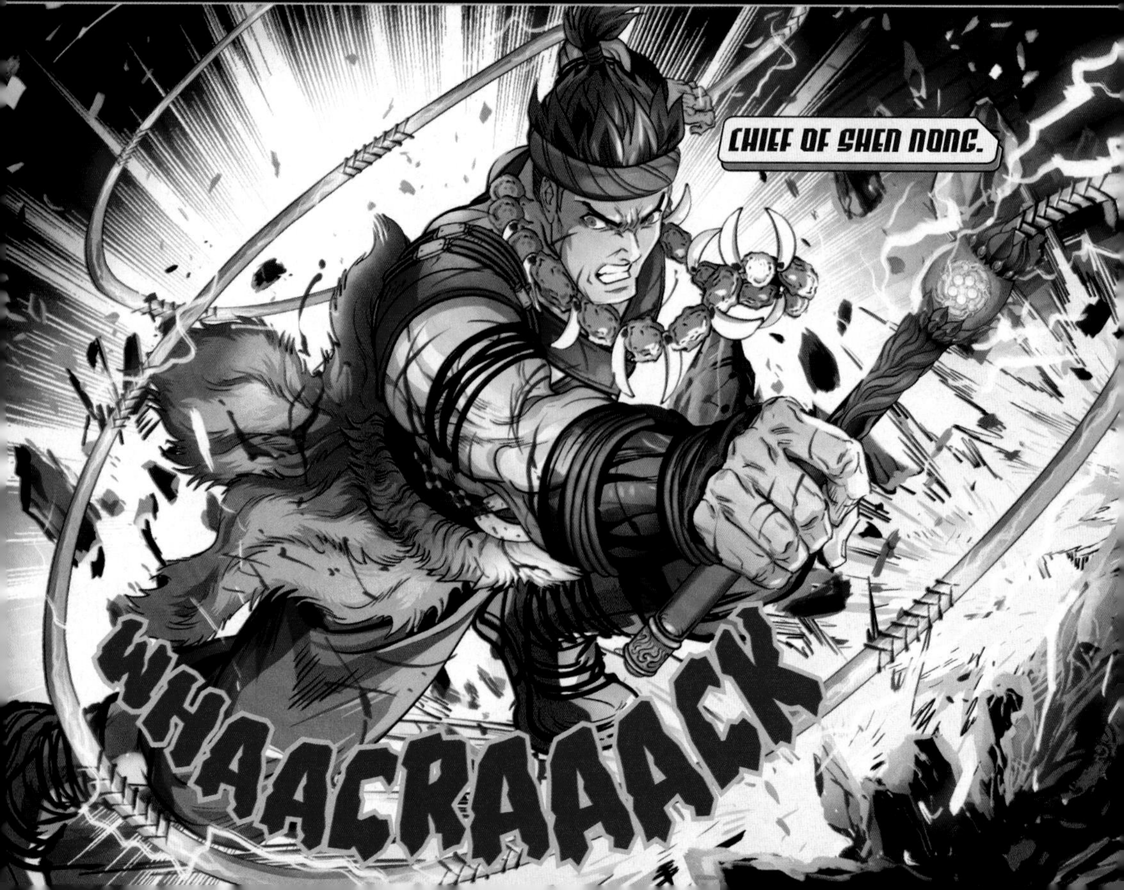
CHIEF OF SHEN NONG.
WHAACRAAACK

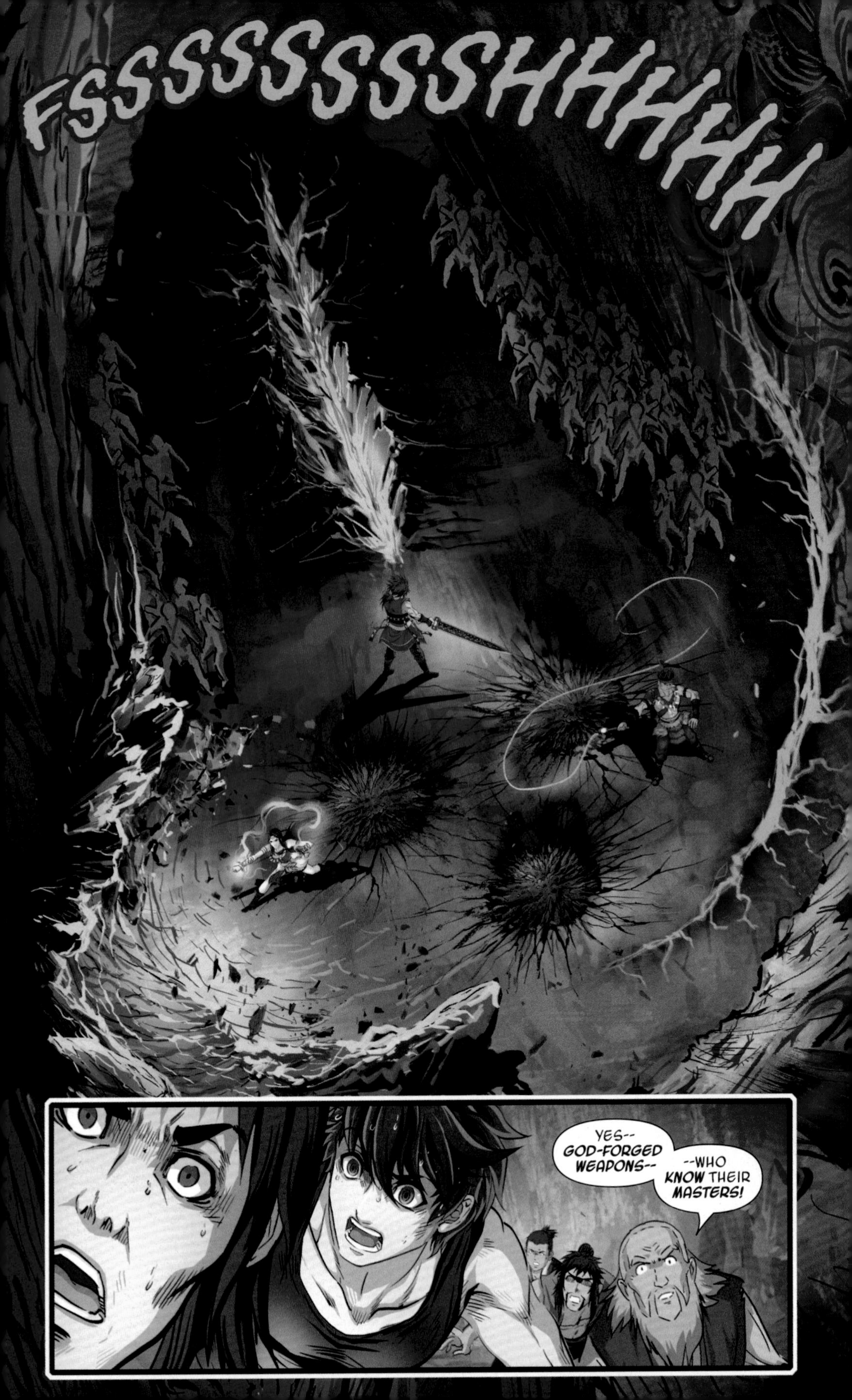
FSSSSSSSSHHHHHH
YES-- GOD-FORGED WEAPONS--
--WHO KNOW THEIR MASTERS!

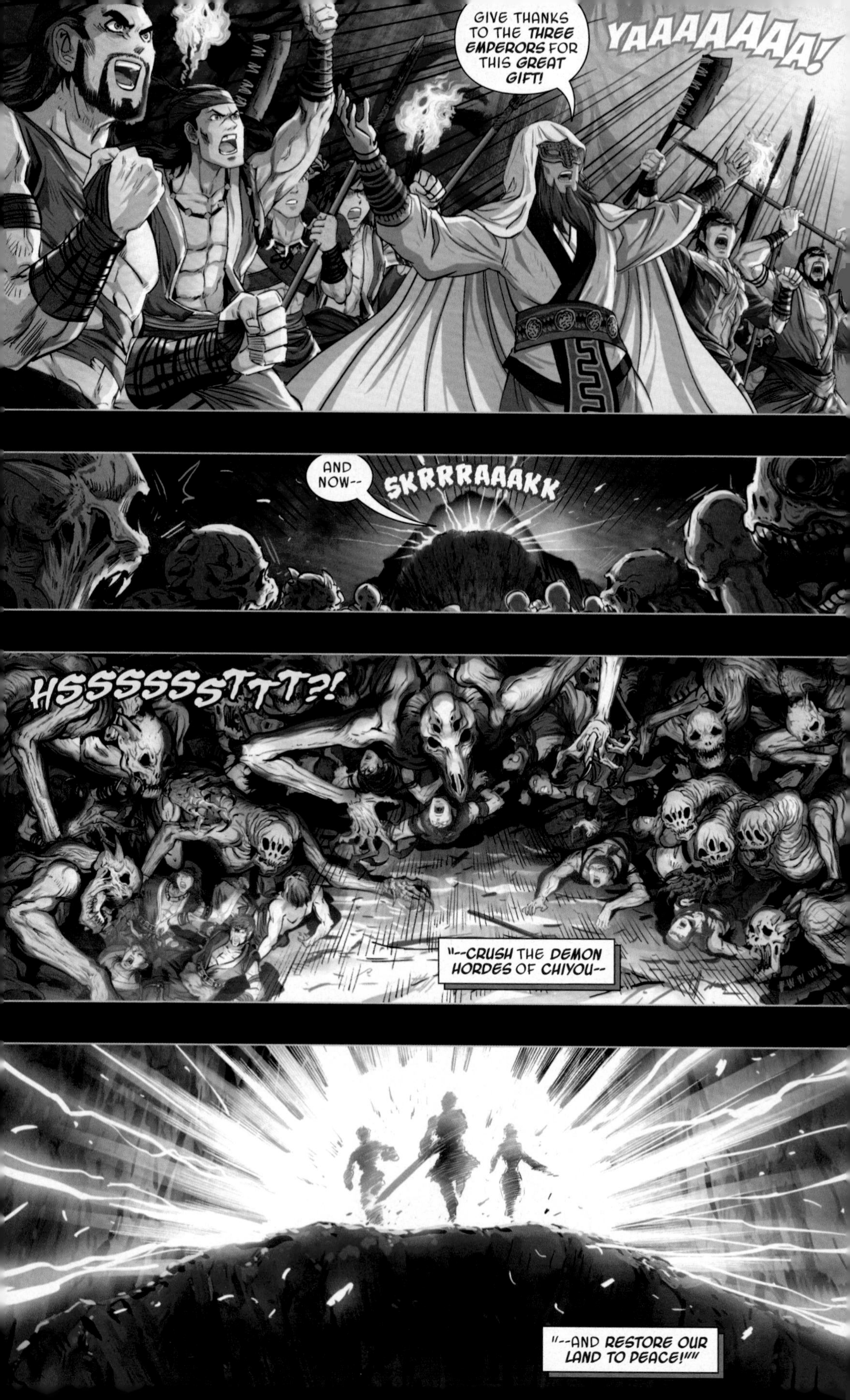
GIVE THANKS TO THE THREE EMPERORS FOR THIS GREAT GIFT!
YAAAAAAA!
AND NOW--
SKRRRAAAKK
HSSSSSSTTTT?!
"--CRUSH THE DEMON HORDES OF CHIYOU--
"--AND RESTORE OUR LAND TO PEACE!'"

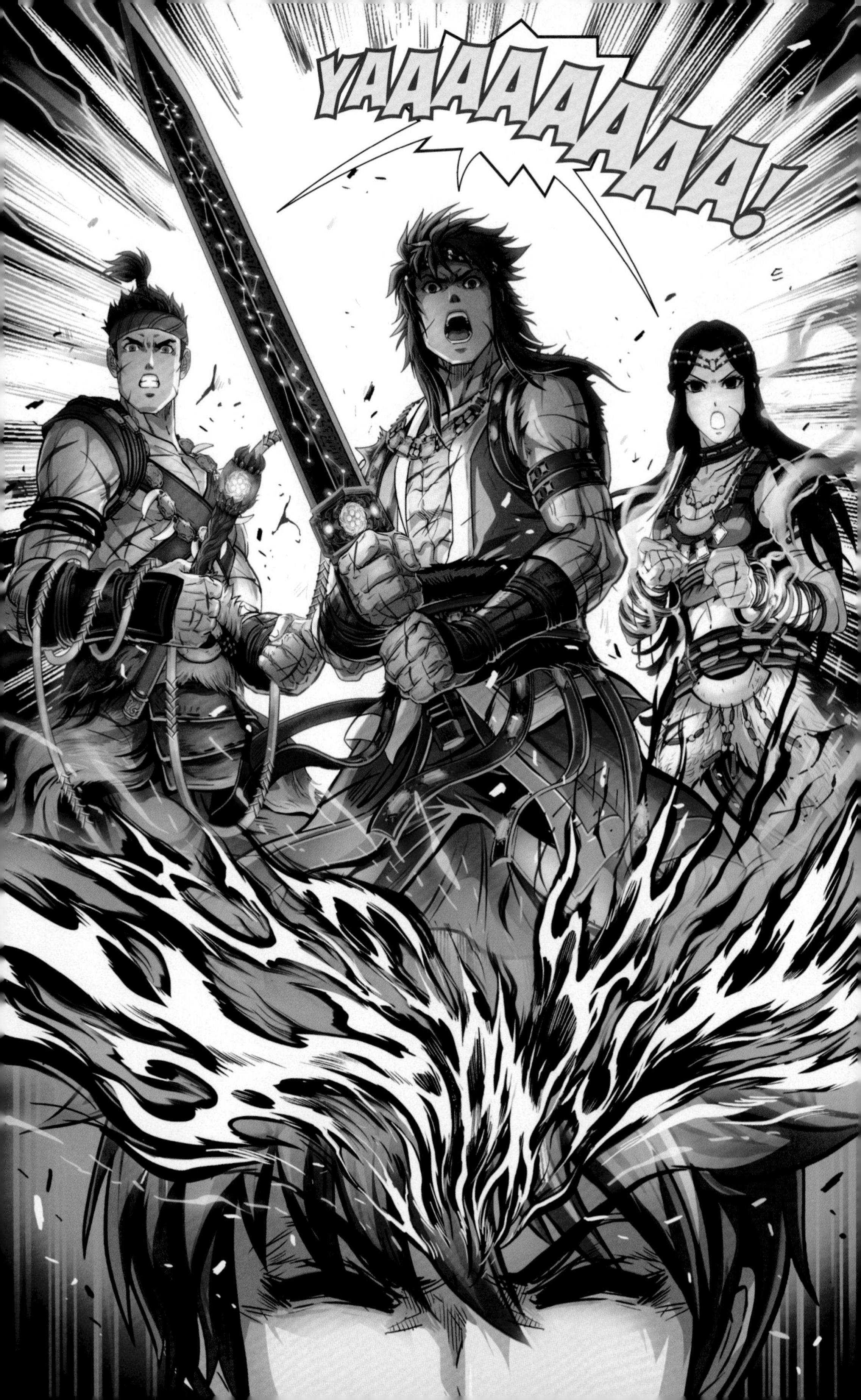
YAAAAAAAAA!

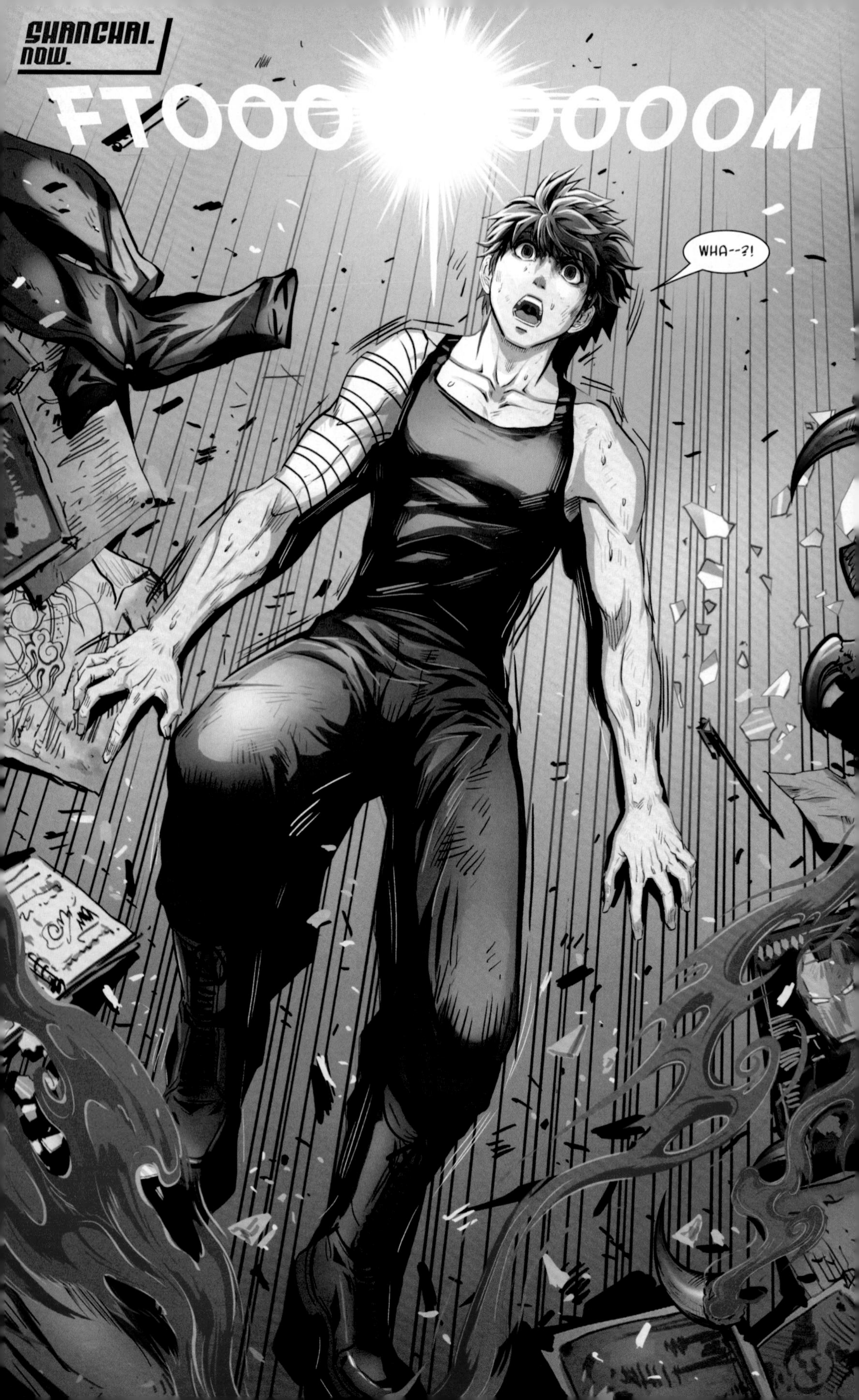
SHANGHAI. NOW.
FTOOO OOOOM
WHA--?!

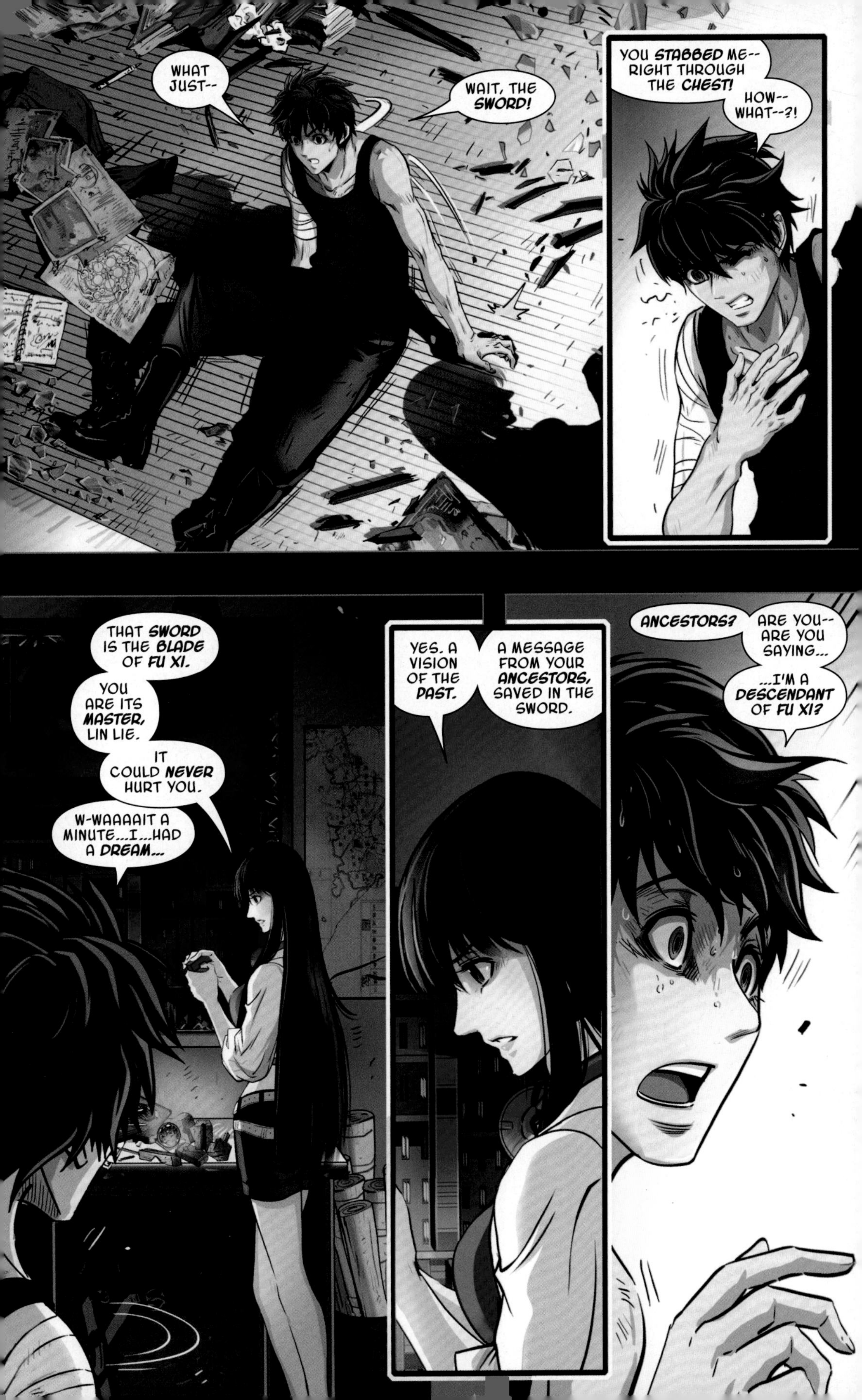
WHAT JUST--
WAIT, THE SWORD!
YOU STABBED ME-- RIGHT THROUGH THE CHEST!
HOW-- WHAT--?!
THAT SWORD IS THE BLADE OF FU XI.
YOU ARE ITS MASTER, LIN LIE.
IT COULD NEVER HURT YOU.
W-WAAAAIT A MINUTE...I...HAD A DREAM...
YES. A VISION OF THE PAST.
A MESSAGE FROM YOUR ANCESTORS, SAVED IN THE SWORD.
ANCESTORS?
ARE YOU-- ARE YOU SAYING...
...I'M A DESCENDANT OF FU XI?

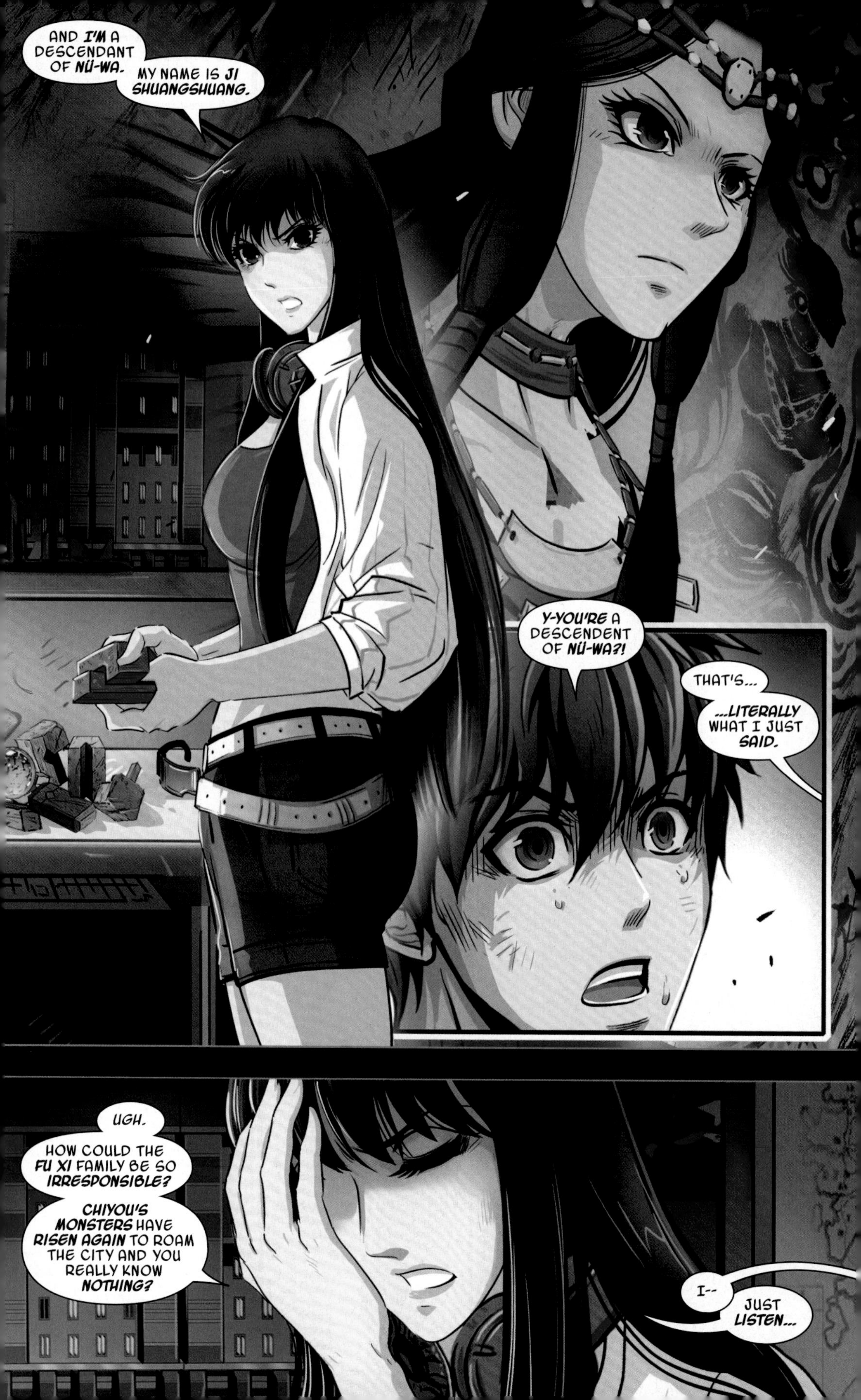
AND I'M A DESCENDANT OF NÜ-WA.
MY NAME IS JI SHUANGSHUANG.
Y-YOU'RE A DESCENDENT OF NÜ-WA?!
THAT'S...
...LITERALLY WHAT I JUST SAID.
UGH.
HOW COULD THE FU XI FAMILY BE SO IRRESPONSIBLE?
CHIYOU'S MONSTERS HAVE RISEN AGAIN TO ROAM THE CITY AND YOU REALLY KNOW NOTHING?
I--
JUST LISTEN...

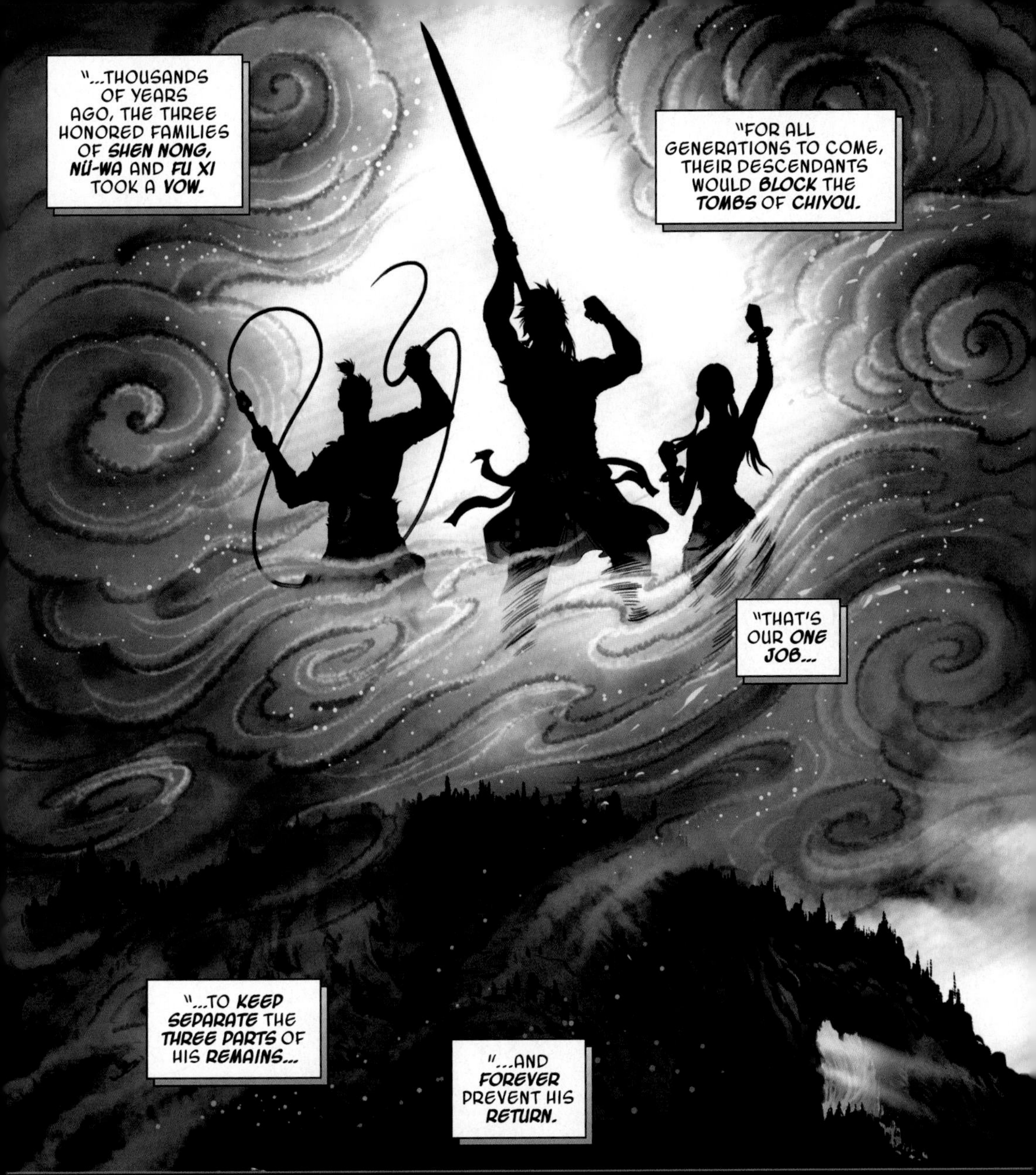
"...THOUSANDS OF YEARS AGO, THE THREE HONORED FAMILIES OF SHEN NONG, NÜ-WA AND FU XI TOOK A VOW.
"FOR ALL GENERATIONS TO COME, THEIR DESCENDANTS WOULD BLOCK THE TOMBS OF CHIYOU.
"THAT'S OUR ONE JOB...
"...TO KEEP SEPARATE THE THREE PARTS OF HIS REMAINS...
"...AND FOREVER PREVENT HIS RETURN.

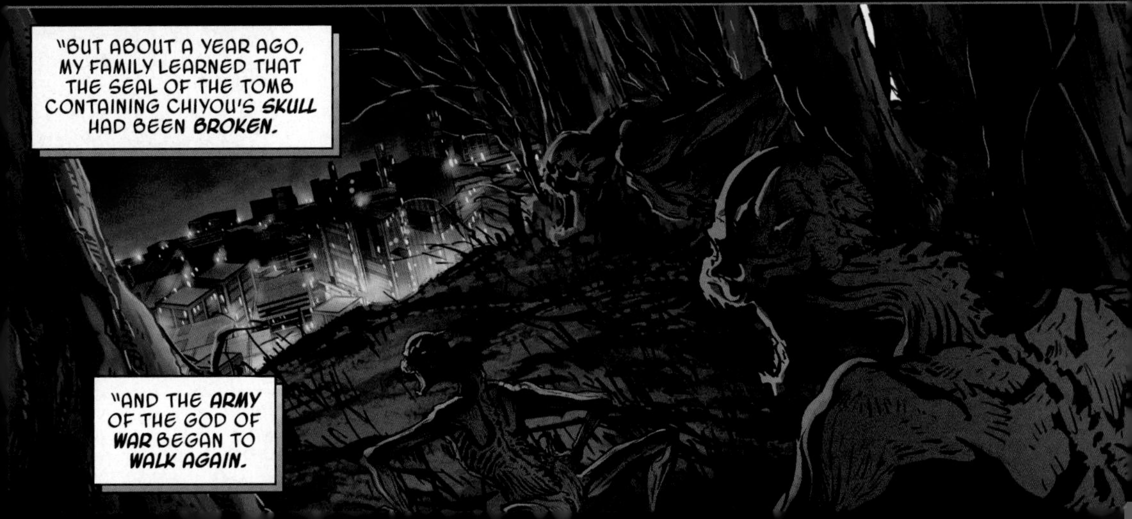
"BUT ABOUT A YEAR AGO, MY FAMILY LEARNED THAT THE SEAL OF THE TOMB CONTAINING CHIYOU'S SKULL HAD BEEN BROKEN.
"AND THE ARMY OF THE GOD OF WAR BEGAN TO WALK AGAIN.

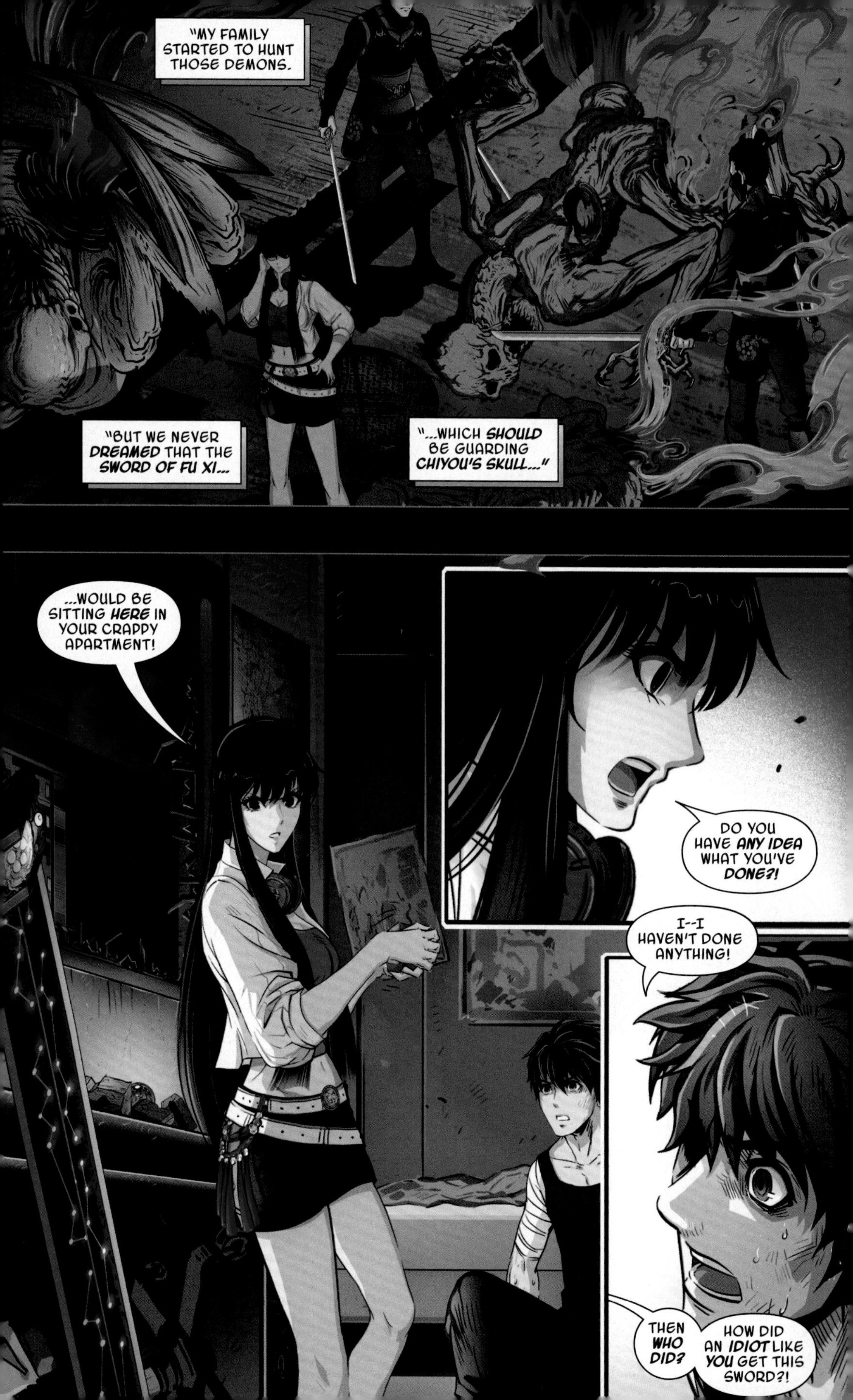
"MY FAMILY STARTED TO HUNT THOSE DEMONS.
"BUT WE NEVER DREAMED THAT THE SWORD OF FU XI...
"...WHICH SHOULD BE GUARDING CHIYOU'S SKULL..."
...WOULD BE SITTING HERE IN YOUR CRAPPY APARTMENT!
DO YOU HAVE ANY IDEA WHAT YOU'VE DONE?!
I--I HAVEN'T DONE ANYTHING!
THEN WHO DID?
HOW DID AN IDIOT LIKE YOU GET THIS SWORD?!

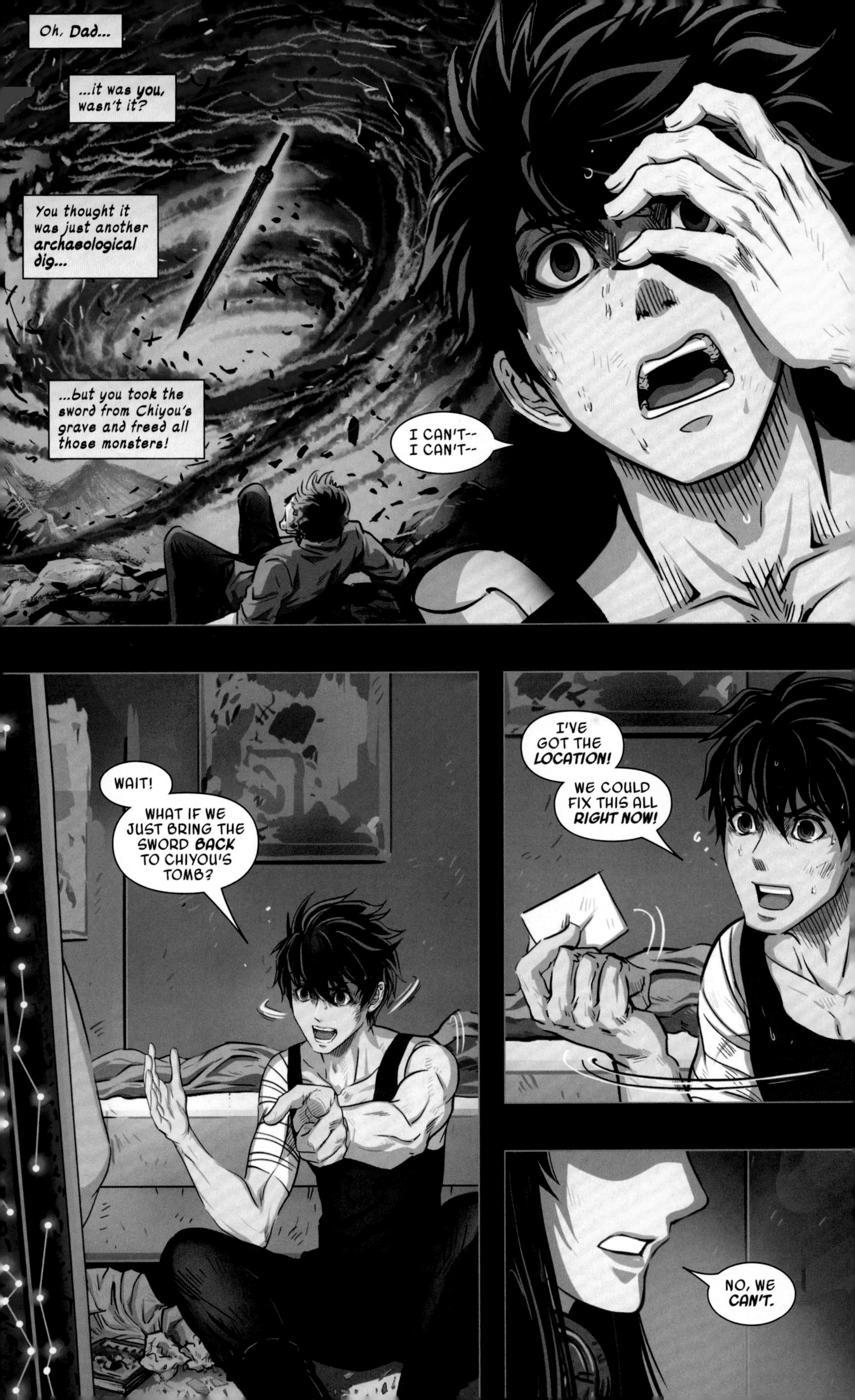

Oh, Dad...
...it was you, wasn't it?
You thought it was just another archaeological dig...
...but you took the sword from Chiyou's grave and freed all those monsters!
I CAN'T-- I CAN'T--
WAIT!
WHAT IF WE JUST BRING THE SWORD BACK TO CHIYOU'S TOMB?
I'VE GOT THE LOCATION!
WE COULD FIX THIS ALL RIGHT NOW!
NO, WE CAN'T.

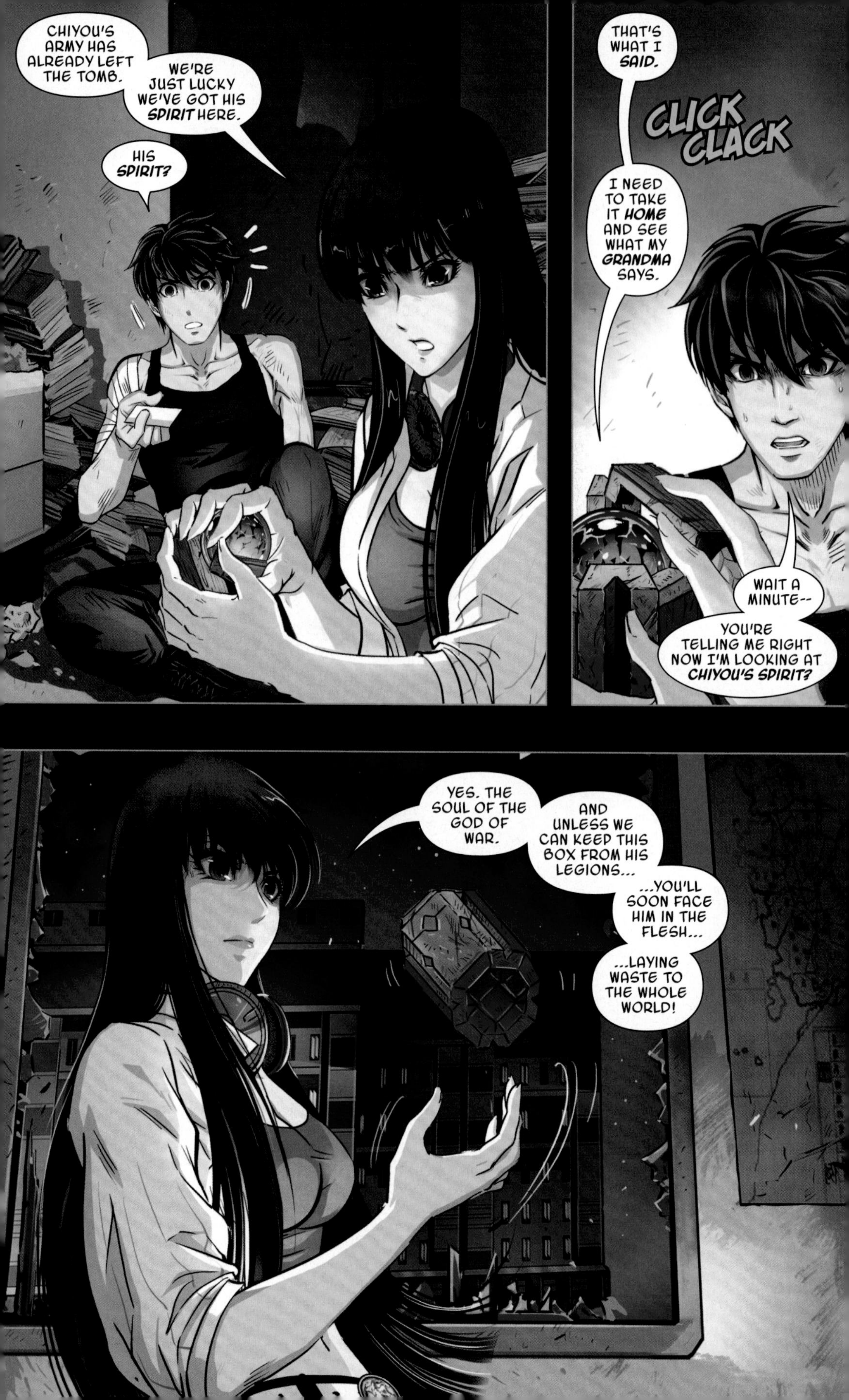
CHIYOU'S ARMY HAS ALREADY LEFT THE TOMB.
WE'RE JUST LUCKY WE'VE GOT HIS SPIRIT HERE.
HIS SPIRIT?
THAT'S WHAT I SAID.
CLICK CLACK
I NEED TO TAKE IT HOME AND SEE WHAT MY GRANDMA SAYS.
WAIT A MINUTE--
YOU'RE TELLING ME RIGHT NOW I'M LOOKING AT CHIYOU'S SPIRIT?
YES. THE SOUL OF THE GOD OF WAR.
AND UNLESS WE CAN KEEP THIS BOX FROM HIS LEGIONS...
...YOU'LL SOON FACE HIM IN THE FLESH...
...LAYING WASTE TO THE WHOLE WORLD!

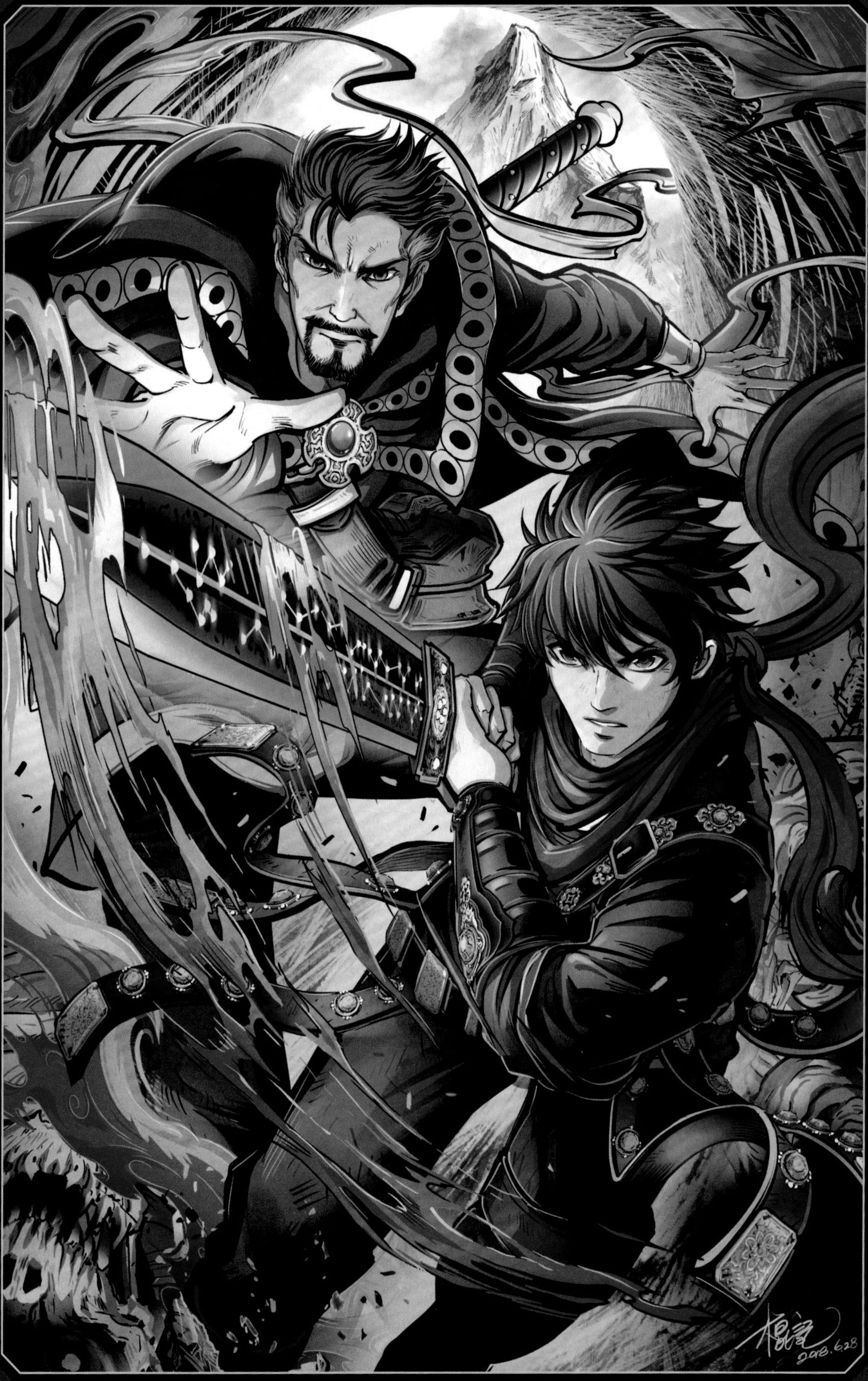

FIVE OBSERVER IN DARKNESS

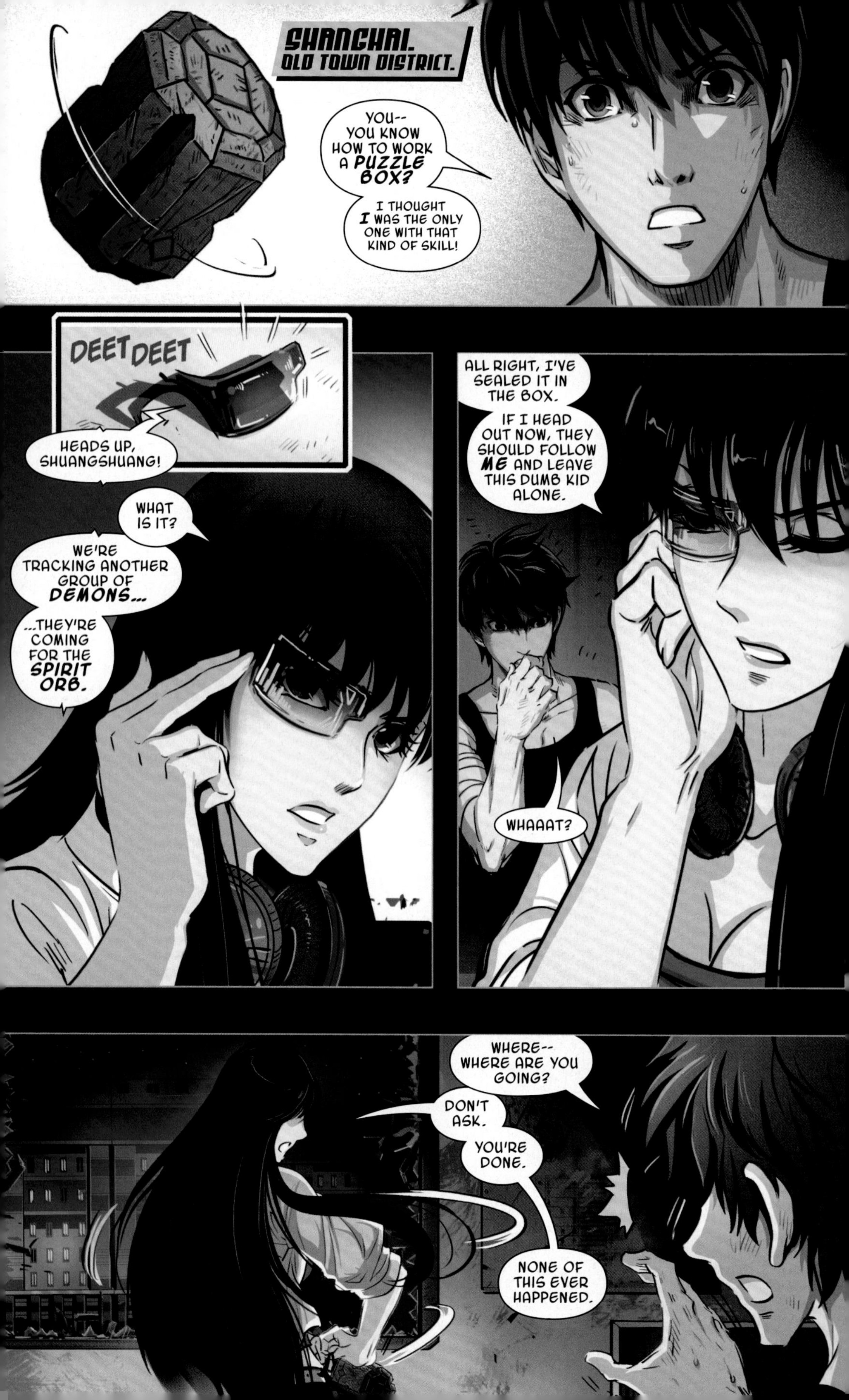
SHANGHAI.
OLD TOWN DISTRICT.
YOU-- YOU KNOW HOW TO WORK A PUZZLE BOX?
I THOUGHT I WAS THE ONLY ONE WITH THAT KIND OF SKILL!
DEET DEET
HEADS UP, SHUANGSHUANG!
WHAT IS IT?
WE'RE TRACKING ANOTHER GROUP OF DEMONS...
...THEY'RE COMING FOR THE SPIRIT ORB.
ALL RIGHT, I'VE SEALED IT IN THE BOX.
IF I HEAD OUT NOW, THEY SHOULD FOLLOW ME AND LEAVE THIS DUMB KID ALONE.
WHAAAT?
WHERE-- WHERE ARE YOU GOING?
DON'T ASK.
YOU'RE DONE.
NONE OF THIS EVER HAPPENED.

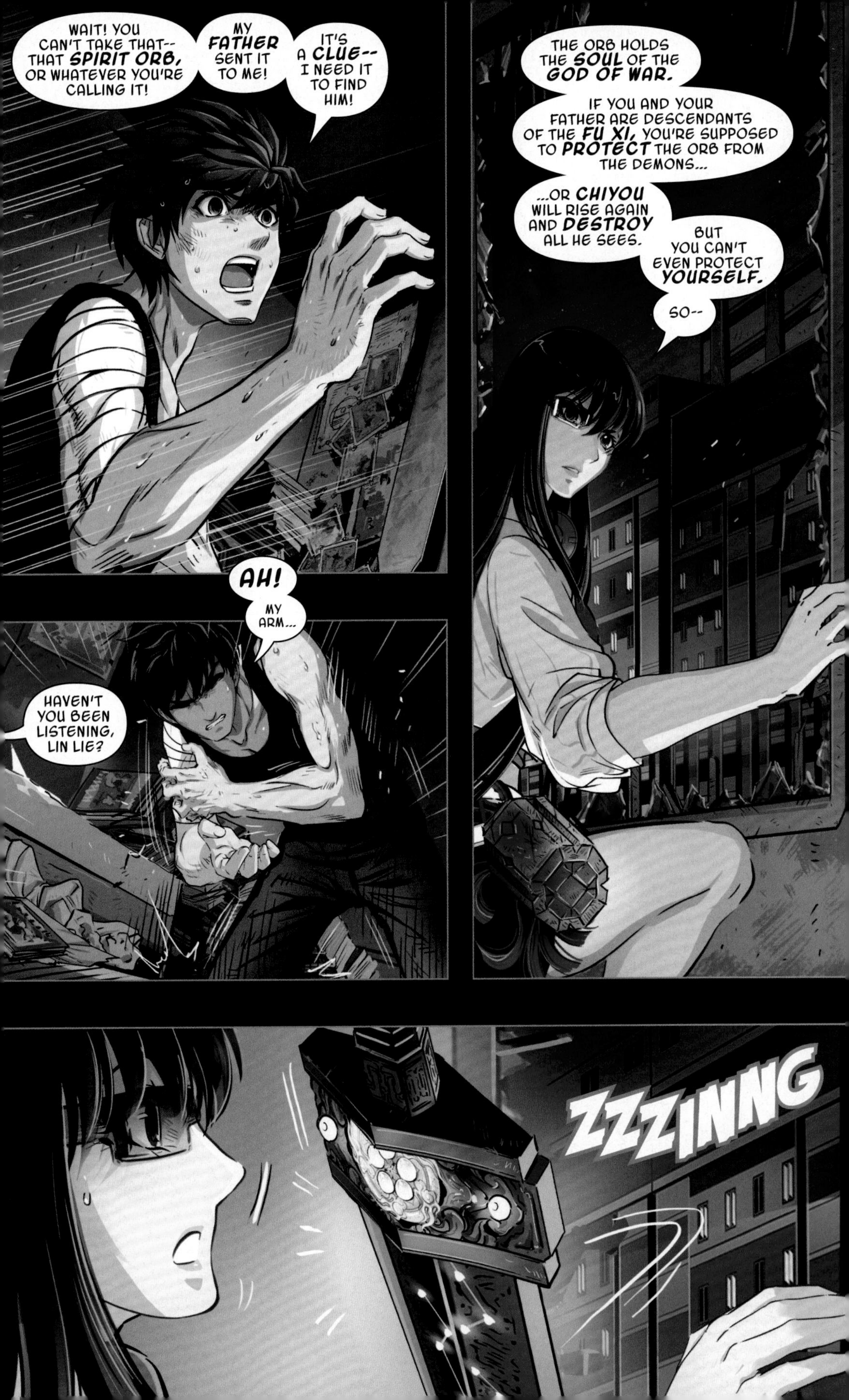
WAIT! YOU CAN'T TAKE THAT-- THAT SPIRIT ORB, OR WHATEVER YOU'RE CALLING IT!
MY FATHER SENT IT TO ME!
IT'S A CLUE-- I NEED IT TO FIND HIM!
THE ORB HOLDS THE SOUL OF THE GOD OF WAR.
IF YOU AND YOUR FATHER ARE DESCENDANTS OF THE FU XI, YOU'RE SUPPOSED TO PROTECT THE ORB FROM THE DEMONS...
...OR CHIYOU WILL RISE AGAIN AND DESTROY ALL HE SEES.
BUT YOU CAN'T EVEN PROTECT YOURSELF.
SO--
AH!
MY ARM...
HAVEN'T YOU BEEN LISTENING, LIN LIE?
ZZZINNG

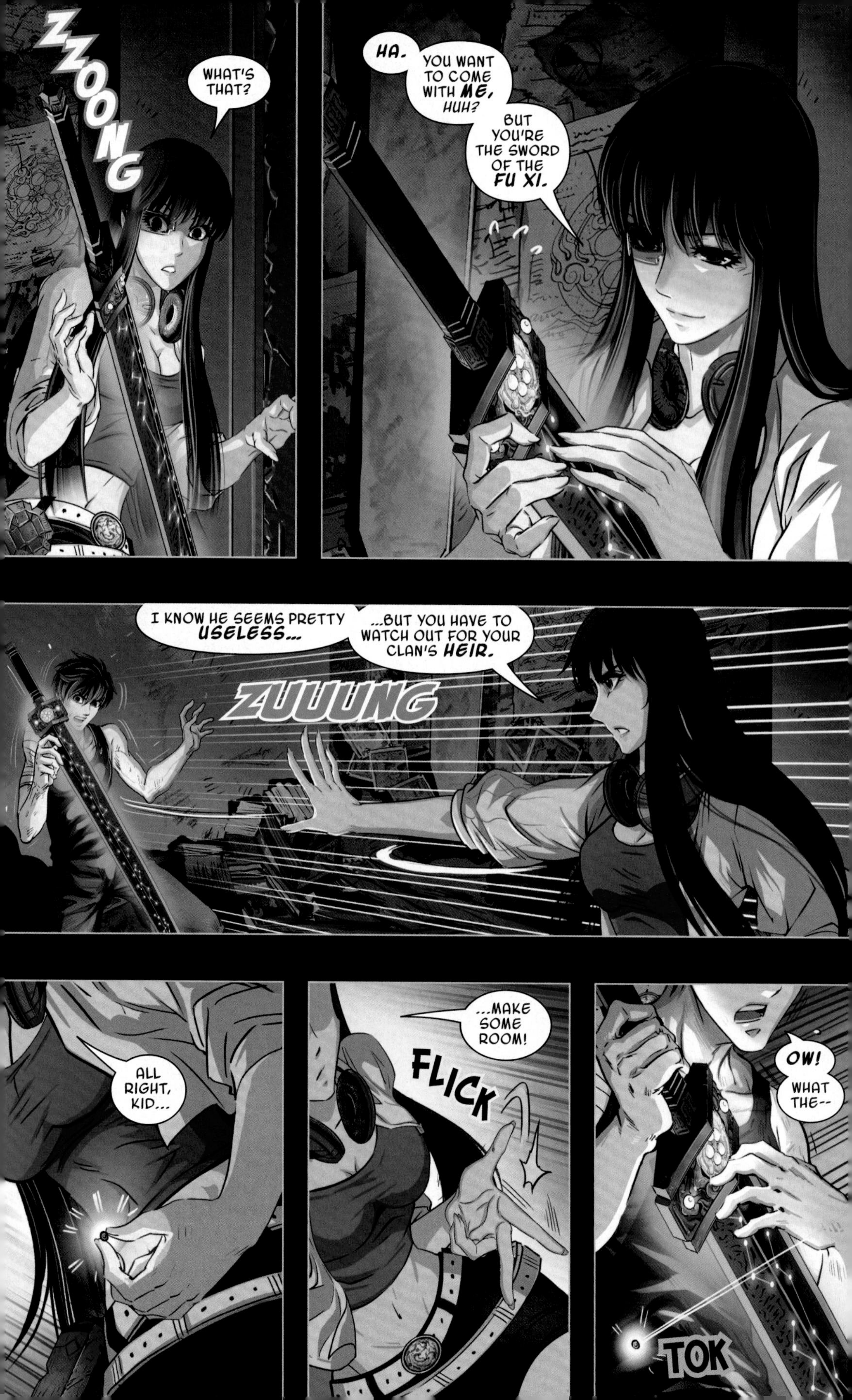
ZZOONG
WHAT'S THAT?
HA.
YOU WANT TO COME WITH ME, HUH?
BUT YOU'RE THE SWORD OF THE FU XI.
I KNOW HE SEEMS PRETTY USELESS...
...BUT YOU HAVE TO WATCH OUT FOR YOUR CLAN'S HEIR.
ZUUUNG
ALL RIGHT, KID...
...MAKE SOME ROOM!
FLICK
OW!
WHAT THE--
TOK

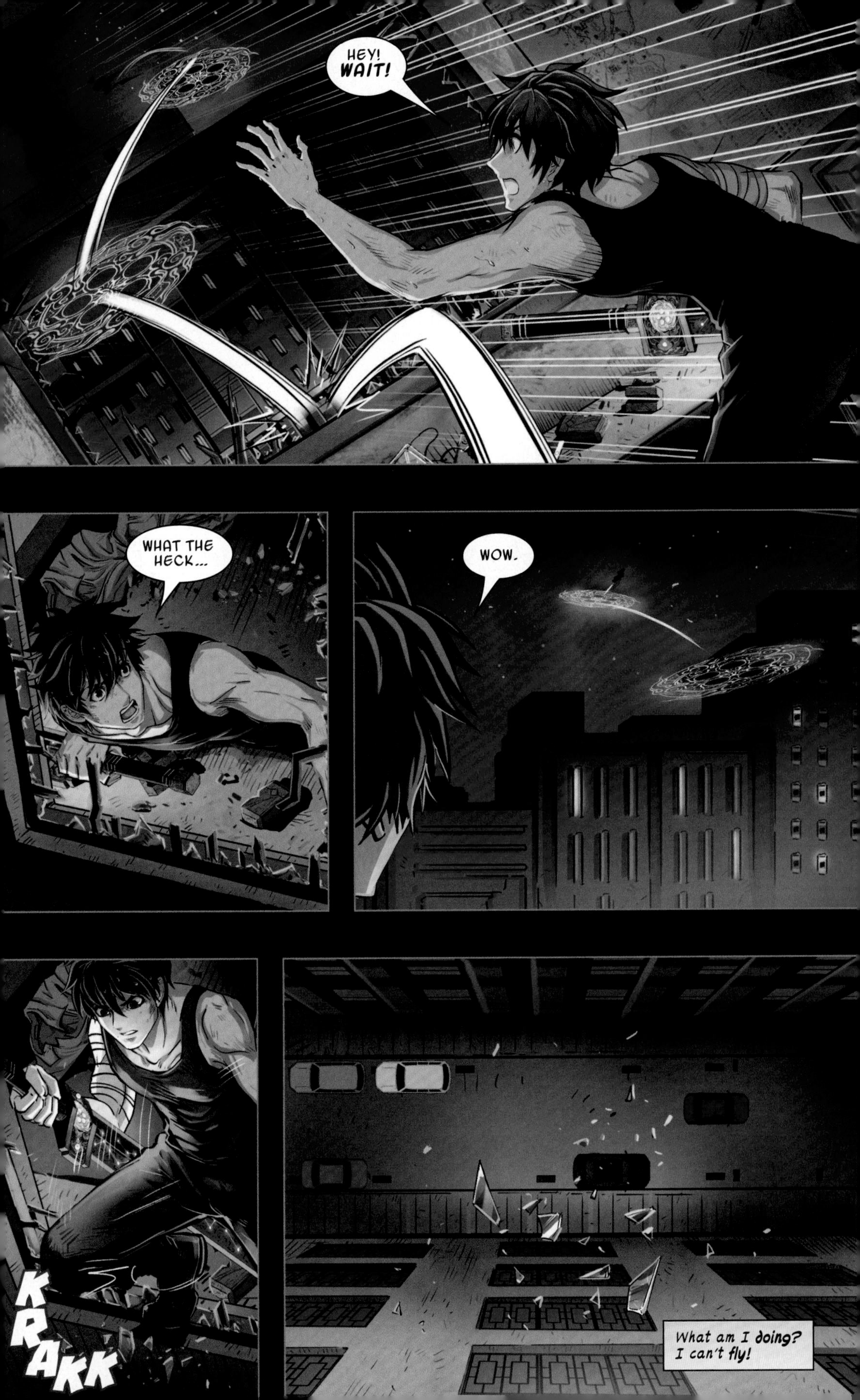
HEY! WAIT!
WHAT THE HECK...
WOW.
KRAKK
What am I doing? I can't fly!

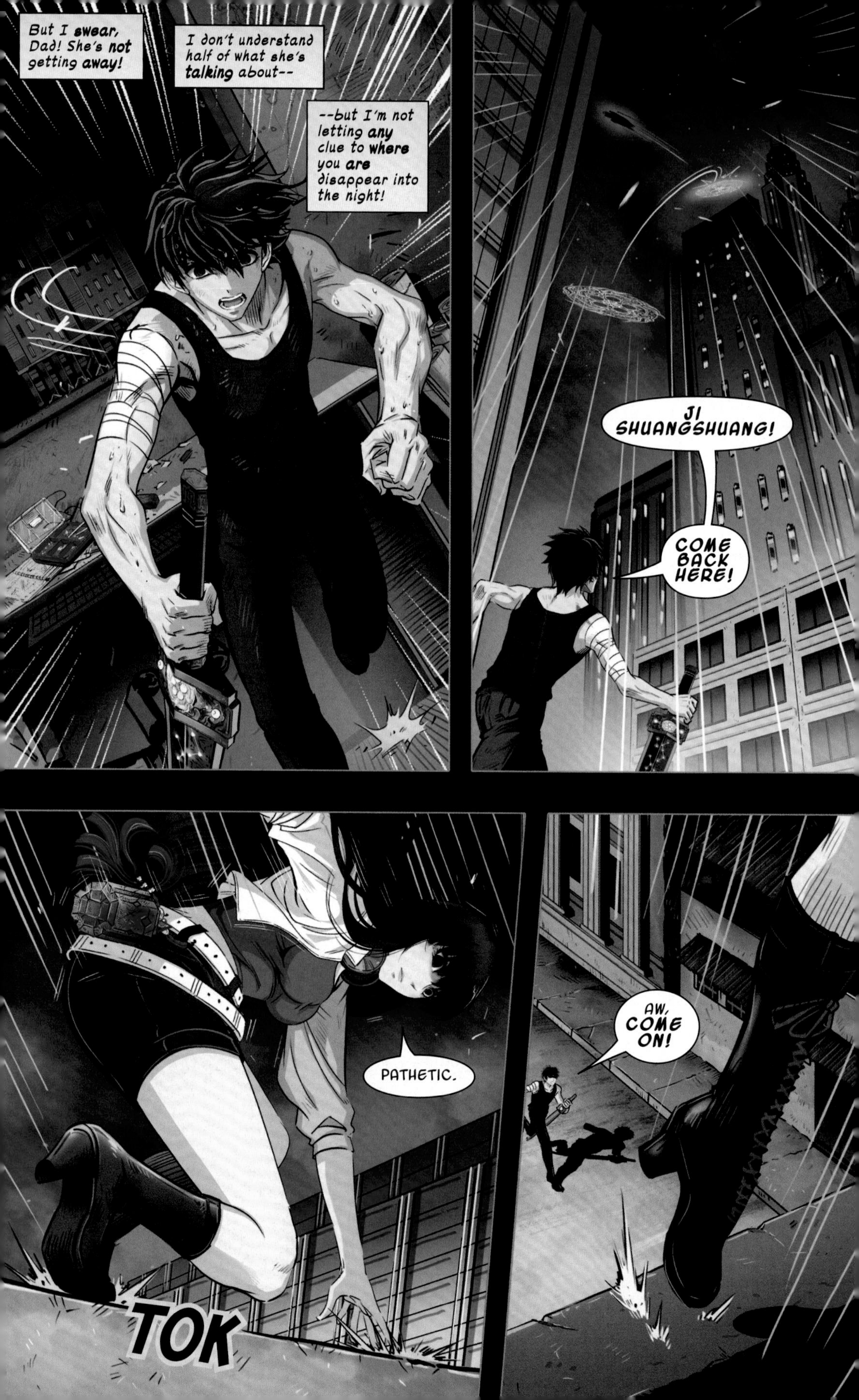

But I swear, Dad! She's not getting away!
I don't understand half of what she's talking about--
--but I'm not letting any clue to where you are disappear into the night!
JI SHUANGSHUANG!
COME BACK HERE!
PATHETIC.
TOK
AW, COME ON!

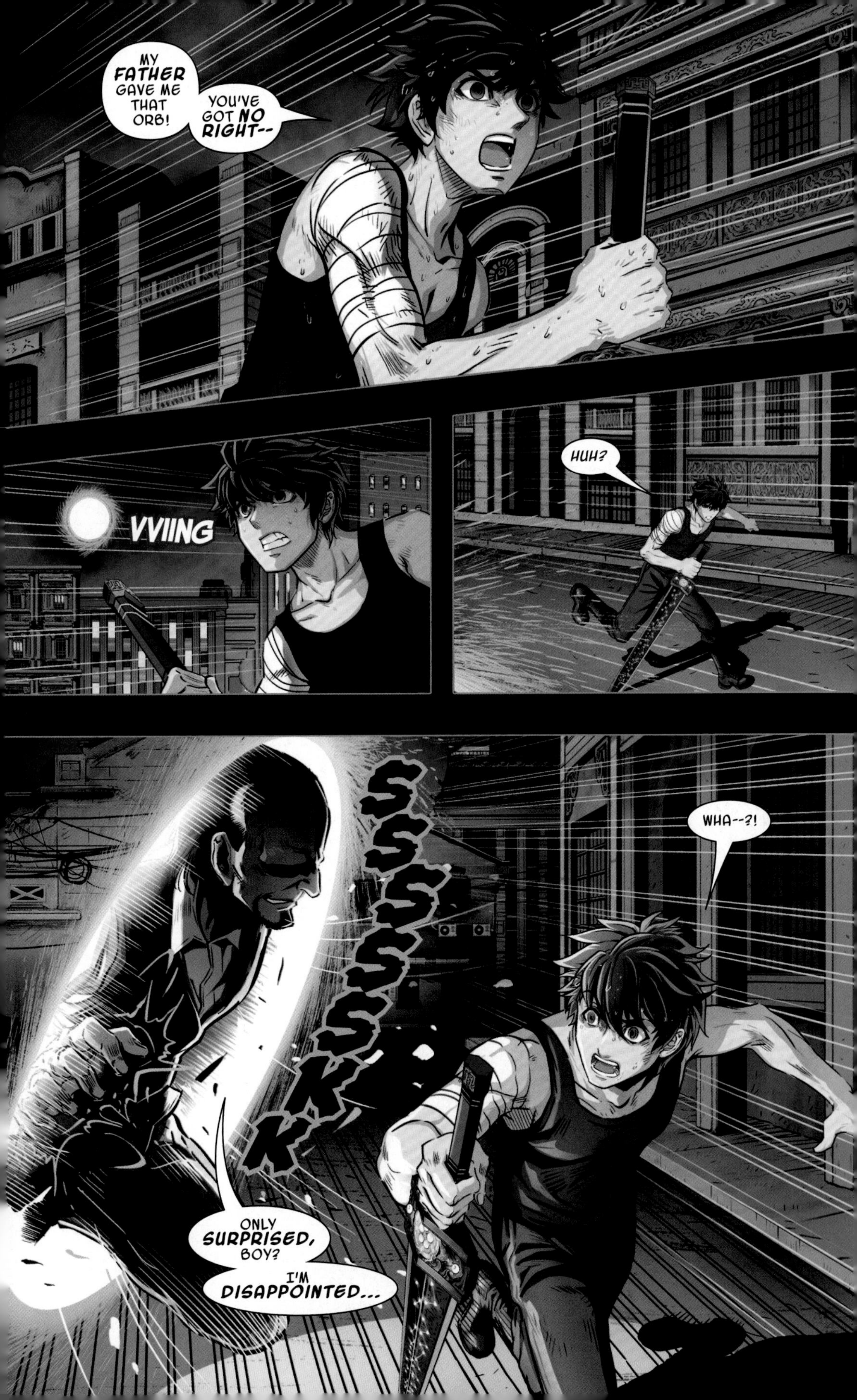
MY FATHER GAVE ME THAT ORB!
YOU'VE GOT NO RIGHT--
VVIING
HUH?
SSSSSSKK
WHA--?!
ONLY SURPRISED, BOY?
I'M DISAPPOINTED...

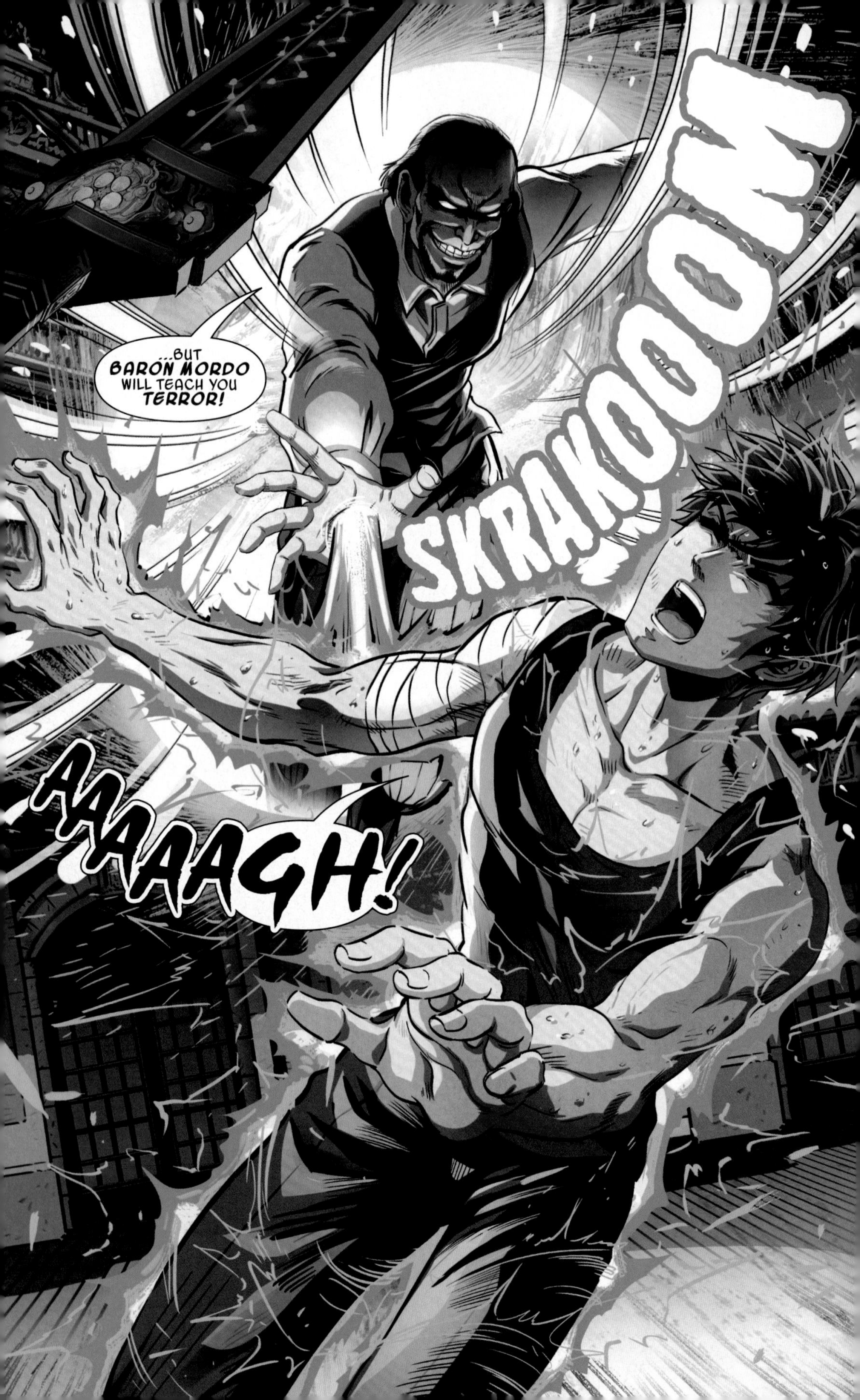
...BUT BARON MORDO WILL TEACH YOU TERROR!
SKRAKOOOM
AAAAAGH!

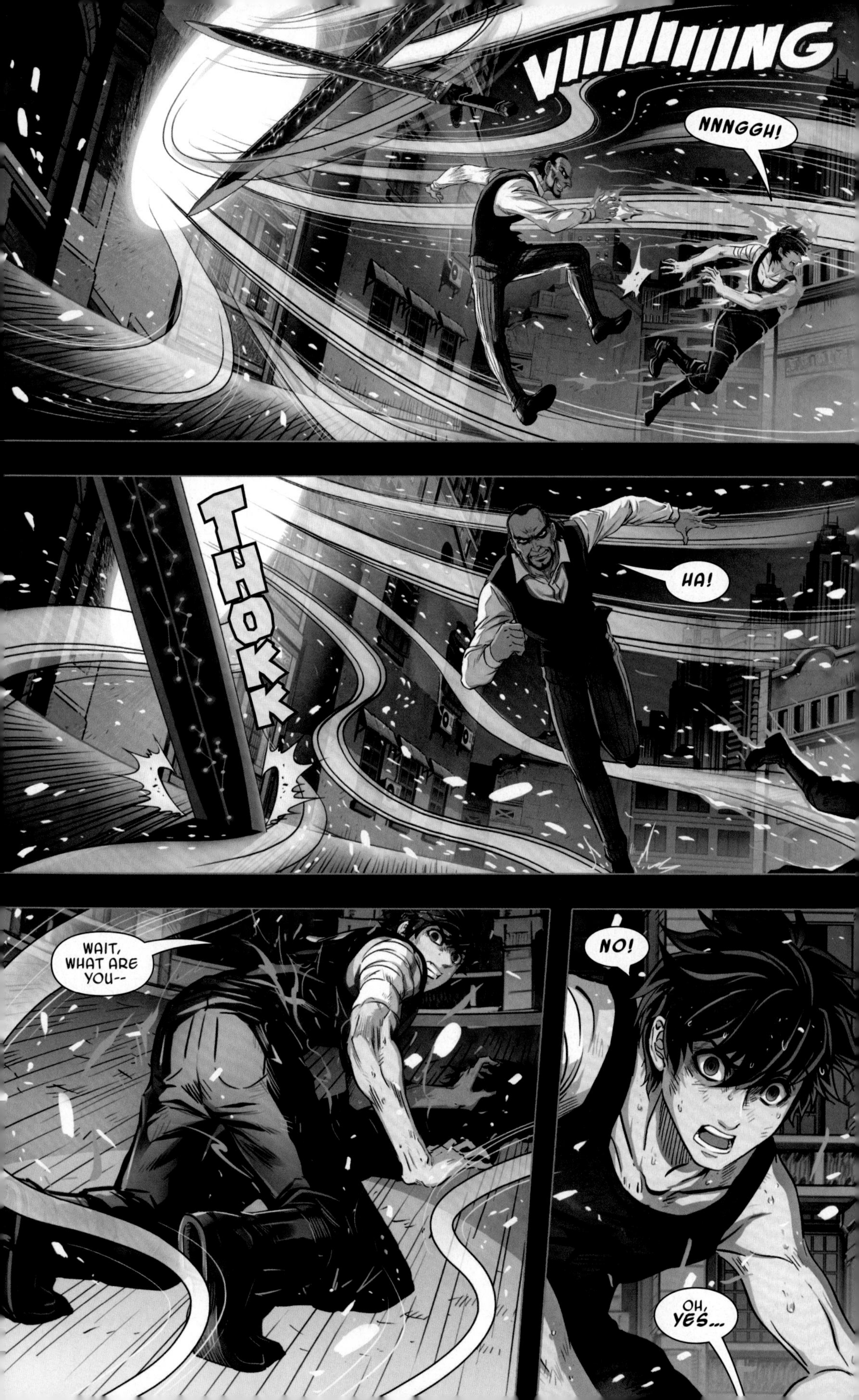
VIIIIIIIING
NNNGGH!
THOKK
HA!
WAIT, WHAT ARE YOU--
NO!
OH, YES...

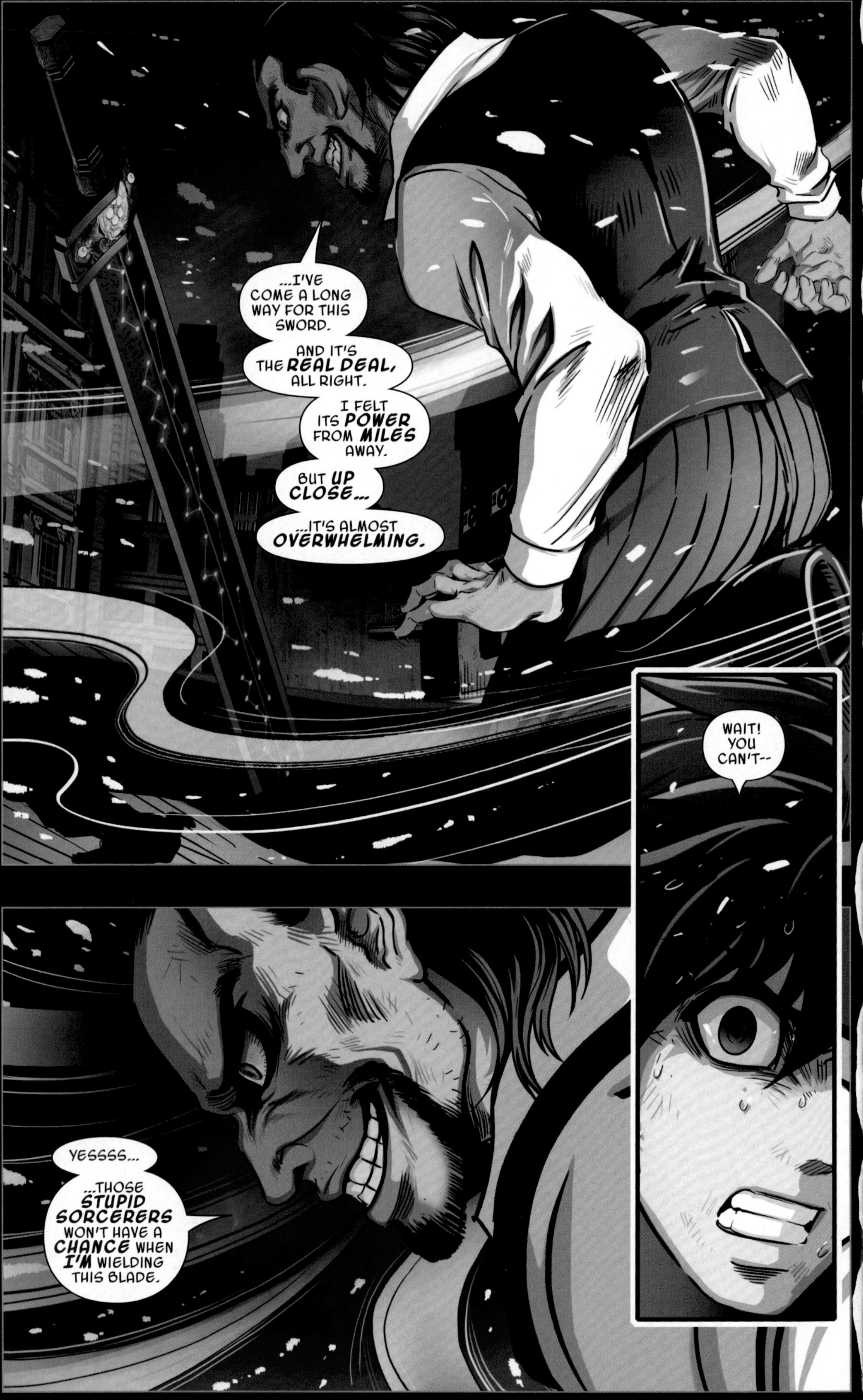
...I'VE COME A LONG WAY FOR THIS SWORD.
AND IT'S THE REAL DEAL, ALL RIGHT.
I FELT ITS POWER FROM MILES AWAY.
BUT UP CLOSE...
...IT'S ALMOST OVERWHELMING.
WAIT! YOU CAN'T--
YESSSS...
...THOSE STUPID SORCERERS WON'T HAVE A CHANCE WHEN I'M WIELDING THIS BLADE.

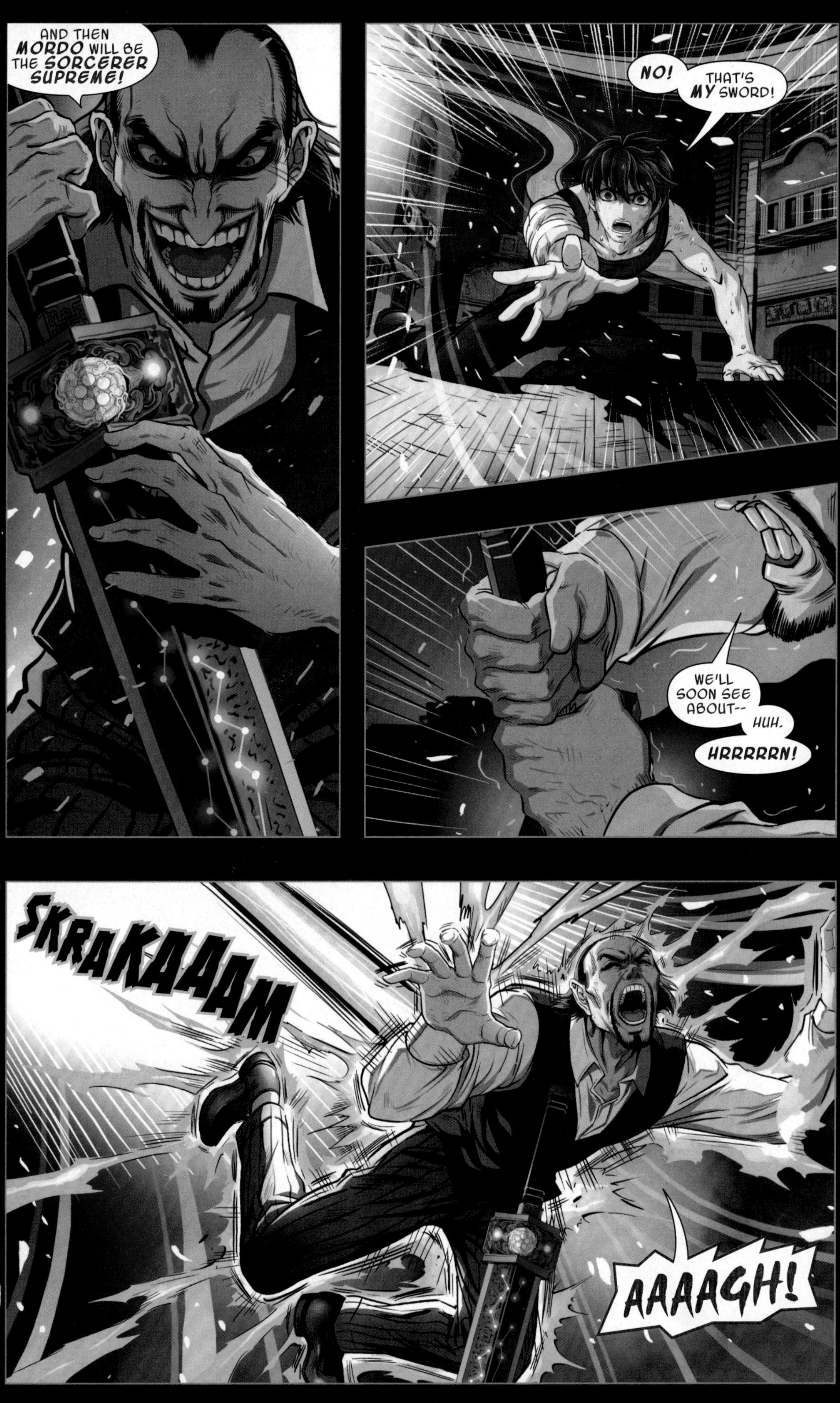
AND THEN MORDO WILL BE THE SORCERER SUPREME!
NO!
THAT'S MY SWORD!
WE'LL SOON SEE ABOUT--
HUH.
HRRRRRN!
SKRAKAAAM
AAAAGH!

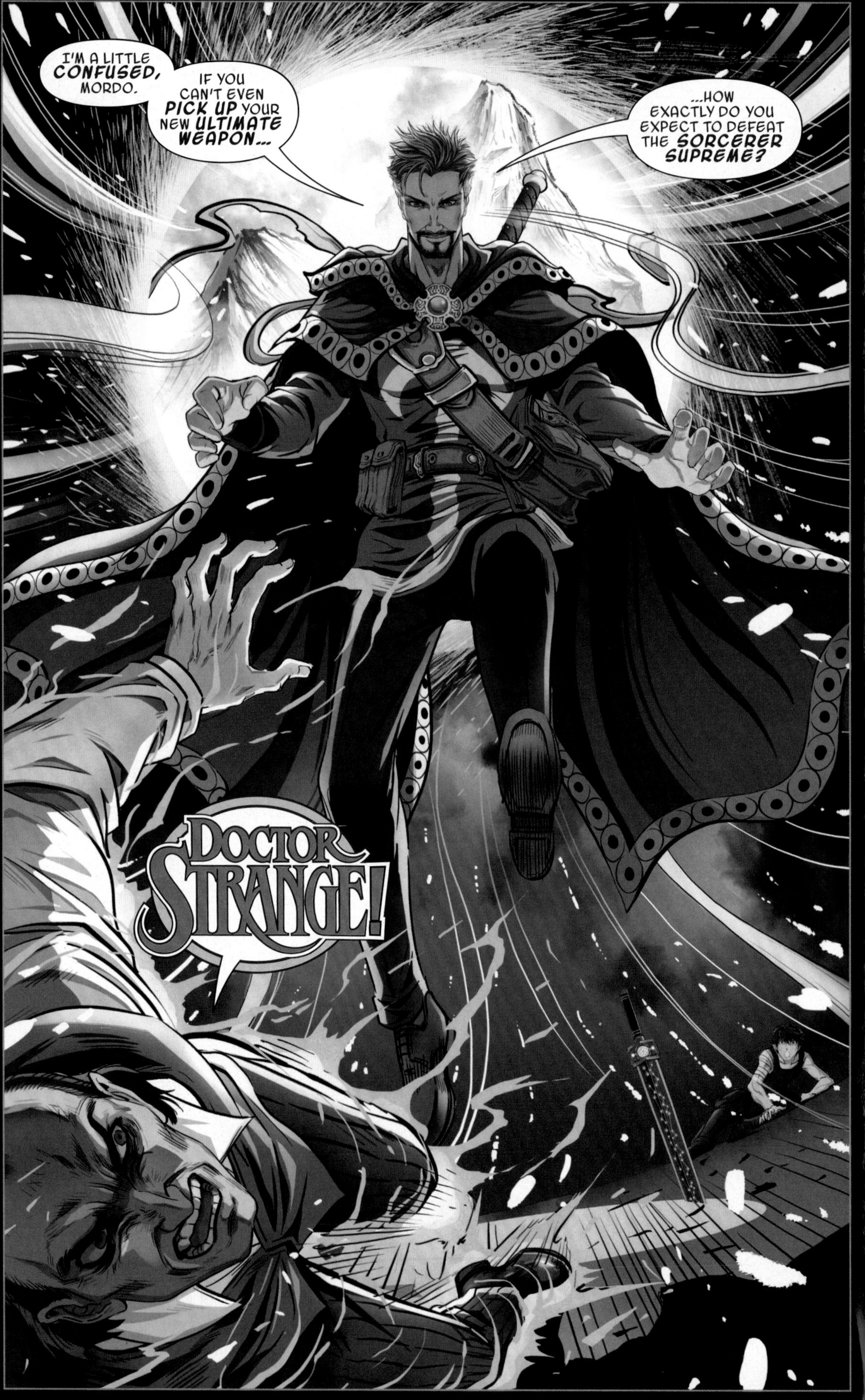
I'M A LITTLE CONFUSED, MORDO.
IF YOU CAN'T EVEN PICK UP YOUR NEW ULTIMATE WEAPON...
...HOW EXACTLY DO YOU EXPECT TO DEFEAT THE SORCERER SUPREME?
DOCTOR STRANGE!

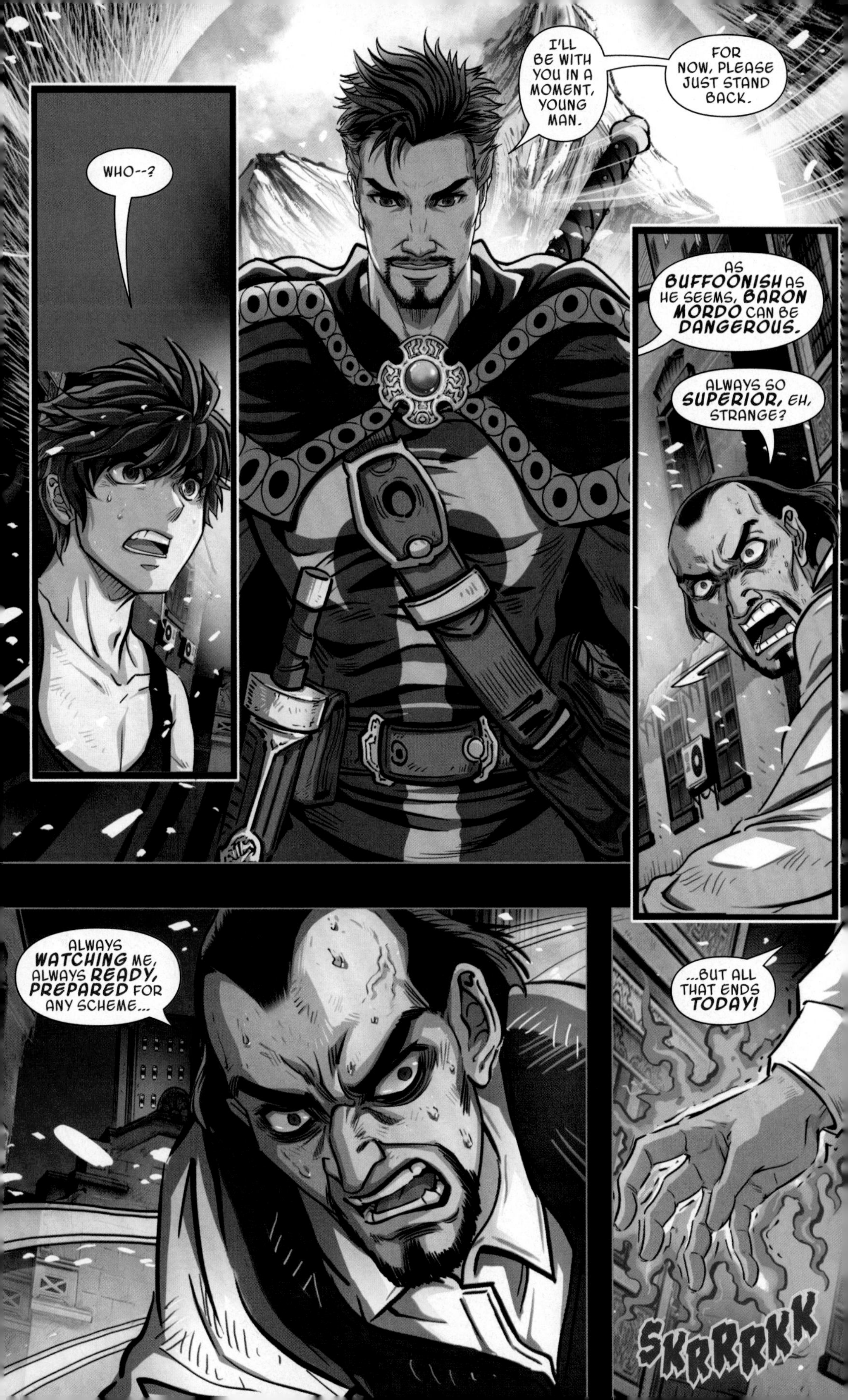
WHO--?
I'LL BE WITH YOU IN A MOMENT, YOUNG MAN.
FOR NOW, PLEASE JUST STAND BACK.
AS BUFFOONISH AS HE SEEMS, BARON MORDO CAN BE DANGEROUS.
ALWAYS SO SUPERIOR, EH, STRANGE?
ALWAYS WATCHING ME, ALWAYS READY, PREPARED FOR ANY SCHEME...
...BUT ALL THAT ENDS TODAY!
SKRRRKK

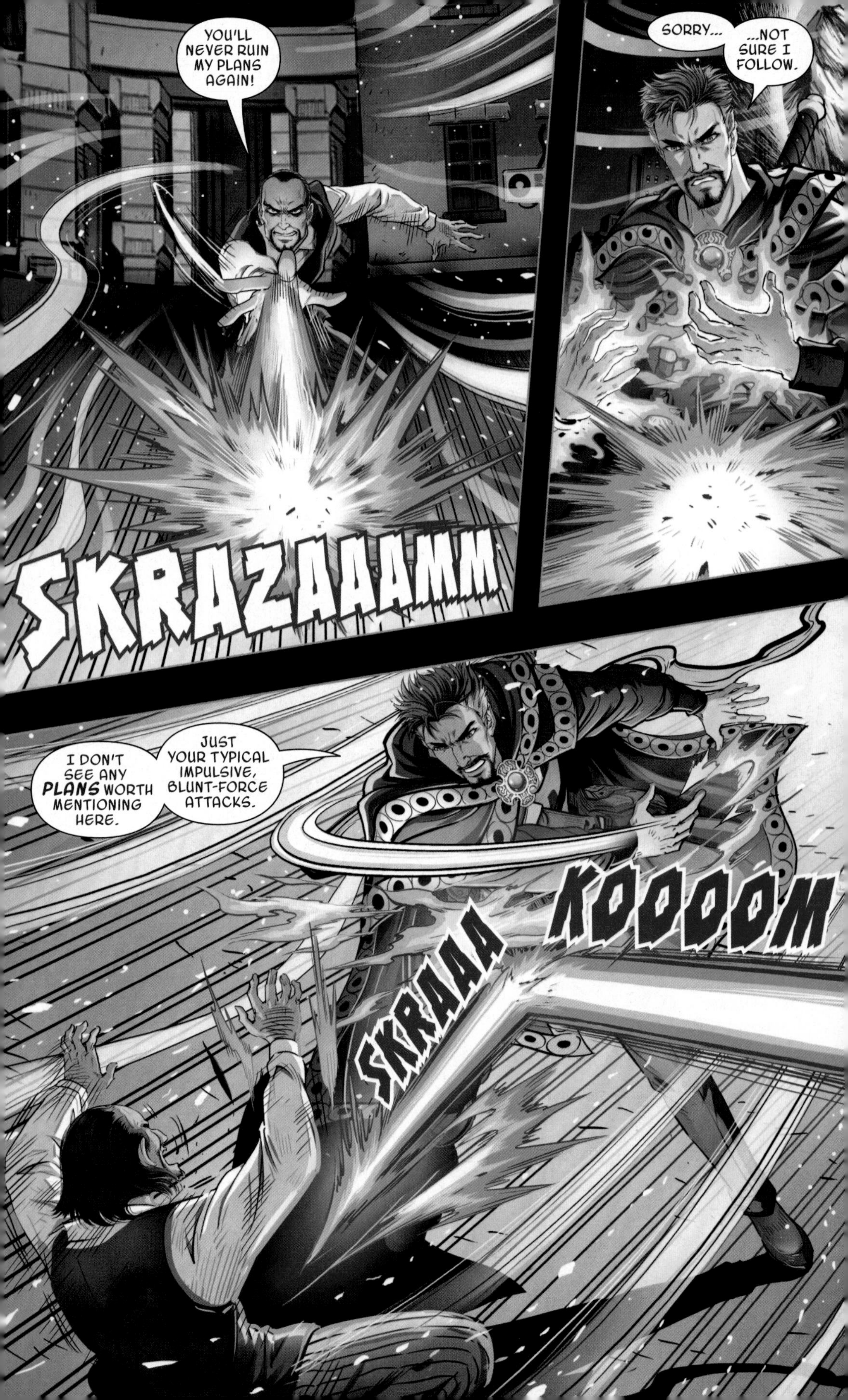
YOU'LL NEVER RUIN MY PLANS AGAIN!
SKRAZAAAMM
SORRY...
...NOT SURE I FOLLOW.
I DON'T SEE ANY PLANS WORTH MENTIONING HERE.
JUST YOUR TYPICAL IMPULSIVE, BLUNT-FORCE ATTACKS.
KOOOOM
SKRAAA

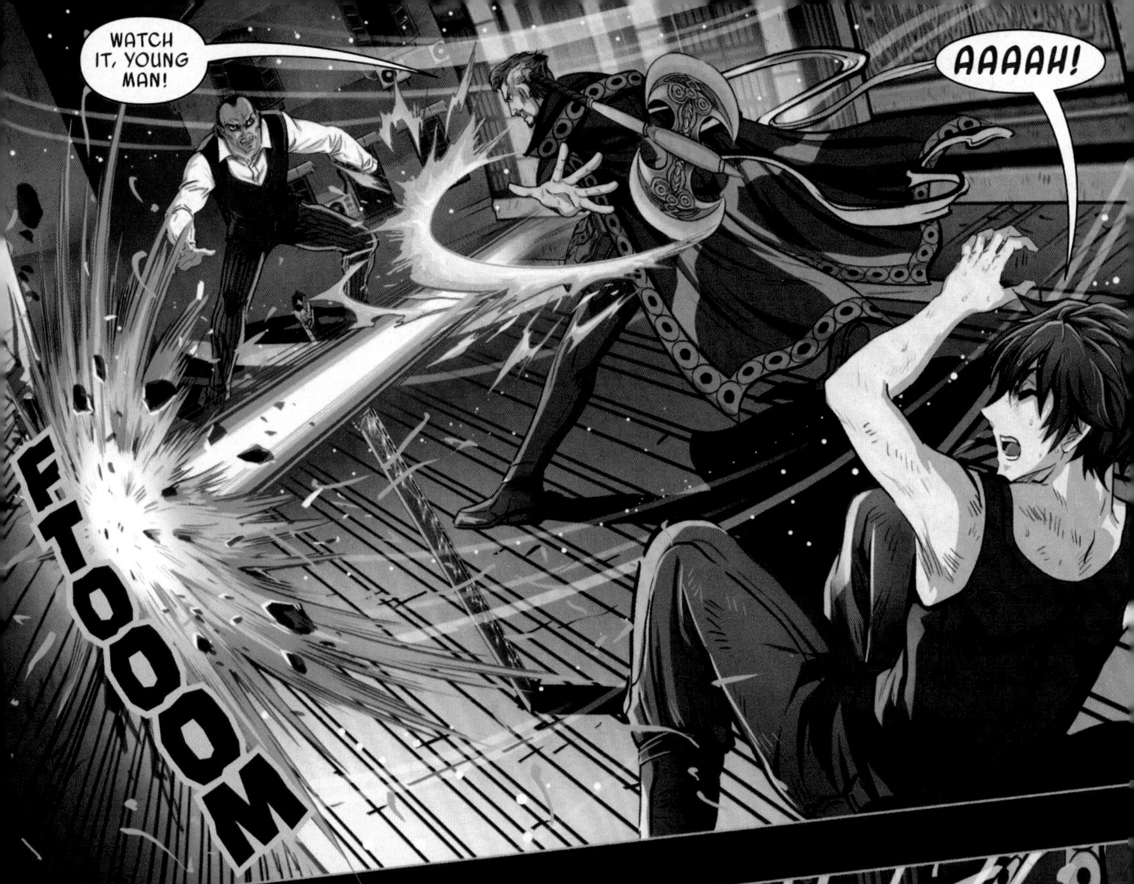
WATCH IT, YOUNG MAN!
AAAAH!
FTOOOM

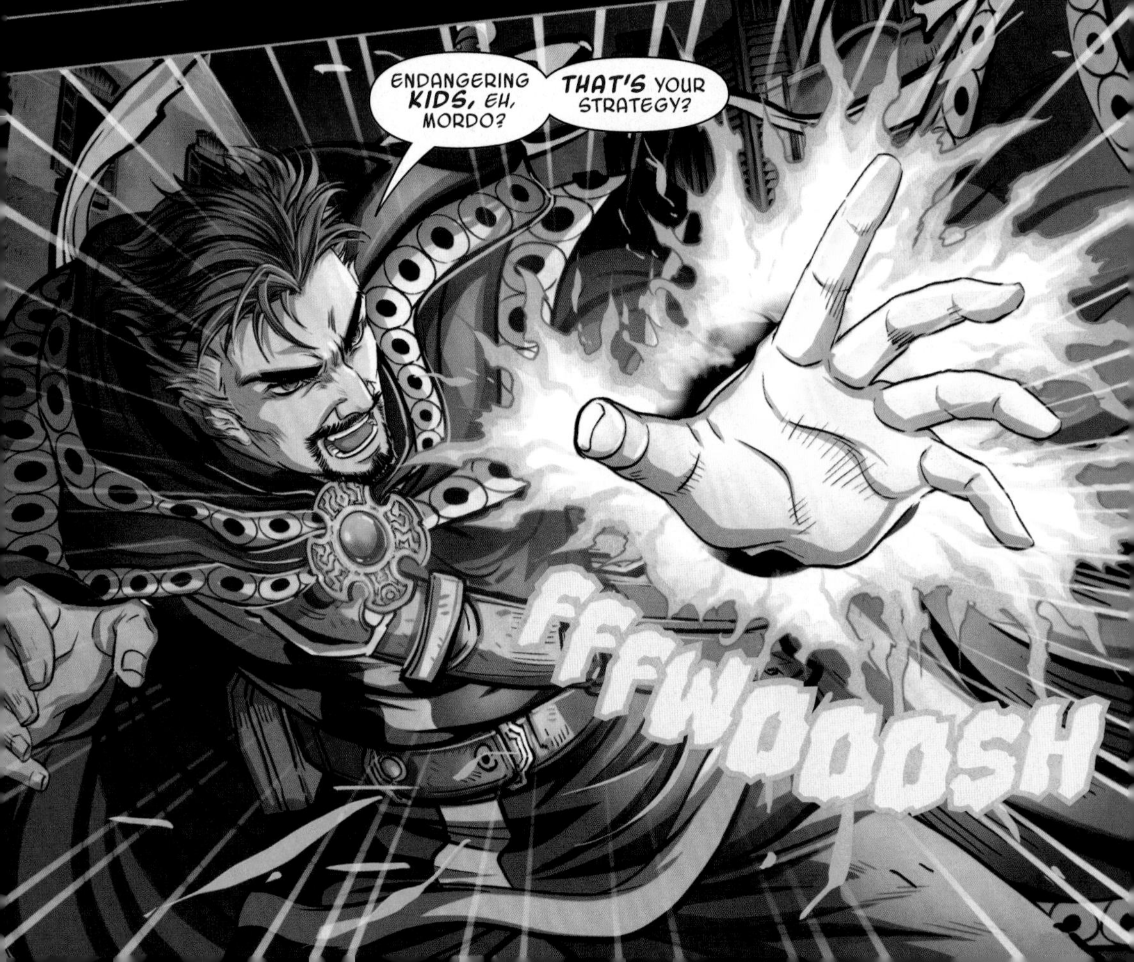
ENDANGERING KIDS, EH, MORDO?
THAT'S YOUR STRATEGY?
FFFWOOOSH

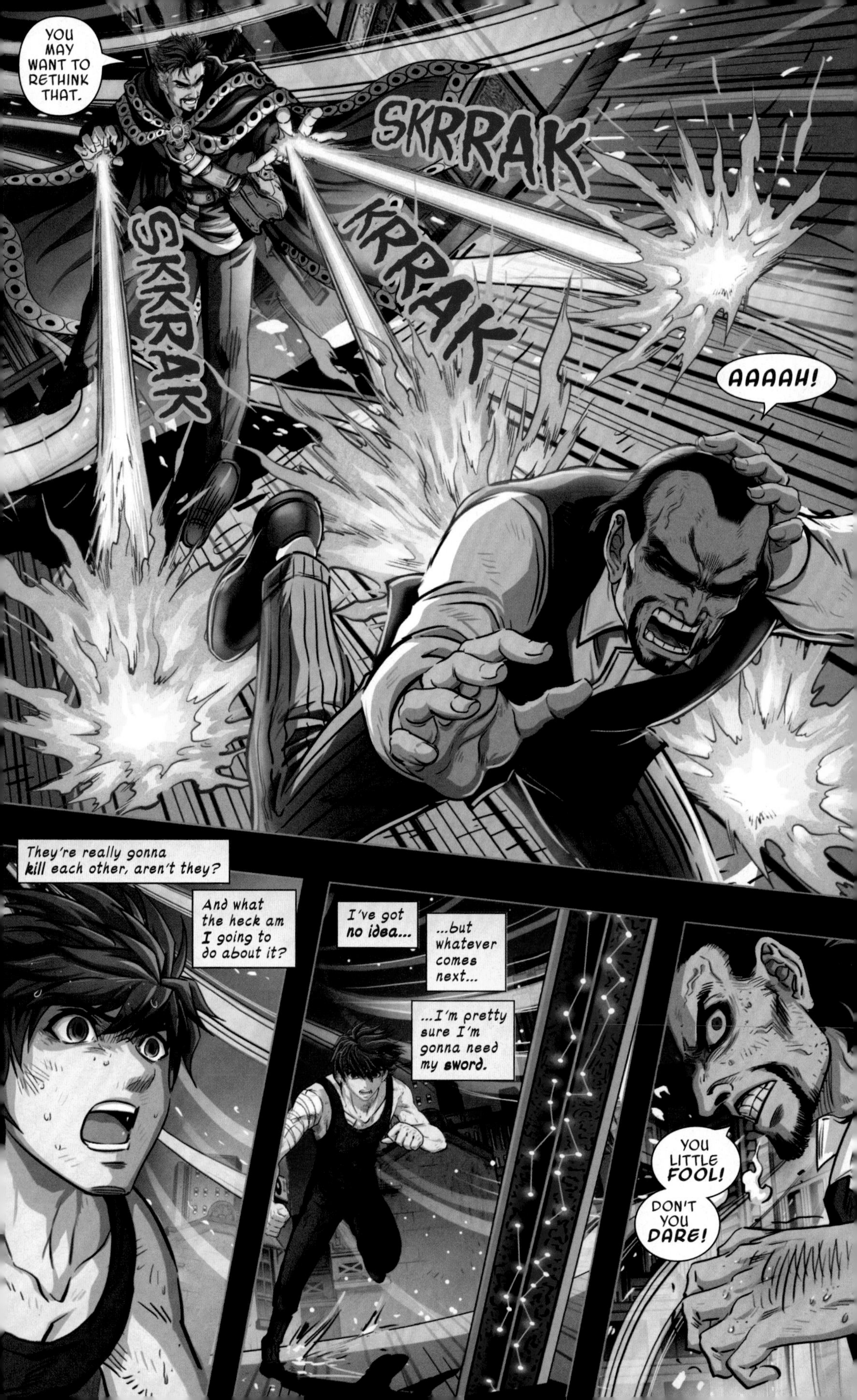

YOU MAY WANT TO RETHINK THAT.
SKRRAK
SKRRAK
KRRAK
AAAAH!
They're really gonna **kill** each other, aren't they?
And what the heck am I going to do about it?
I've got **no idea...**
...but whatever comes next...
...I'm pretty sure I'm gonna need my **sword.**
YOU LITTLE **FOOL!**
DON'T YOU **DARE!**

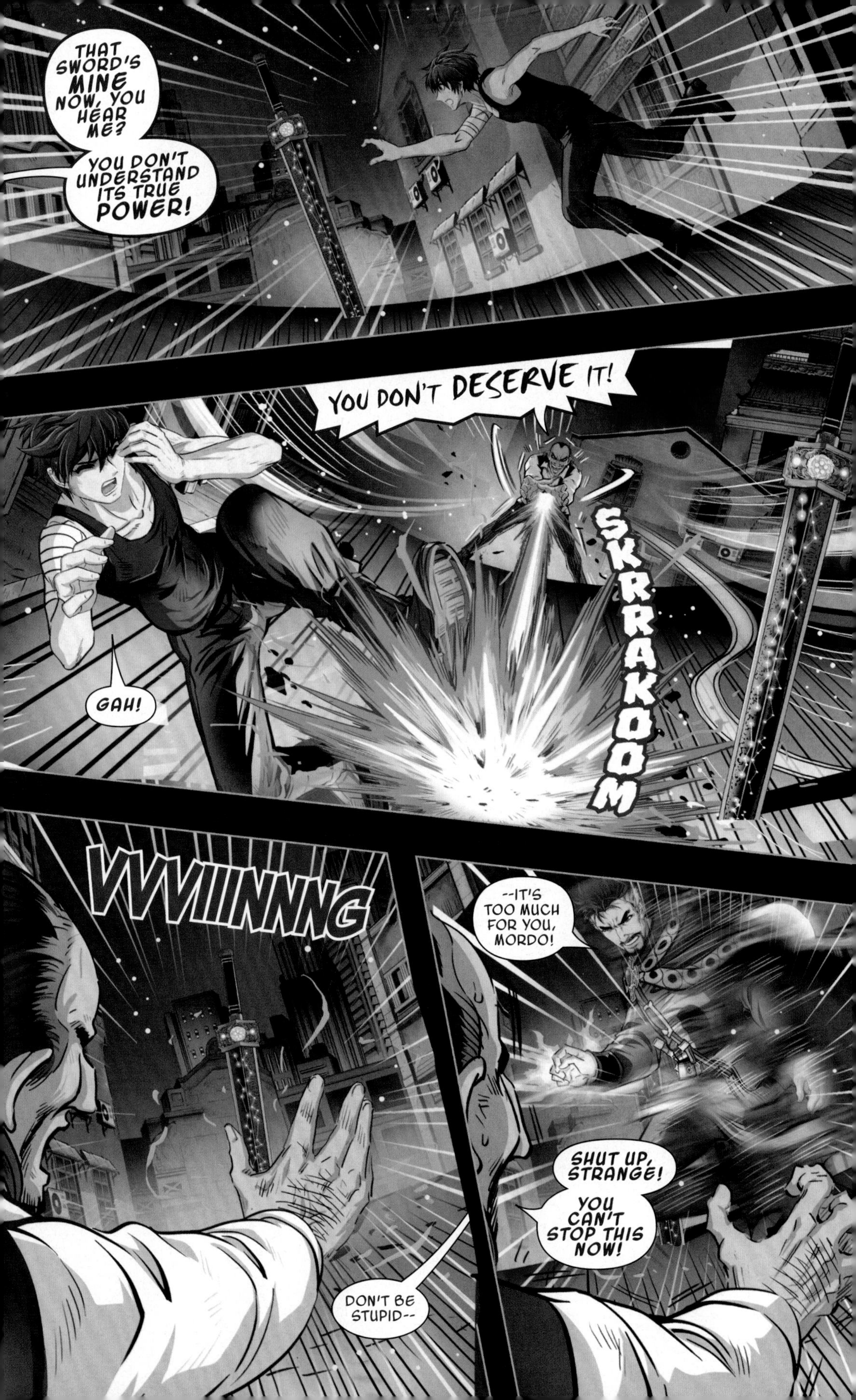
THAT SWORD'S MINE NOW, YOU HEAR ME?
YOU DON'T UNDERSTAND ITS TRUE POWER!
YOU DON'T DESERVE IT!
GAH!
SKRRAKOOM
VVVIIINNNG
DON'T BE STUPID--
--IT'S TOO MUCH FOR YOU, MORDO!
SHUT UP, STRANGE!
YOU CAN'T STOP THIS NOW!

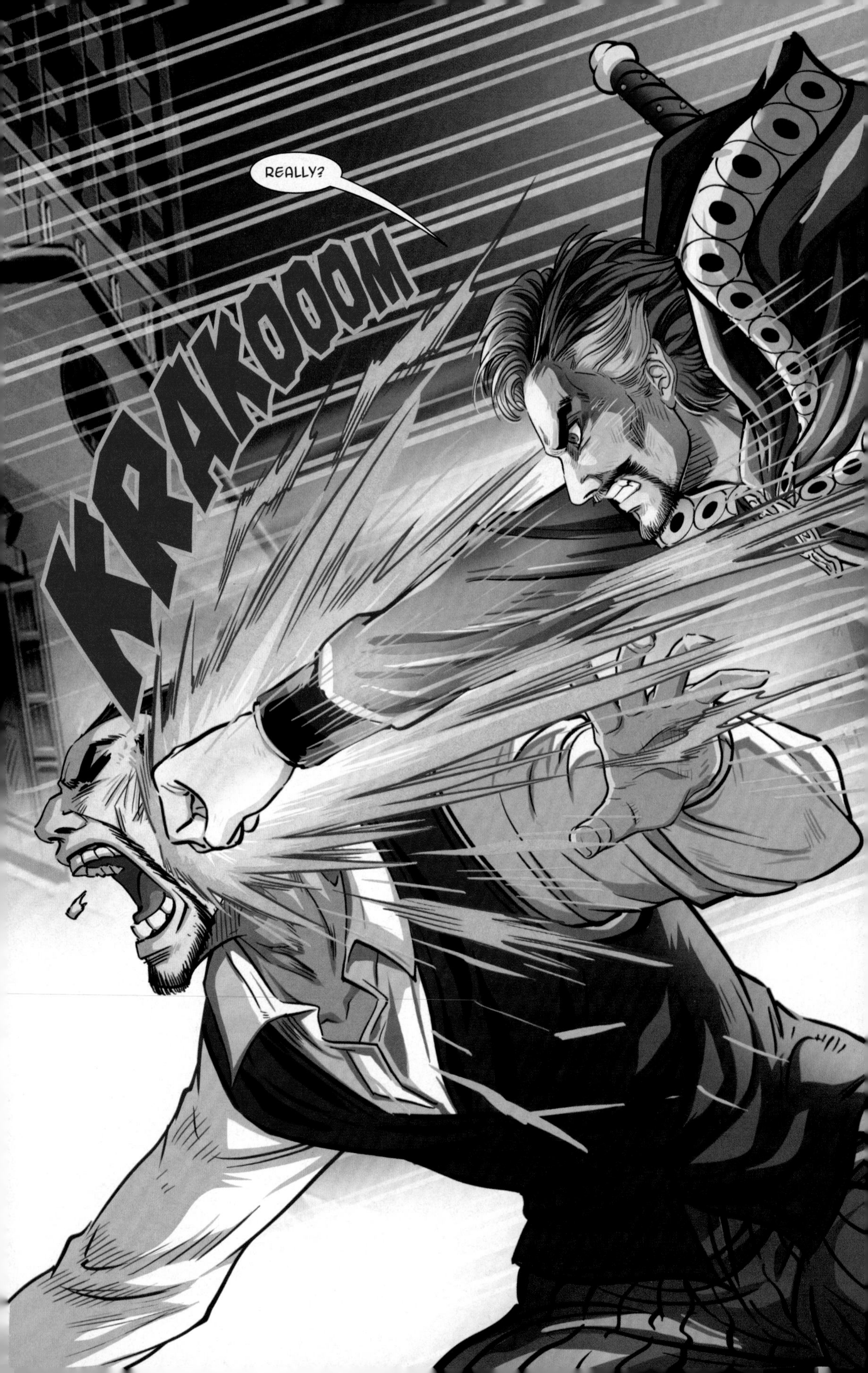
REALLY?
KRAKOOOM

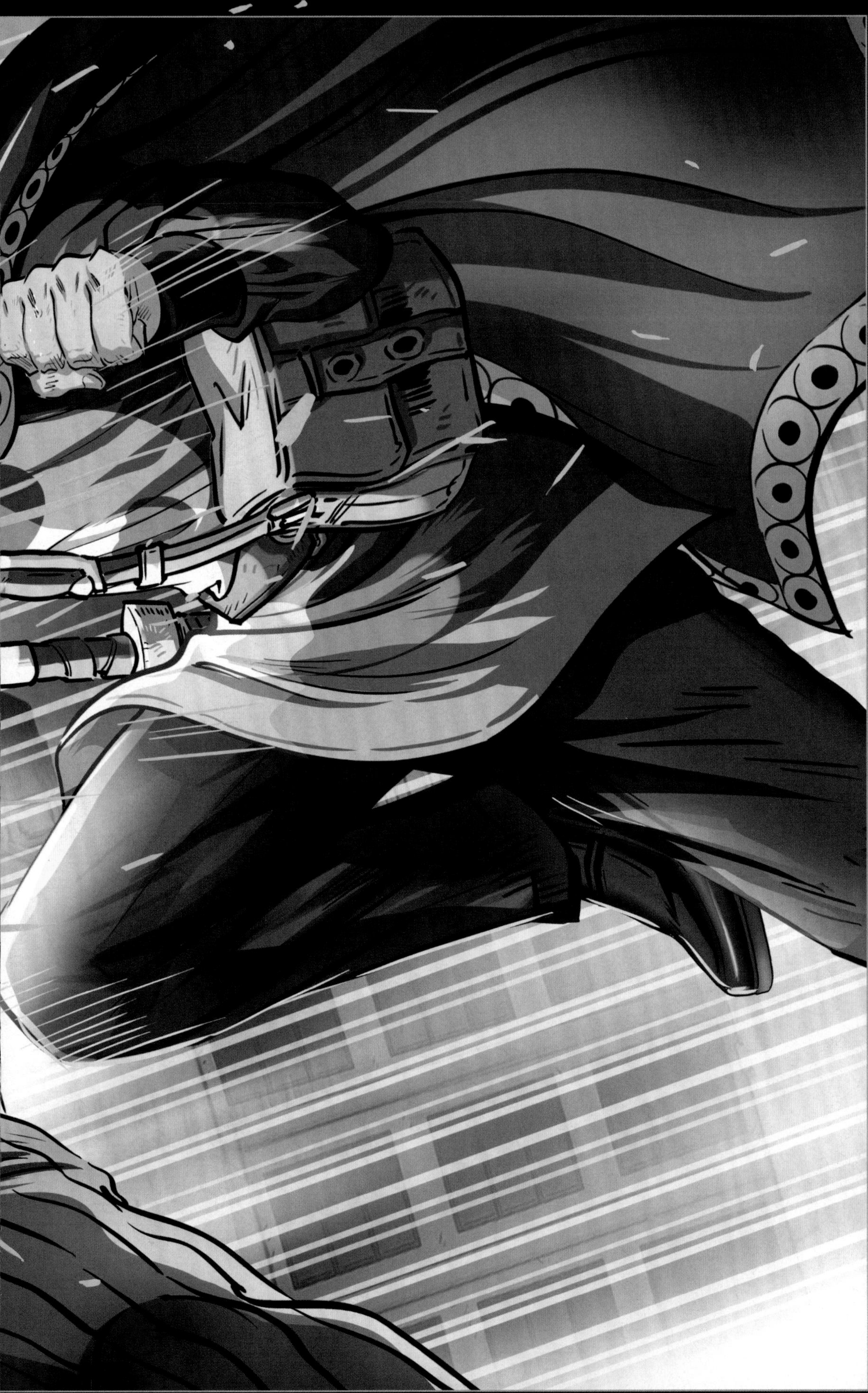

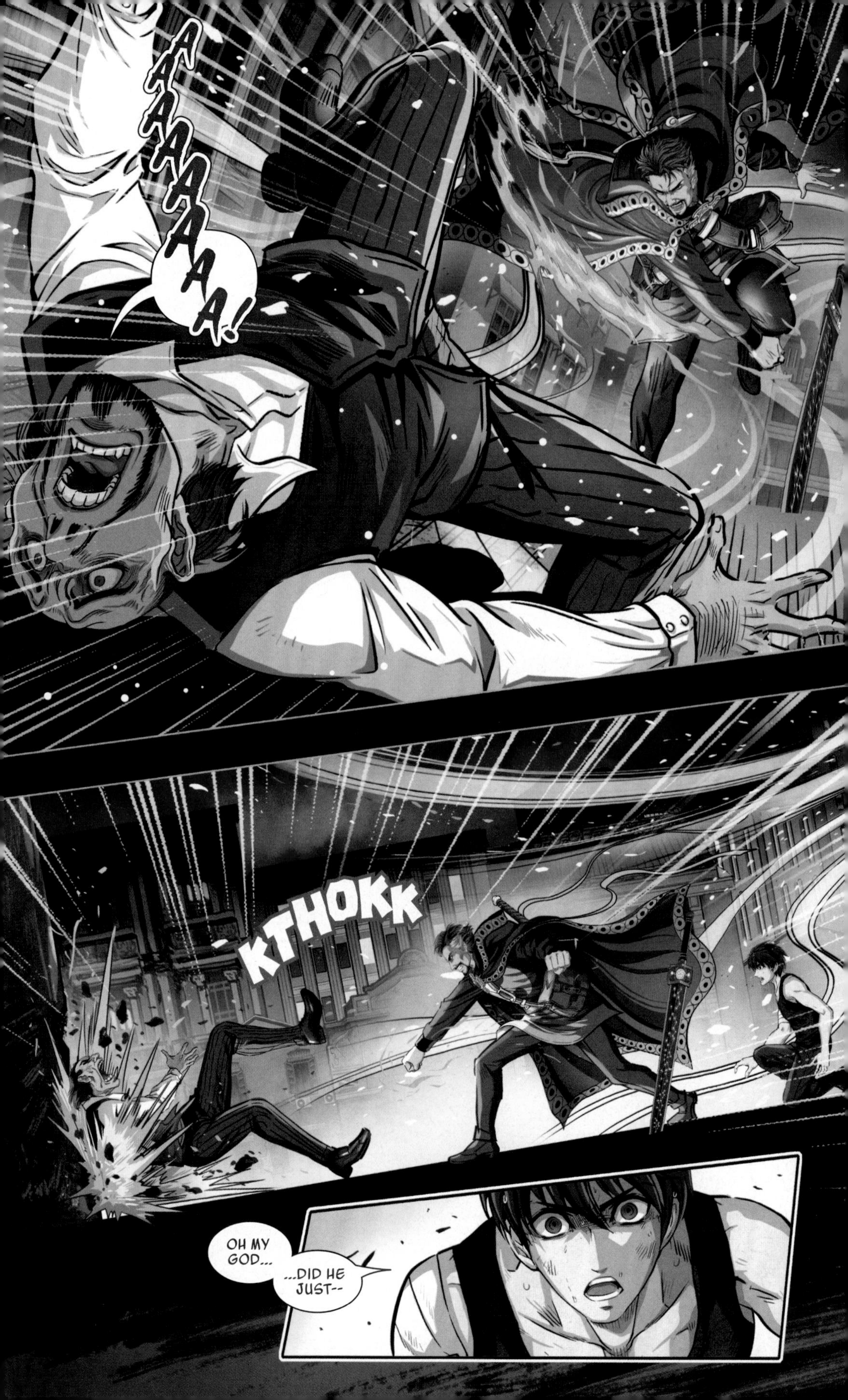
AAAAAAAAA!
KTHOKK
OH MY GOD...
...DID HE JUST--

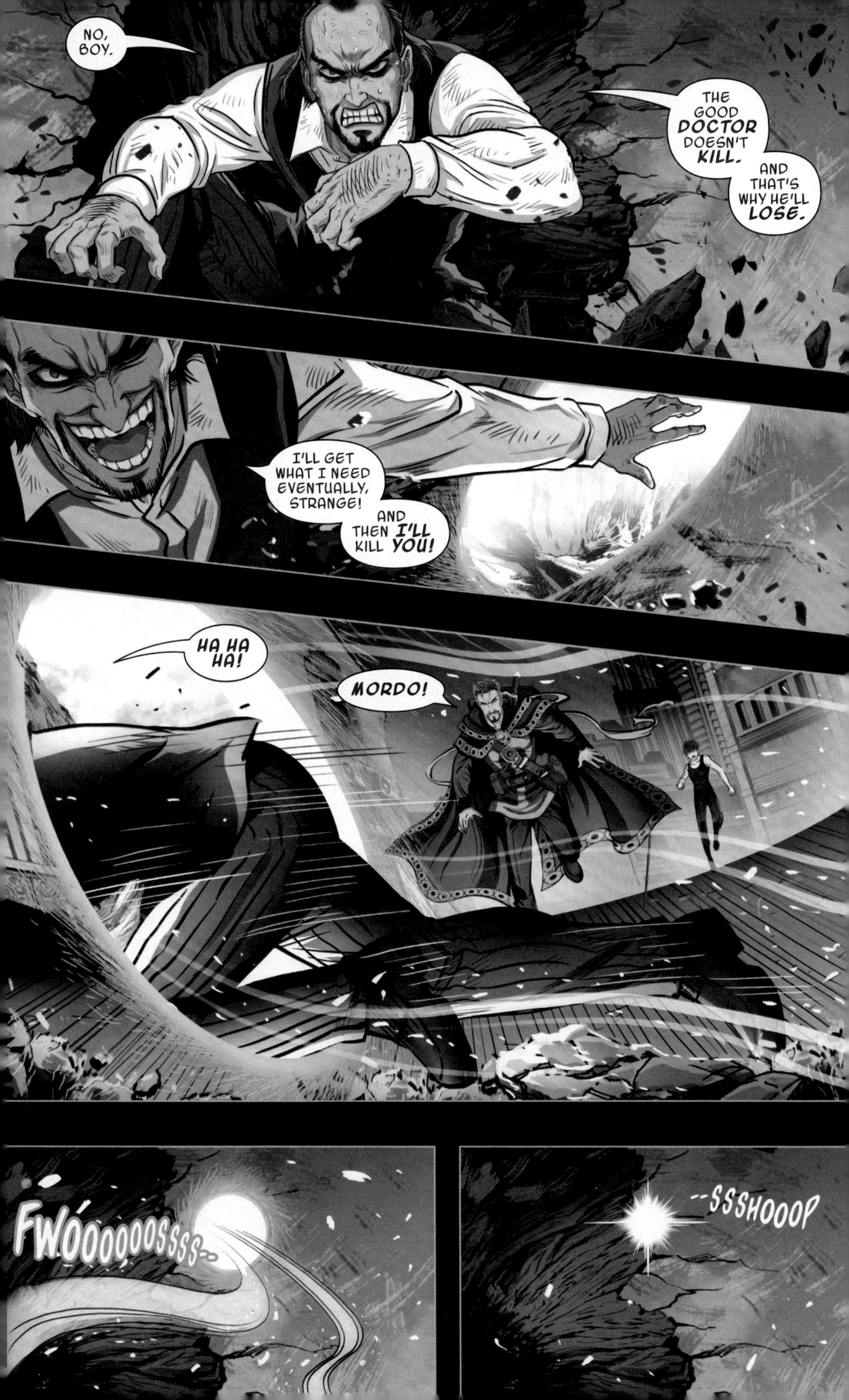
NO, BOY.
THE GOOD DOCTOR DOESN'T KILL.
AND THAT'S WHY HE'LL LOSE.
I'LL GET WHAT I NEED EVENTUALLY, STRANGE!
AND THEN I'LL KILL YOU!
HA HA HA!
MORDO!
FWOOOOOOSSSS--
--SSSHOOOP

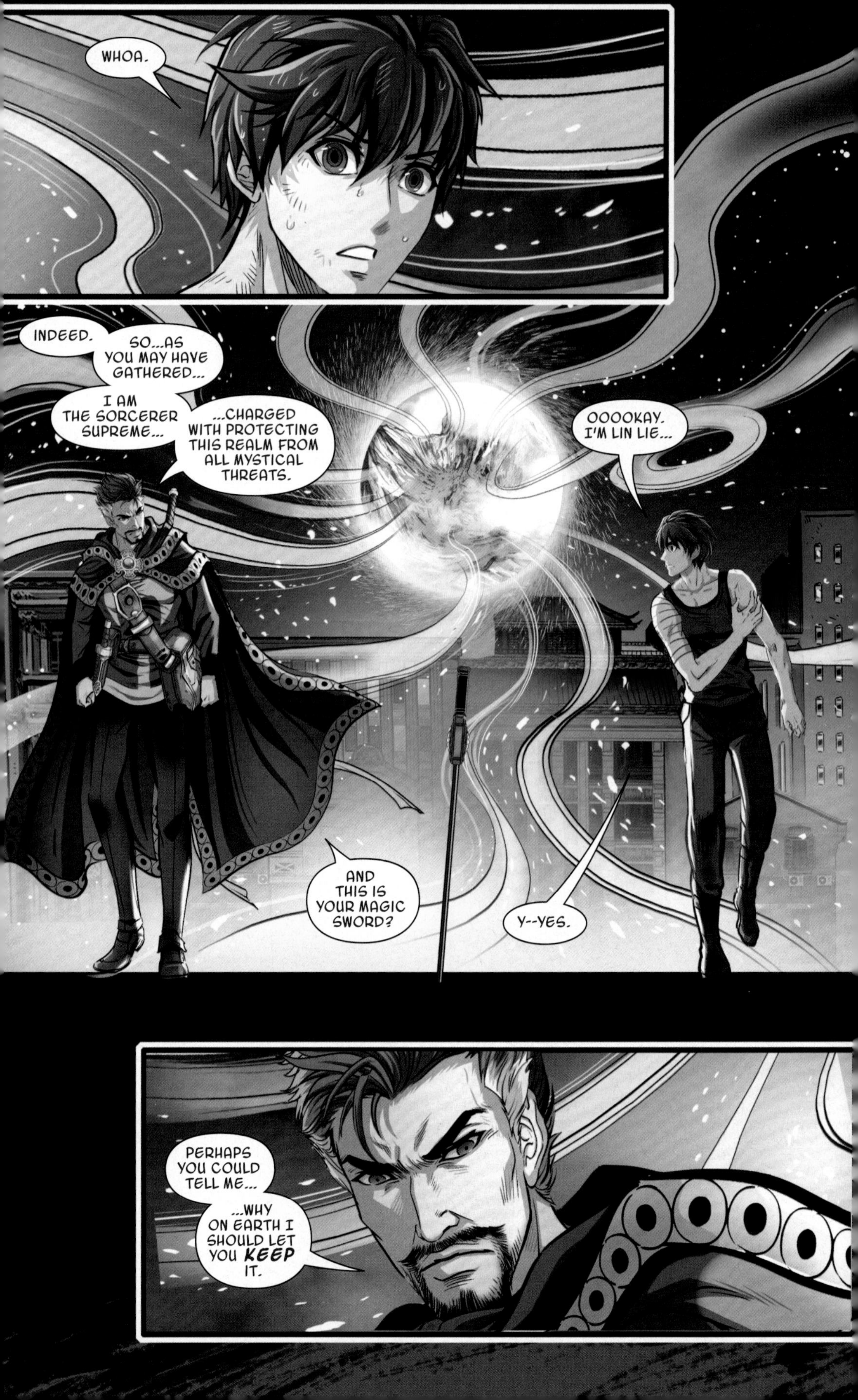
WHOA.
INDEED.
SO...AS YOU MAY HAVE GATHERED...
I AM THE SORCERER SUPREME...
...CHARGED WITH PROTECTING THIS REALM FROM ALL MYSTICAL THREATS.
OOOOKAY. I'M LIN LIE...
AND THIS IS YOUR MAGIC SWORD?
Y--YES.
PERHAPS YOU COULD TELL ME...
...WHY ON EARTH I SHOULD LET YOU **KEEP** IT.

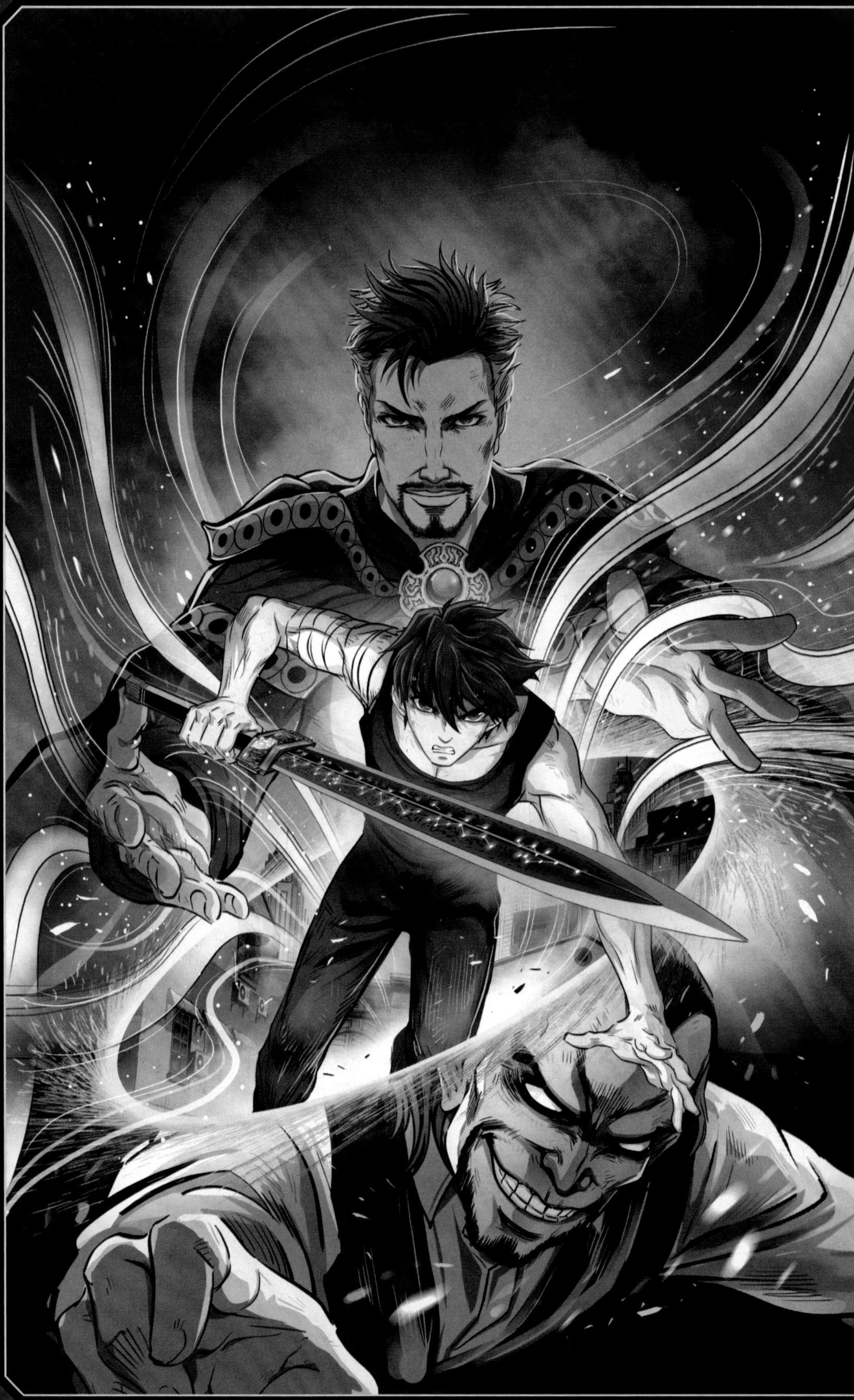

SIX A STRANGE ENCOUNTER

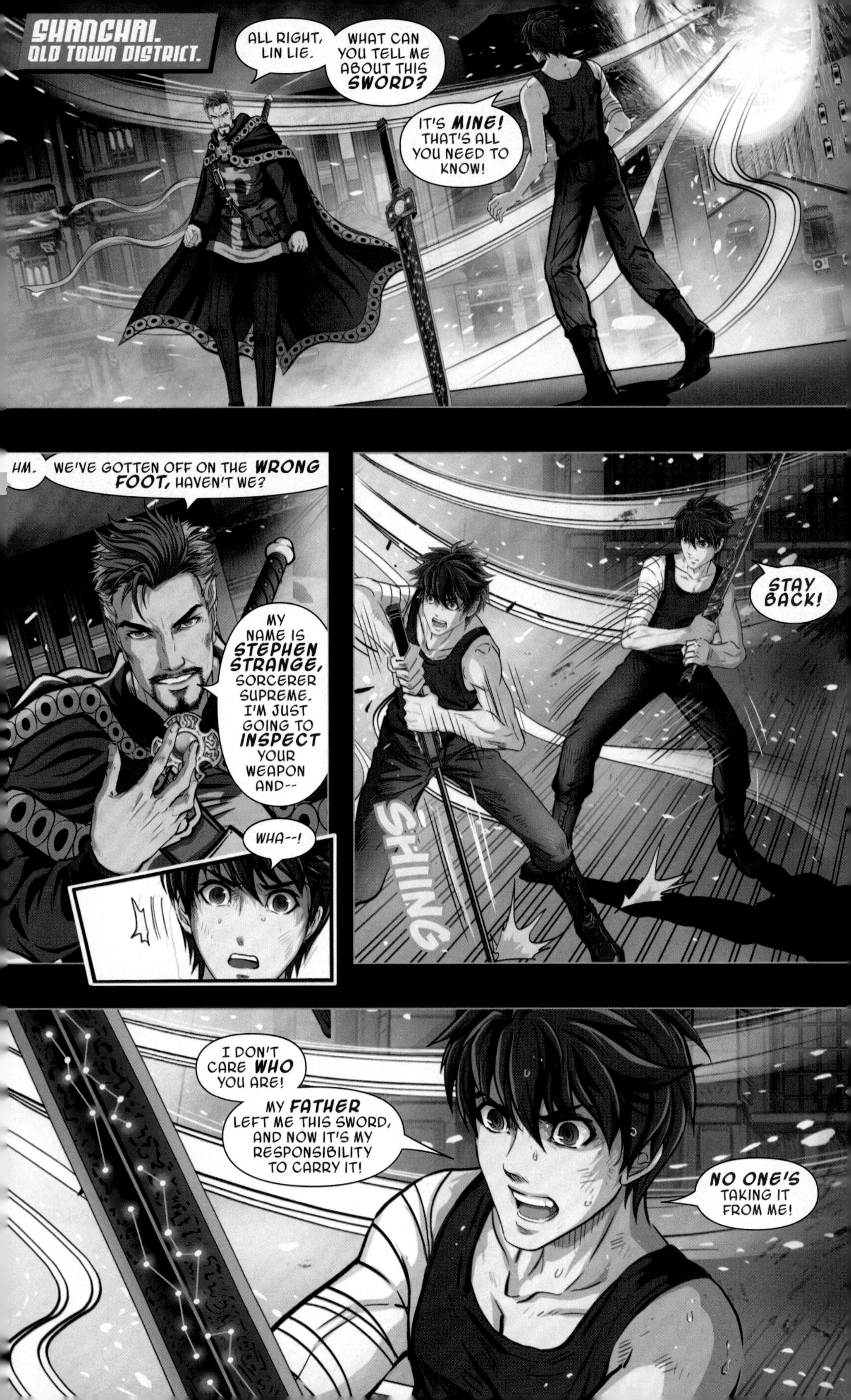
SHANGHAI.
OLD TOWN DISTRICT.
ALL RIGHT, LIN LIE.
WHAT CAN YOU TELL ME ABOUT THIS SWORD?
IT'S MINE! THAT'S ALL YOU NEED TO KNOW!
HM.
WE'VE GOTTEN OFF ON THE WRONG FOOT, HAVEN'T WE?
MY NAME IS STEPHEN STRANGE, SORCERER SUPREME. I'M JUST GOING TO INSPECT YOUR WEAPON AND--
WHA--!
STAY BACK!
SHING
I DON'T CARE WHO YOU ARE!
MY FATHER LEFT ME THIS SWORD, AND NOW IT'S MY RESPONSIBILITY TO CARRY IT!
NO ONE'S TAKING IT FROM ME!

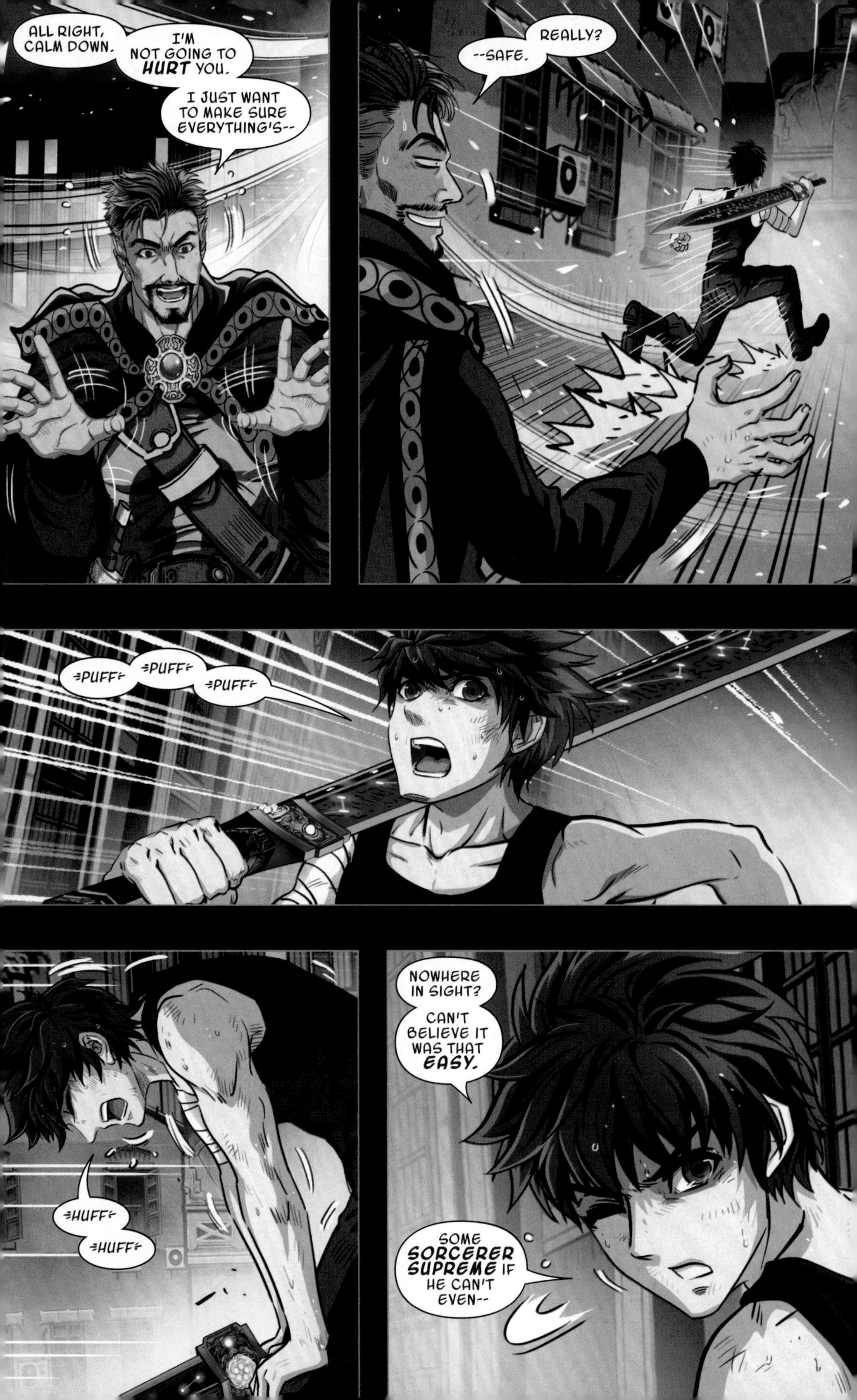
ALL RIGHT, CALM DOWN.
I'M NOT GOING TO HURT YOU.
I JUST WANT TO MAKE SURE EVERYTHING'S--
--SAFE.
REALLY?
=PUFF= =PUFF= =PUFF=
=HUFF= =HUFF=
NOWHERE IN SIGHT?
CAN'T BELIEVE IT WAS THAT EASY.
SOME SORCERER SUPREME IF HE CAN'T EVEN--

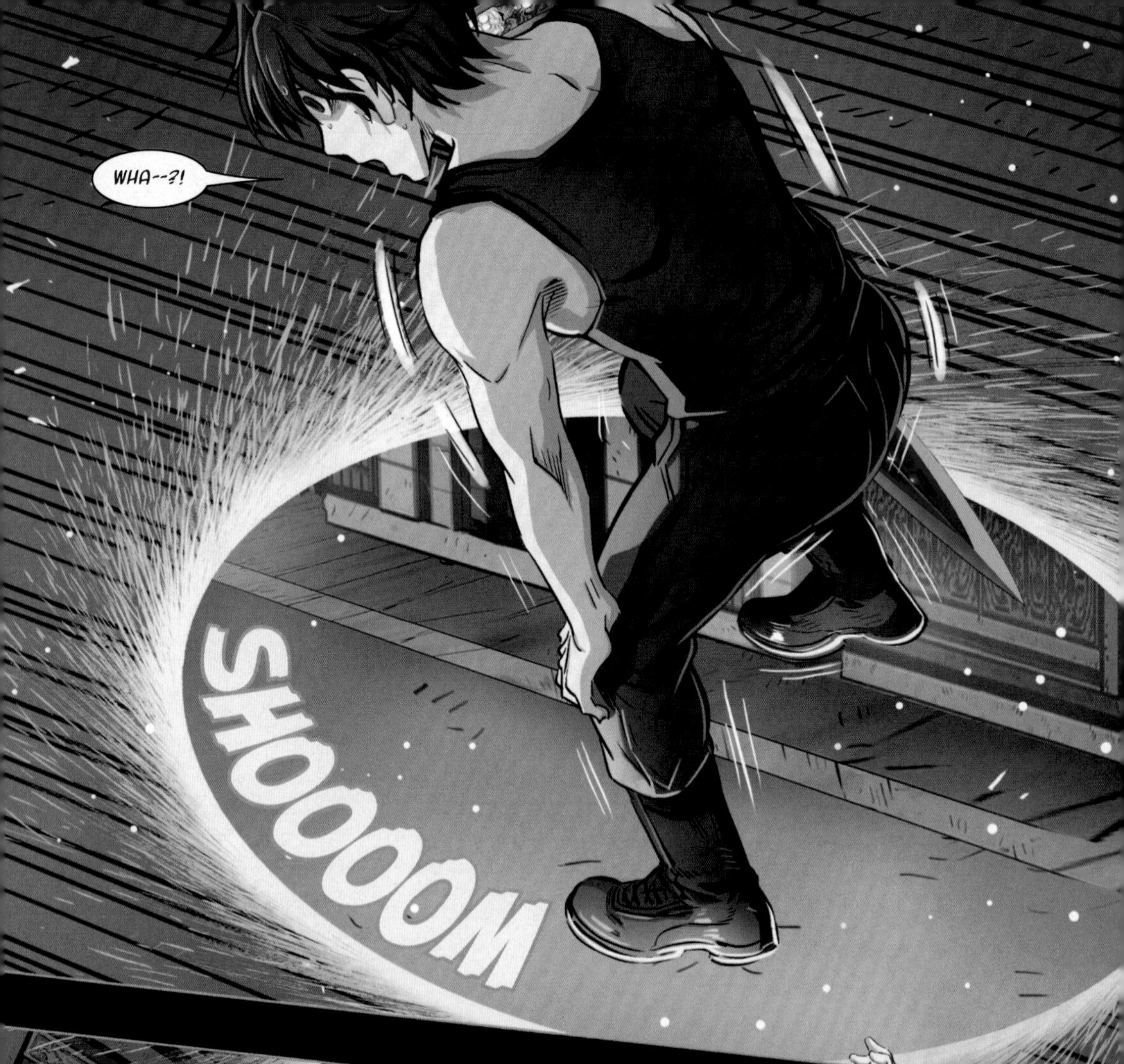
WHA--?!
SHOOOOOM

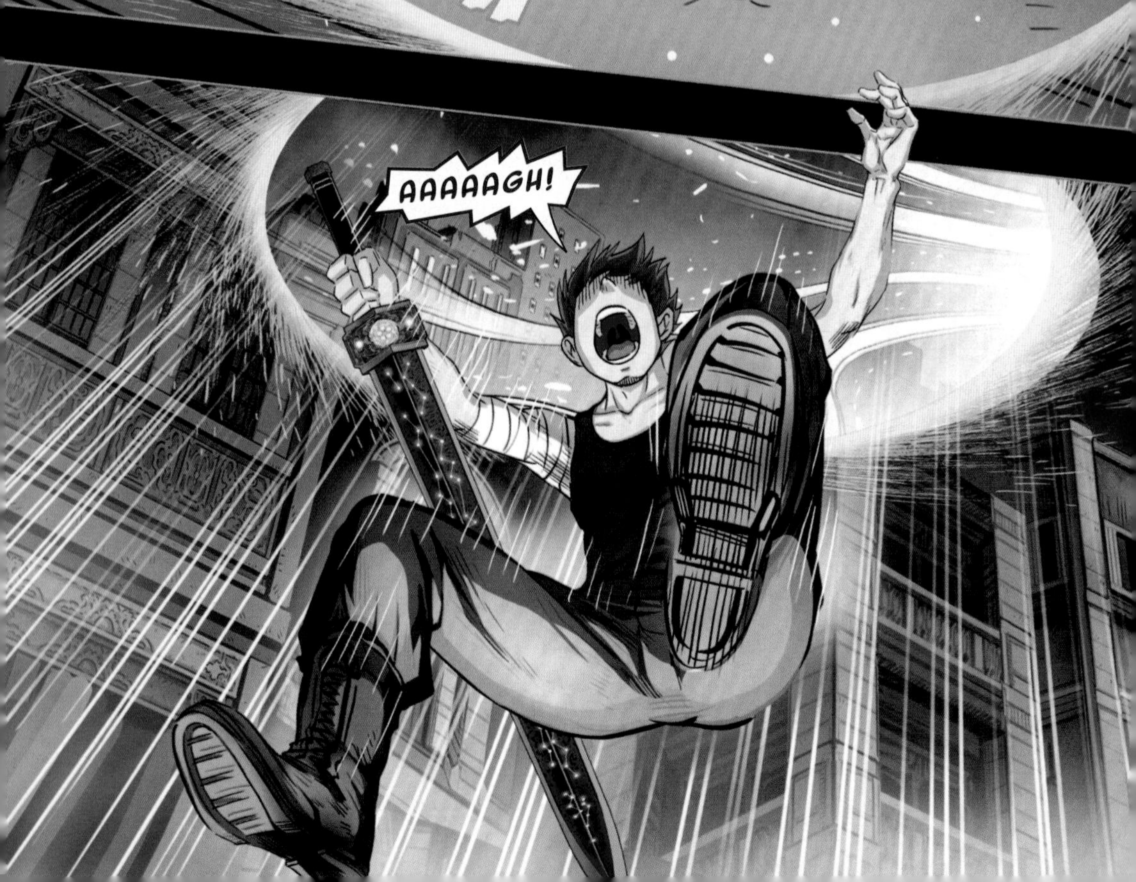
AAAAAGH!

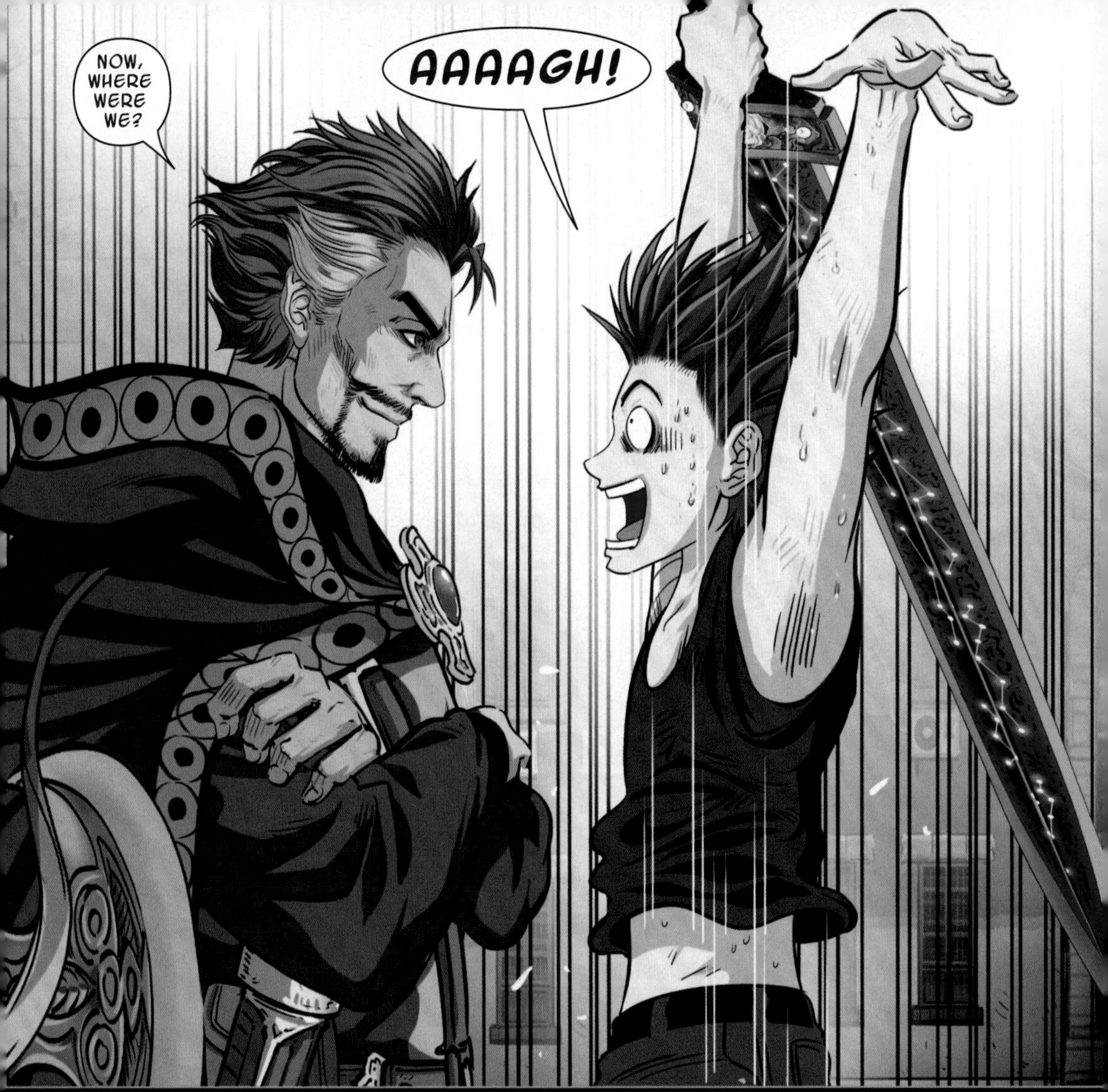
NOW, WHERE WERE WE?
AAAAGH!

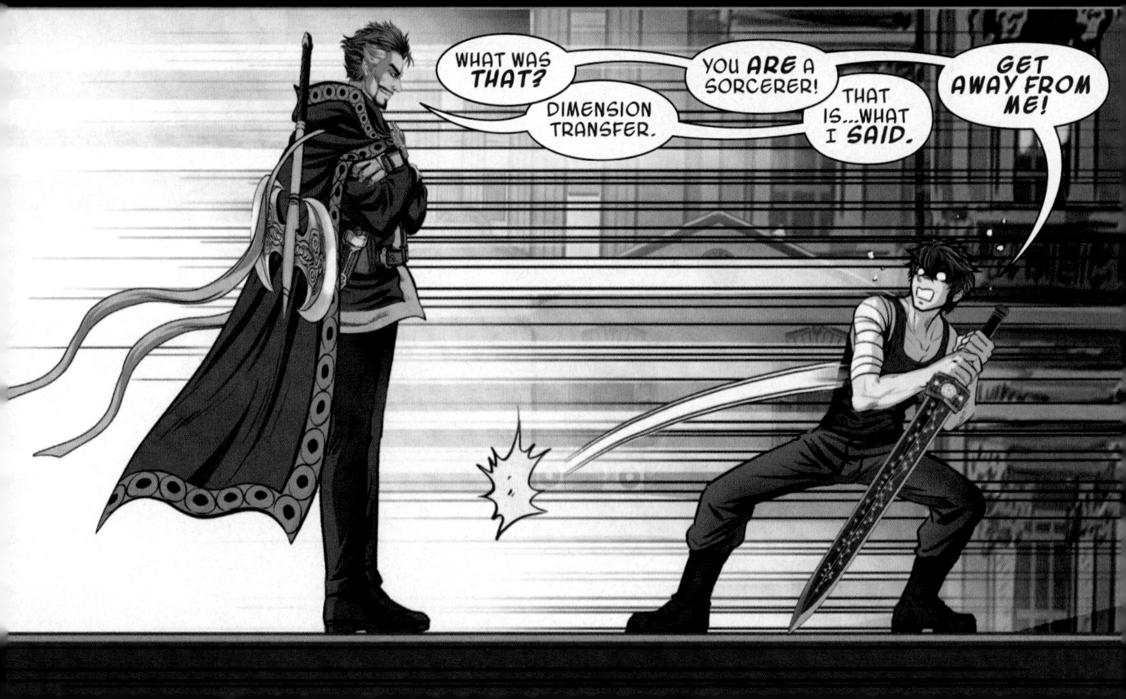
WHAT WAS THAT?
DIMENSION TRANSFER.
YOU ARE A SORCERER!
THAT IS...WHAT I SAID.
GET AWAY FROM ME!

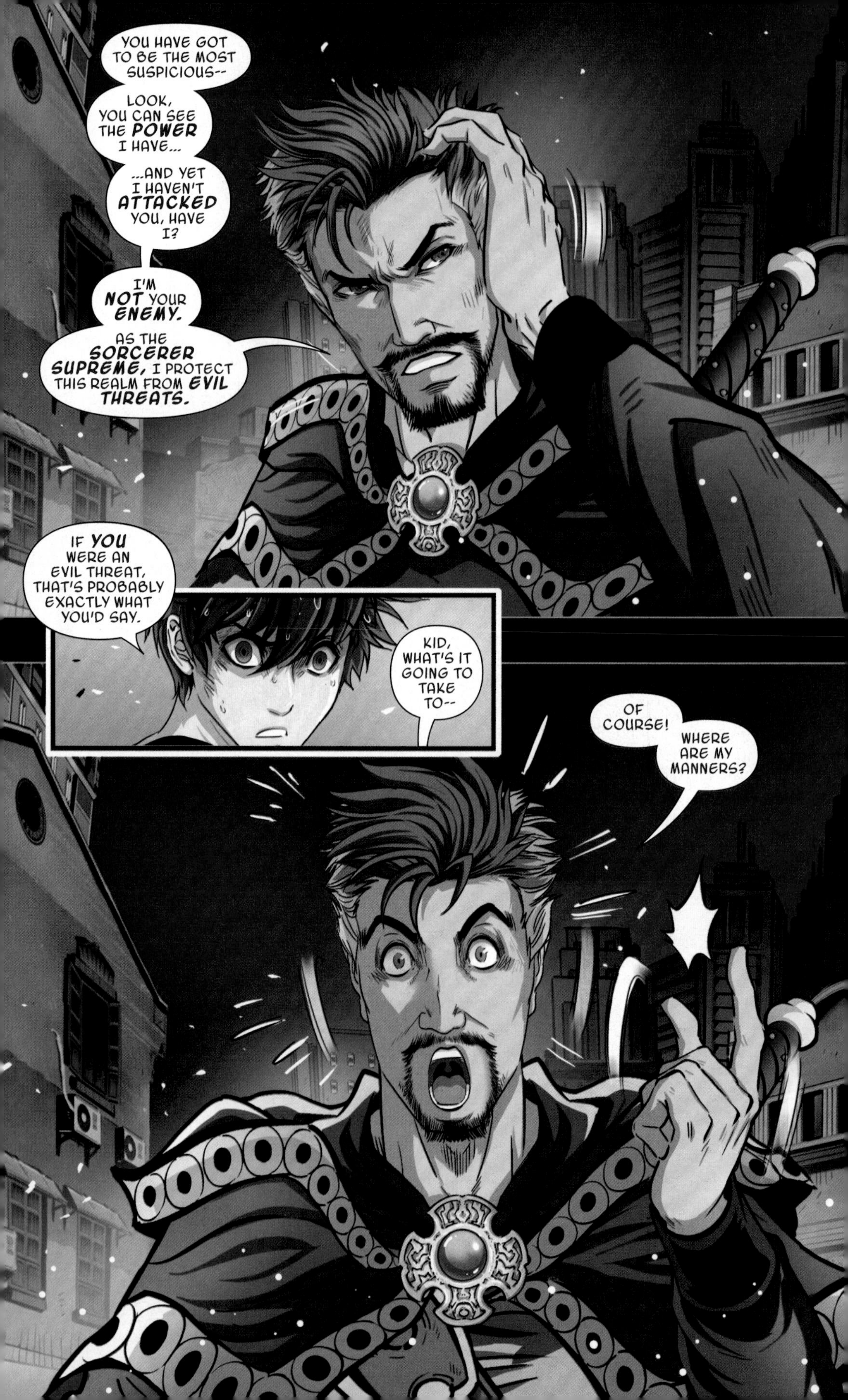
YOU HAVE GOT TO BE THE MOST SUSPICIOUS--
LOOK, YOU CAN SEE THE POWER I HAVE...
...AND YET I HAVEN'T ATTACKED YOU, HAVE I?
I'M NOT YOUR ENEMY.
AS THE SORCERER SUPREME, I PROTECT THIS REALM FROM EVIL THREATS.
IF YOU WERE AN EVIL THREAT, THAT'S PROBABLY EXACTLY WHAT YOU'D SAY.
KID, WHAT'S IT GOING TO TAKE TO--
OF COURSE!
WHERE ARE MY MANNERS?

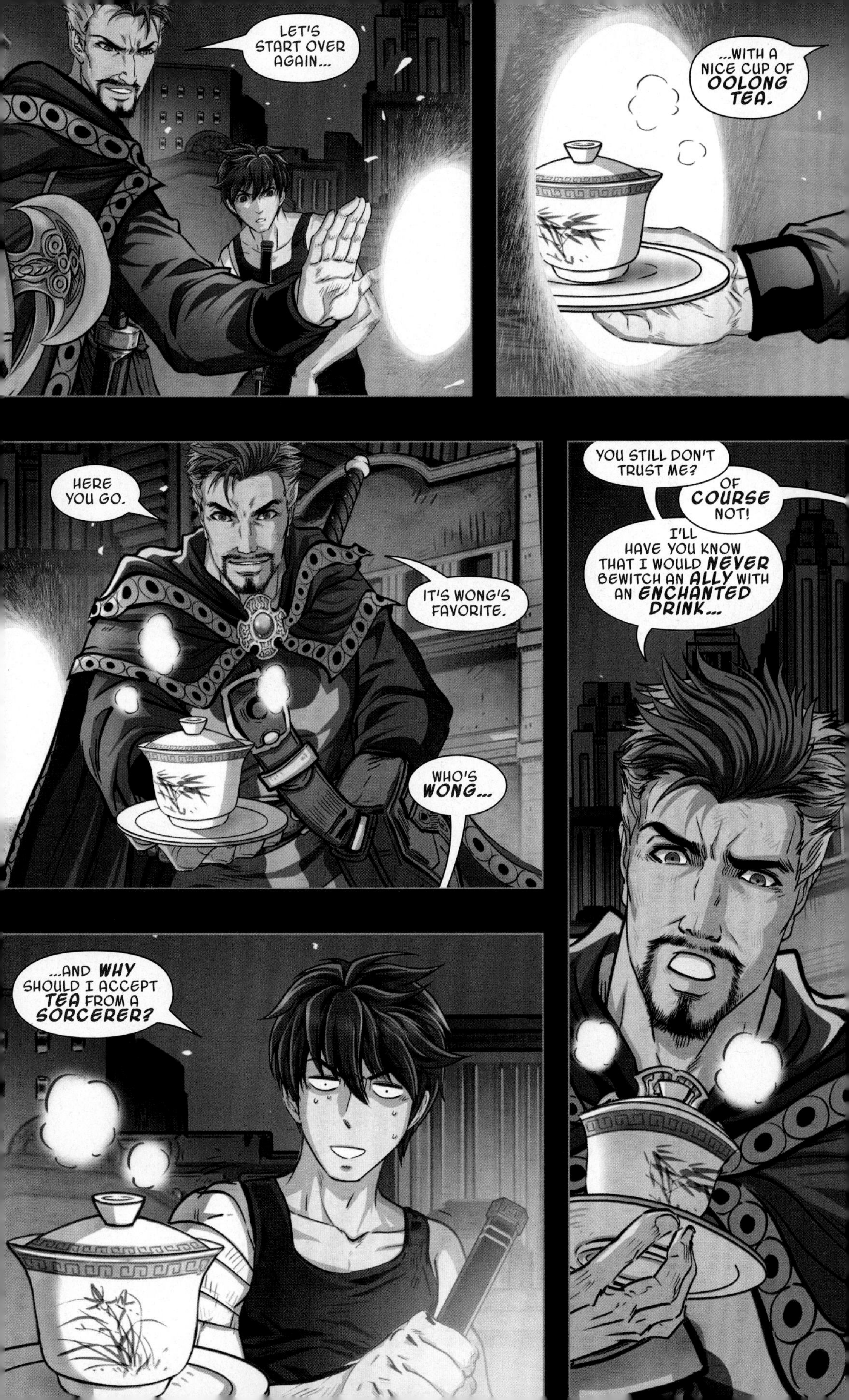
LET'S START OVER AGAIN...
...WITH A NICE CUP OF OOLONG TEA.
HERE YOU GO.
IT'S WONG'S FAVORITE.
WHO'S WONG...
...AND WHY SHOULD I ACCEPT TEA FROM A SORCERER?
YOU STILL DON'T TRUST ME?
OF COURSE NOT!
I'LL HAVE YOU KNOW THAT I WOULD NEVER BEWITCH AN ALLY WITH AN ENCHANTED DRINK...

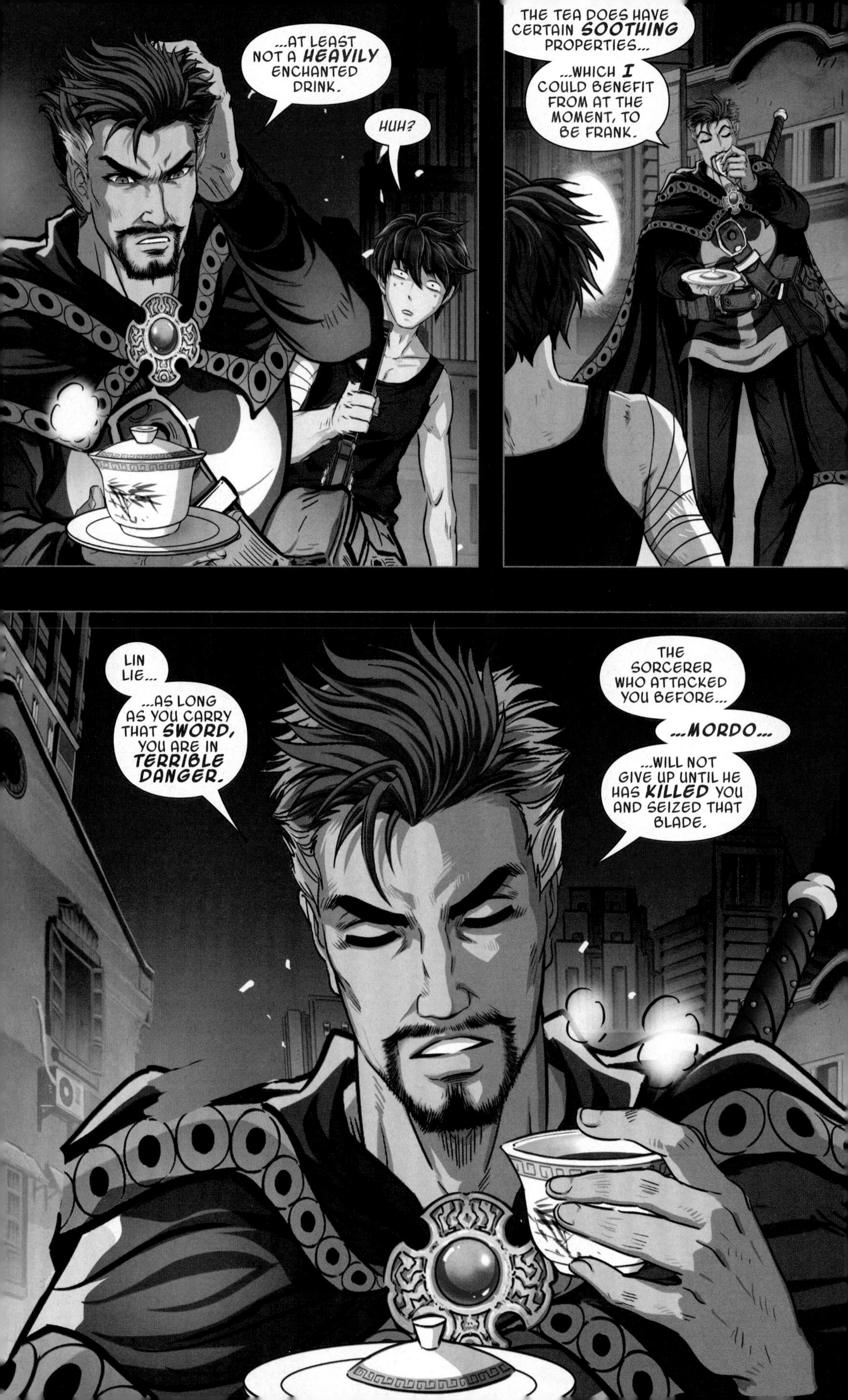
...AT LEAST NOT A HEAVILY ENCHANTED DRINK.
HUH?
THE TEA DOES HAVE CERTAIN SOOTHING PROPERTIES...
...WHICH I COULD BENEFIT FROM AT THE MOMENT, TO BE FRANK.
LIN LIE...
...AS LONG AS YOU CARRY THAT SWORD, YOU ARE IN TERRIBLE DANGER.
THE SORCERER WHO ATTACKED YOU BEFORE...
...MORDO...
...WILL NOT GIVE UP UNTIL HE HAS KILLED YOU AND SEIZED THAT BLADE.

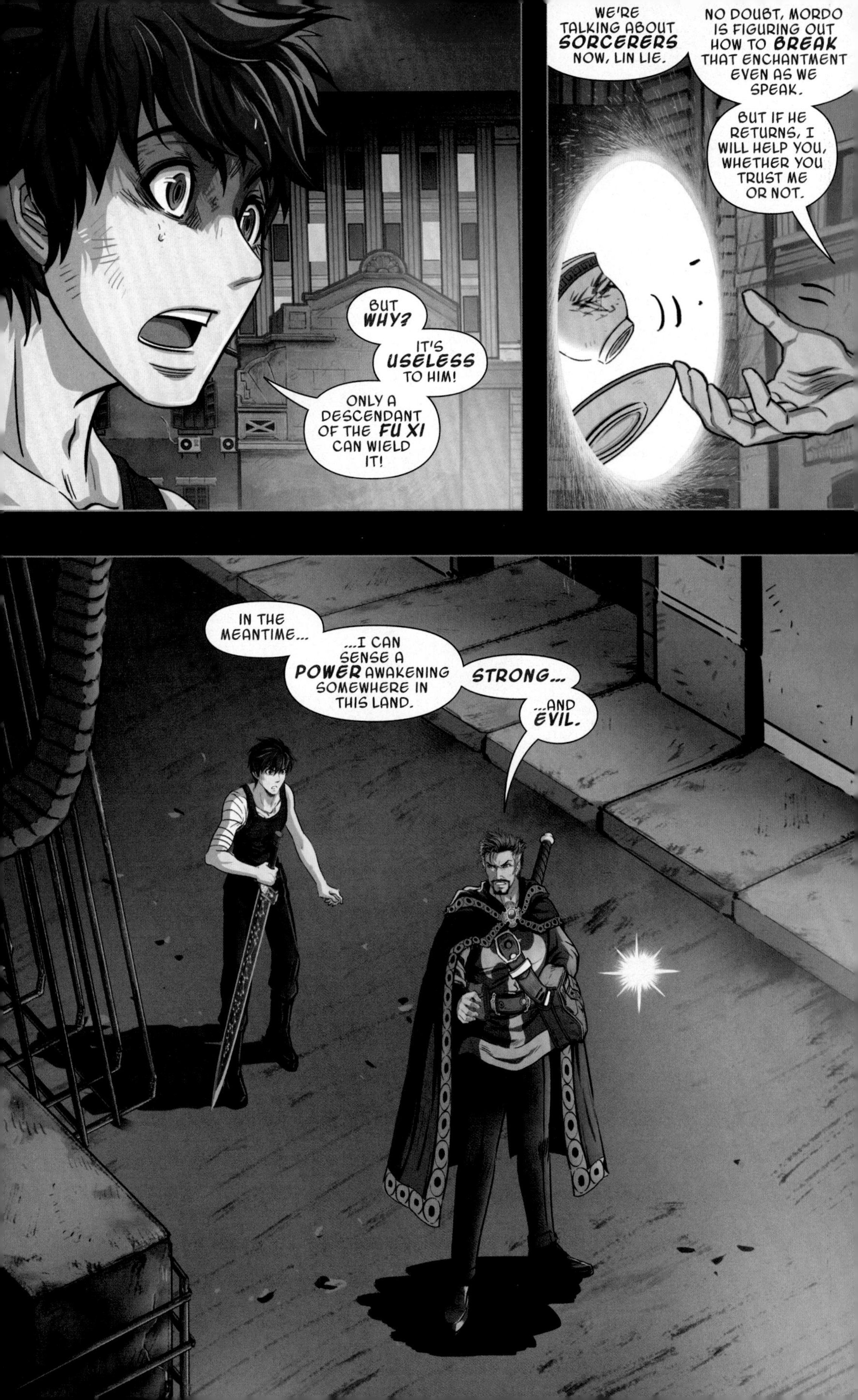
BUT WHY?
IT'S USELESS TO HIM!
ONLY A DESCENDANT OF THE FU XI CAN WIELD IT!
WE'RE TALKING ABOUT SORCERERS NOW, LIN LIE.
NO DOUBT, MORDO IS FIGURING OUT HOW TO BREAK THAT ENCHANTMENT EVEN AS WE SPEAK.
BUT IF HE RETURNS, I WILL HELP YOU, WHETHER YOU TRUST ME OR NOT.
IN THE MEANTIME...
...I CAN SENSE A POWER AWAKENING SOMEWHERE IN THIS LAND.
STRONG...
...AND EVIL.

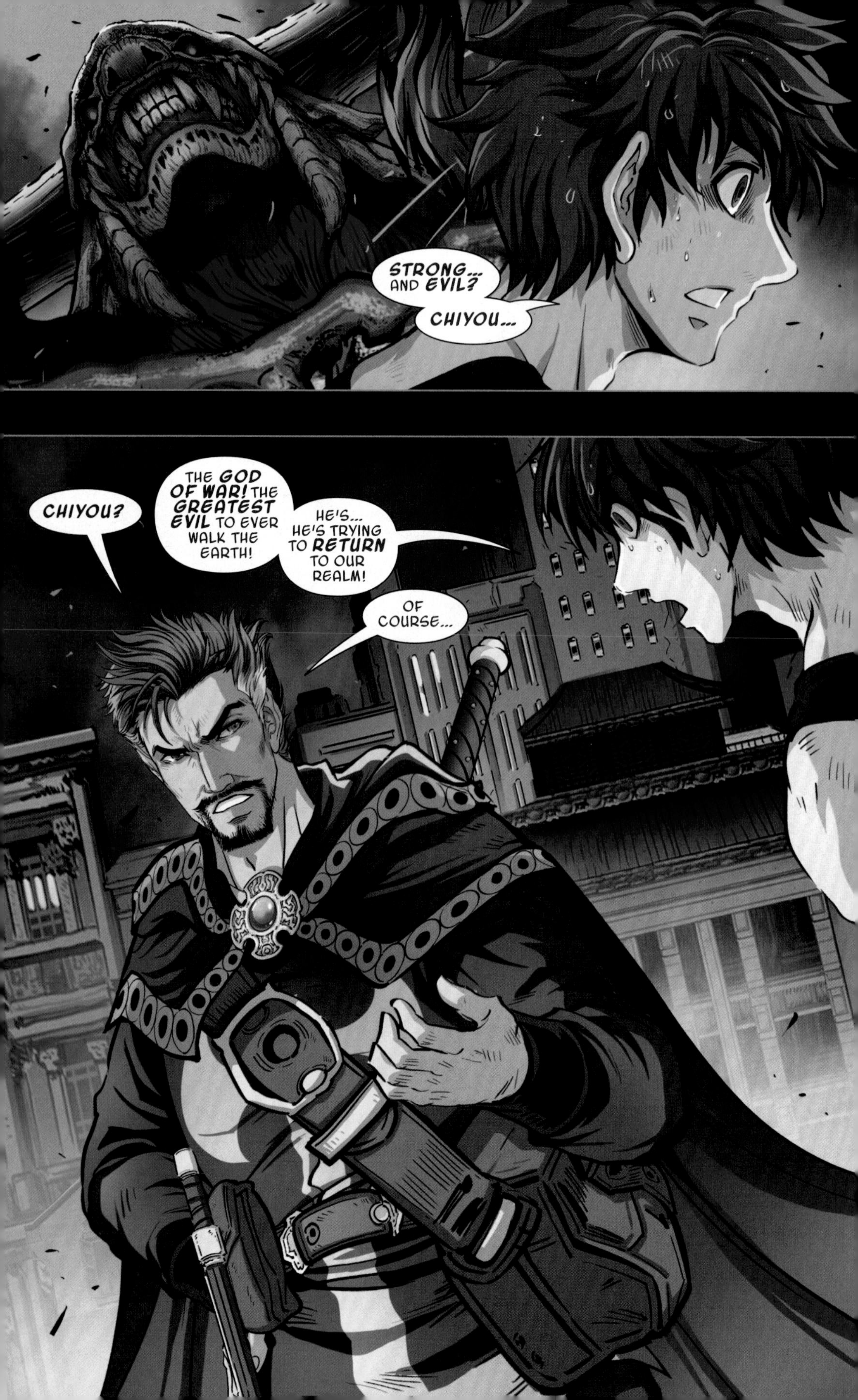
STRONG... AND EVIL?
CHIYOU...
CHIYOU?
THE GOD OF WAR! THE GREATEST EVIL TO EVER WALK THE EARTH!
HE'S... HE'S TRYING TO RETURN TO OUR REALM!
OF COURSE...

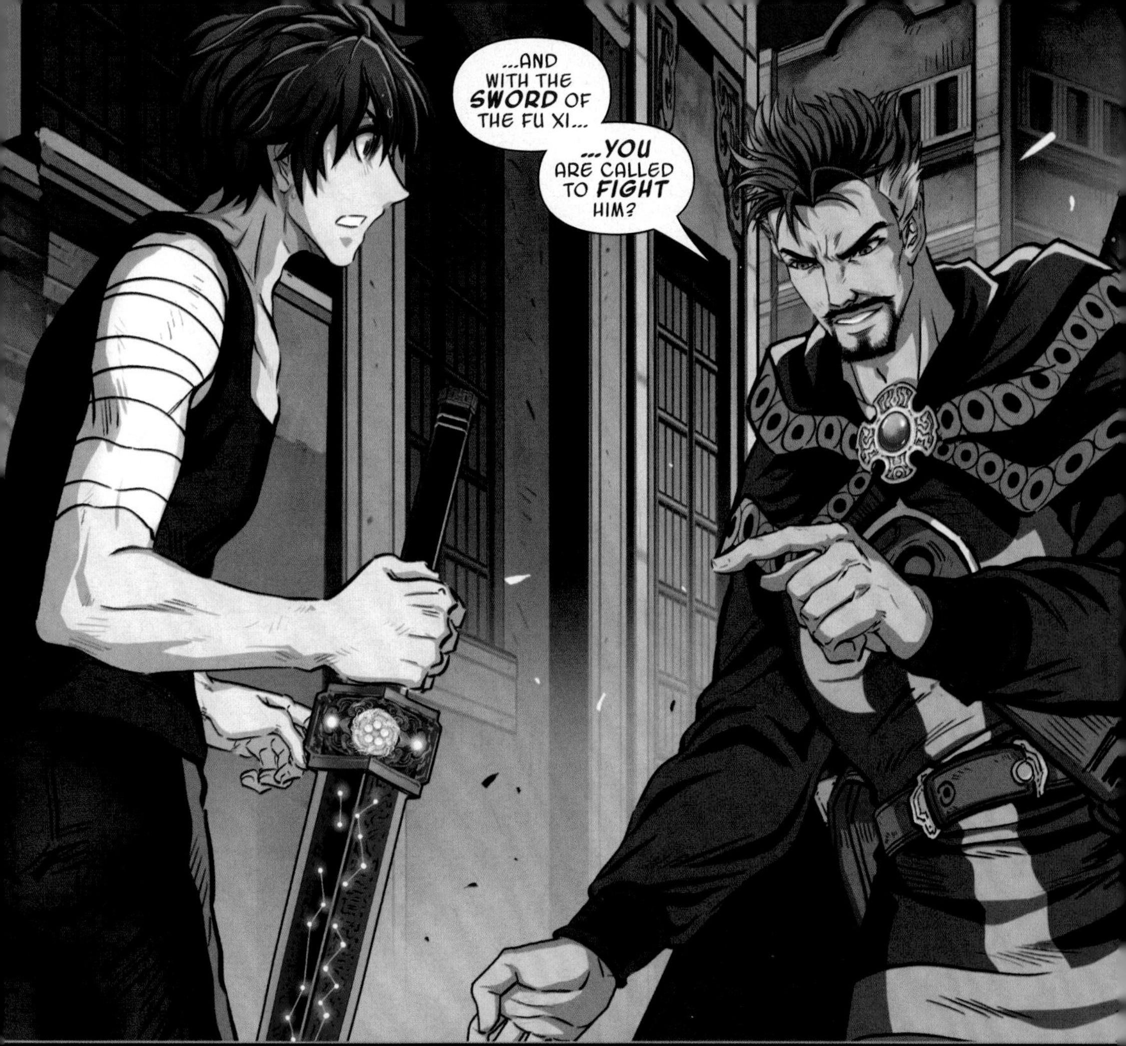
...AND WITH THE SWORD OF THE FU XI...
...YOU ARE CALLED TO FIGHT HIM?

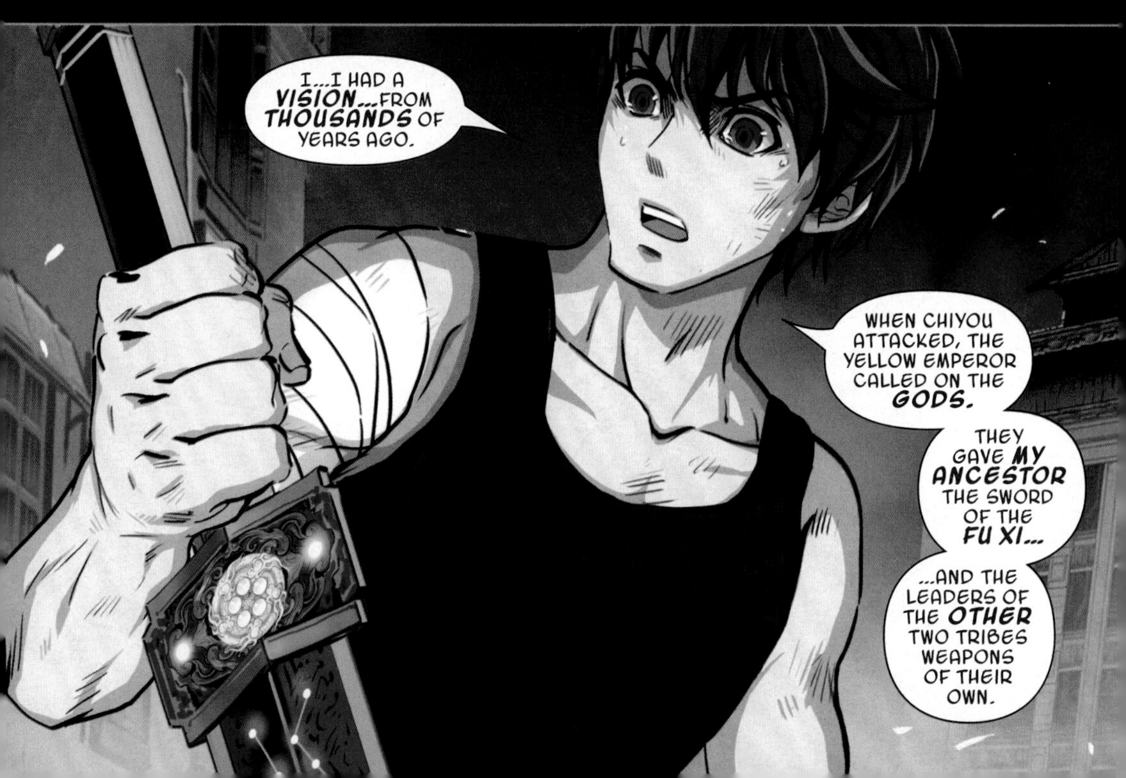
I...I HAD A VISION...FROM THOUSANDS OF YEARS AGO.
WHEN CHIYOU ATTACKED, THE YELLOW EMPEROR CALLED ON THE GODS.
THEY GAVE MY ANCESTOR THE SWORD OF THE FU XI...
...AND THE LEADERS OF THE OTHER TWO TRIBES WEAPONS OF THEIR OWN.

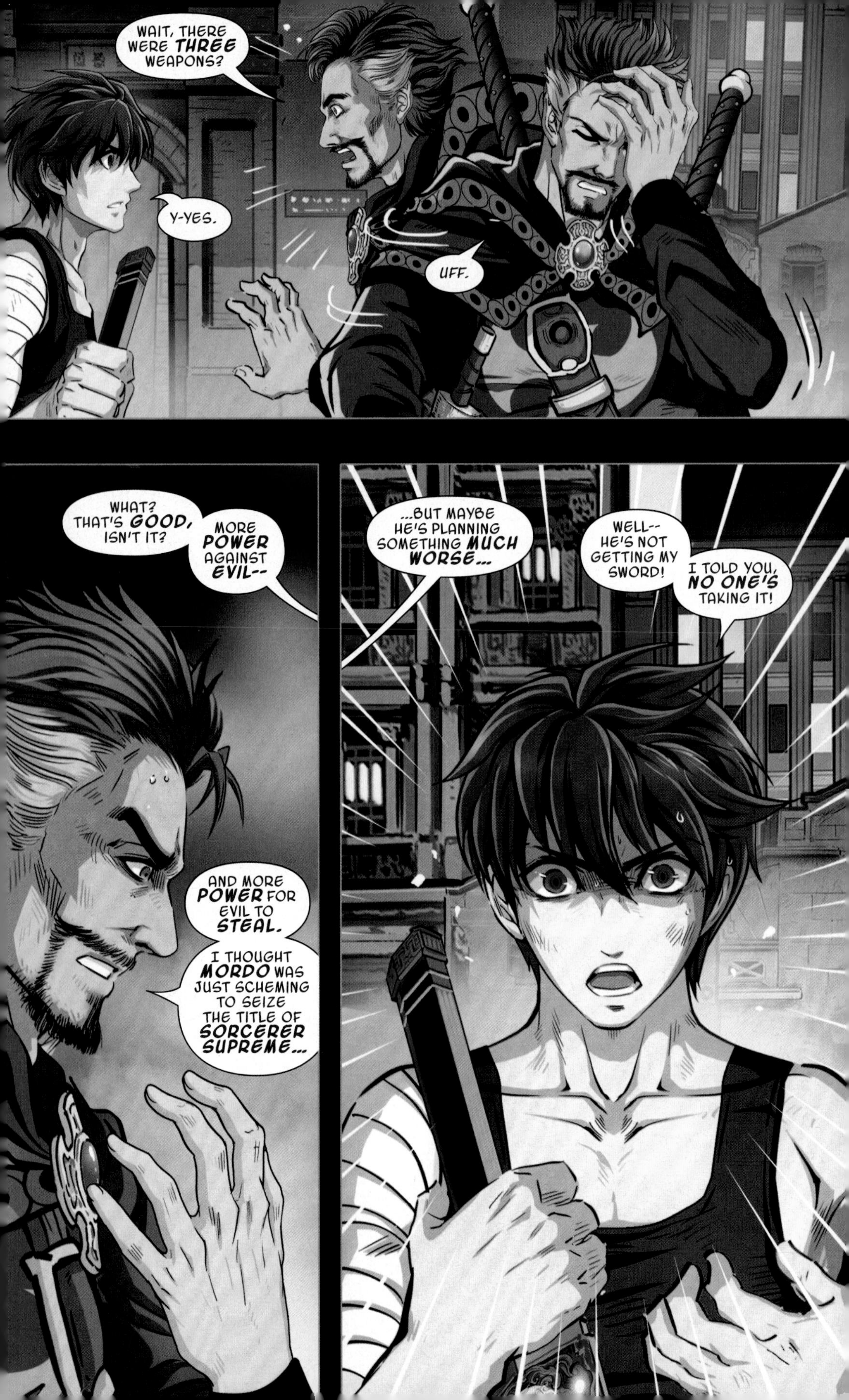
WAIT, THERE WERE THREE WEAPONS?
Y-YES.
UFF.
WHAT? THAT'S GOOD, ISN'T IT?
MORE POWER AGAINST EVIL--
AND MORE POWER FOR EVIL TO STEAL.
I THOUGHT MORDO WAS JUST SCHEMING TO SEIZE THE TITLE OF SORCERER SUPREME...
...BUT MAYBE HE'S PLANNING SOMETHING MUCH WORSE...
WELL-- HE'S NOT GETTING MY SWORD!
I TOLD YOU, NO ONE'S TAKING IT!

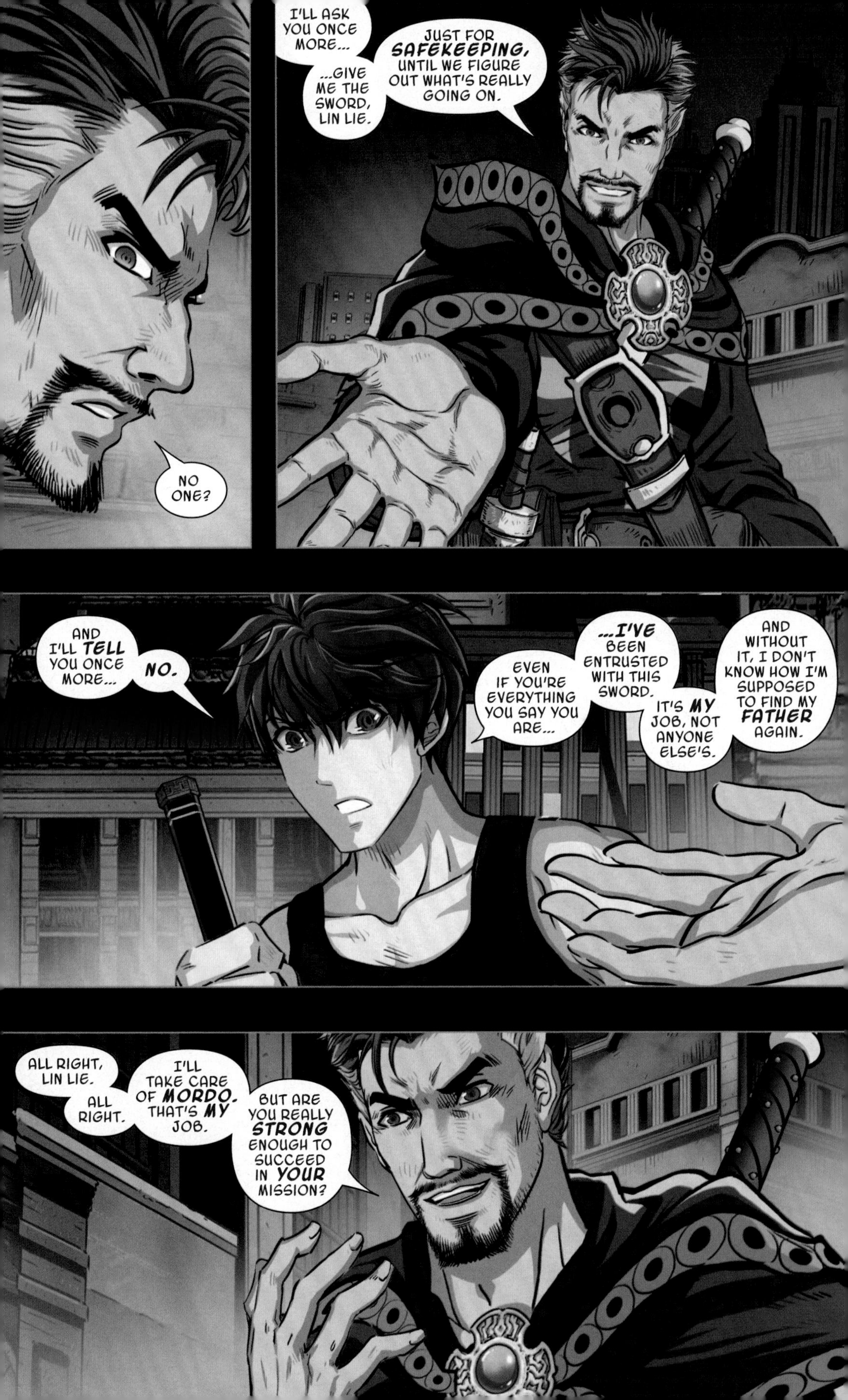
NO ONE?
I'LL ASK YOU ONCE MORE...
...GIVE ME THE SWORD, LIN LIE.
JUST FOR SAFEKEEPING, UNTIL WE FIGURE OUT WHAT'S REALLY GOING ON.
AND I'LL TELL YOU ONCE MORE...
NO.
EVEN IF YOU'RE EVERYTHING YOU SAY YOU ARE...
...I'VE BEEN ENTRUSTED WITH THIS SWORD.
IT'S MY JOB, NOT ANYONE ELSE'S.
AND WITHOUT IT, I DON'T KNOW HOW I'M SUPPOSED TO FIND MY FATHER AGAIN.
ALL RIGHT, LIN LIE.
ALL RIGHT.
I'LL TAKE CARE OF MORDO. THAT'S MY JOB.
BUT ARE YOU REALLY STRONG ENOUGH TO SUCCEED IN YOUR MISSION?

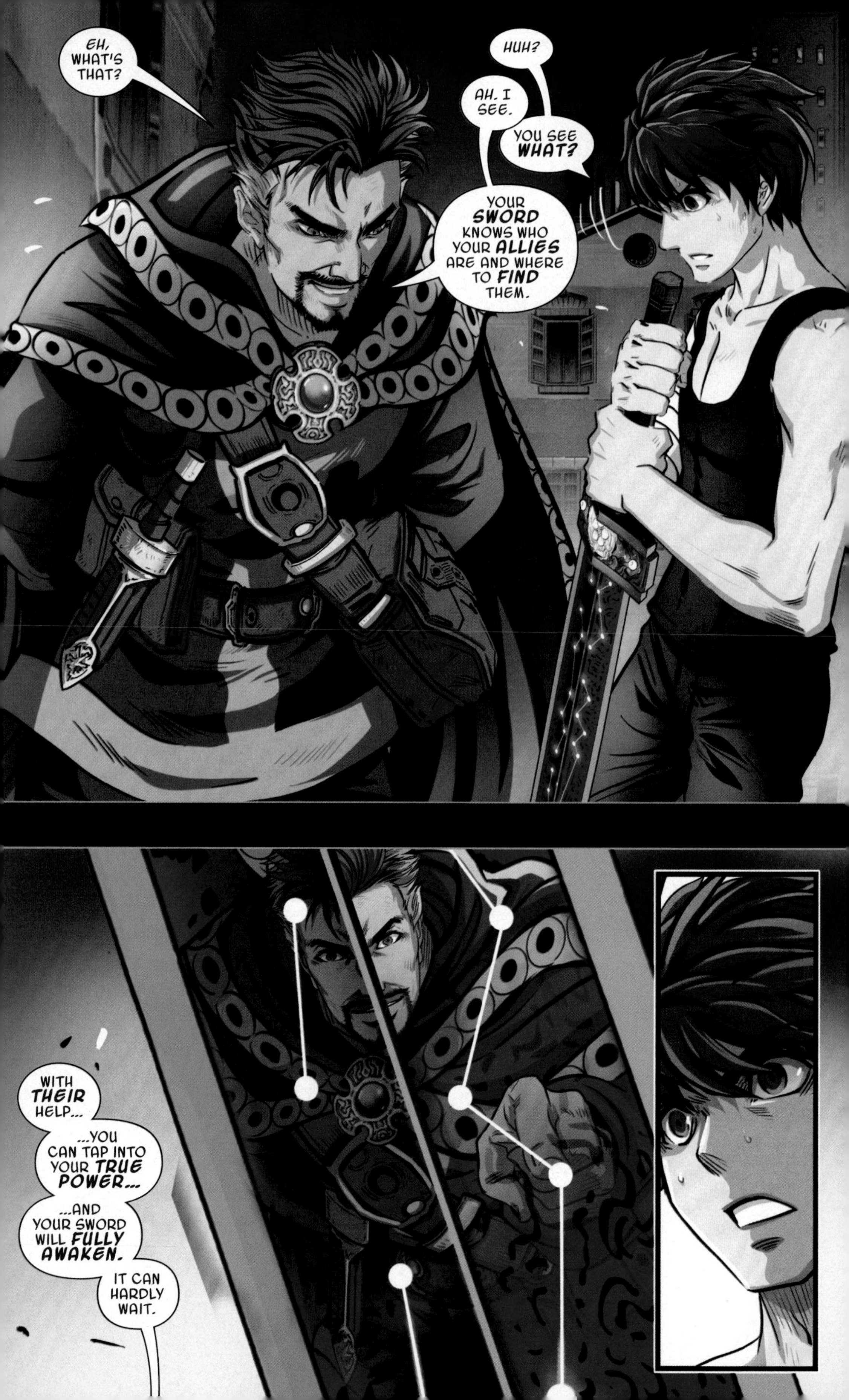
EH, WHAT'S THAT?
HUH?
AH. I SEE.
YOU SEE WHAT?
YOUR SWORD KNOWS WHO YOUR ALLIES ARE AND WHERE TO FIND THEM.
WITH THEIR HELP...
...YOU CAN TAP INTO YOUR TRUE POWER...
...AND YOUR SWORD WILL FULLY AWAKEN.
IT CAN HARDLY WAIT.

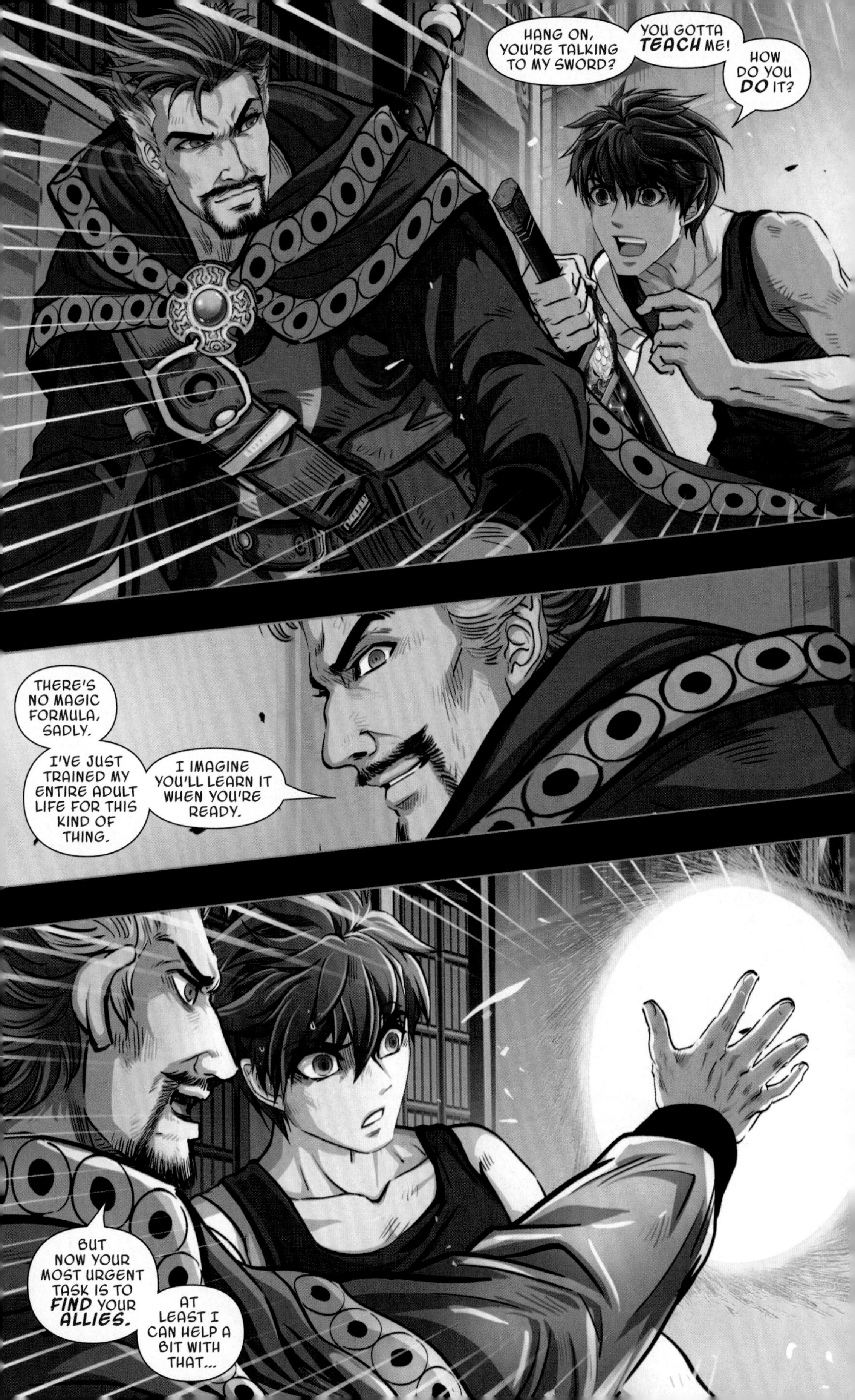
HANG ON, YOU'RE TALKING TO MY SWORD?
YOU GOTTA TEACH ME!
HOW DO YOU DO IT?
THERE'S NO MAGIC FORMULA, SADLY.
I'VE JUST TRAINED MY ENTIRE ADULT LIFE FOR THIS KIND OF THING.
I IMAGINE YOU'LL LEARN IT WHEN YOU'RE READY.
BUT NOW YOUR MOST URGENT TASK IS TO FIND YOUR ALLIES.
AT LEAST I CAN HELP A BIT WITH THAT...

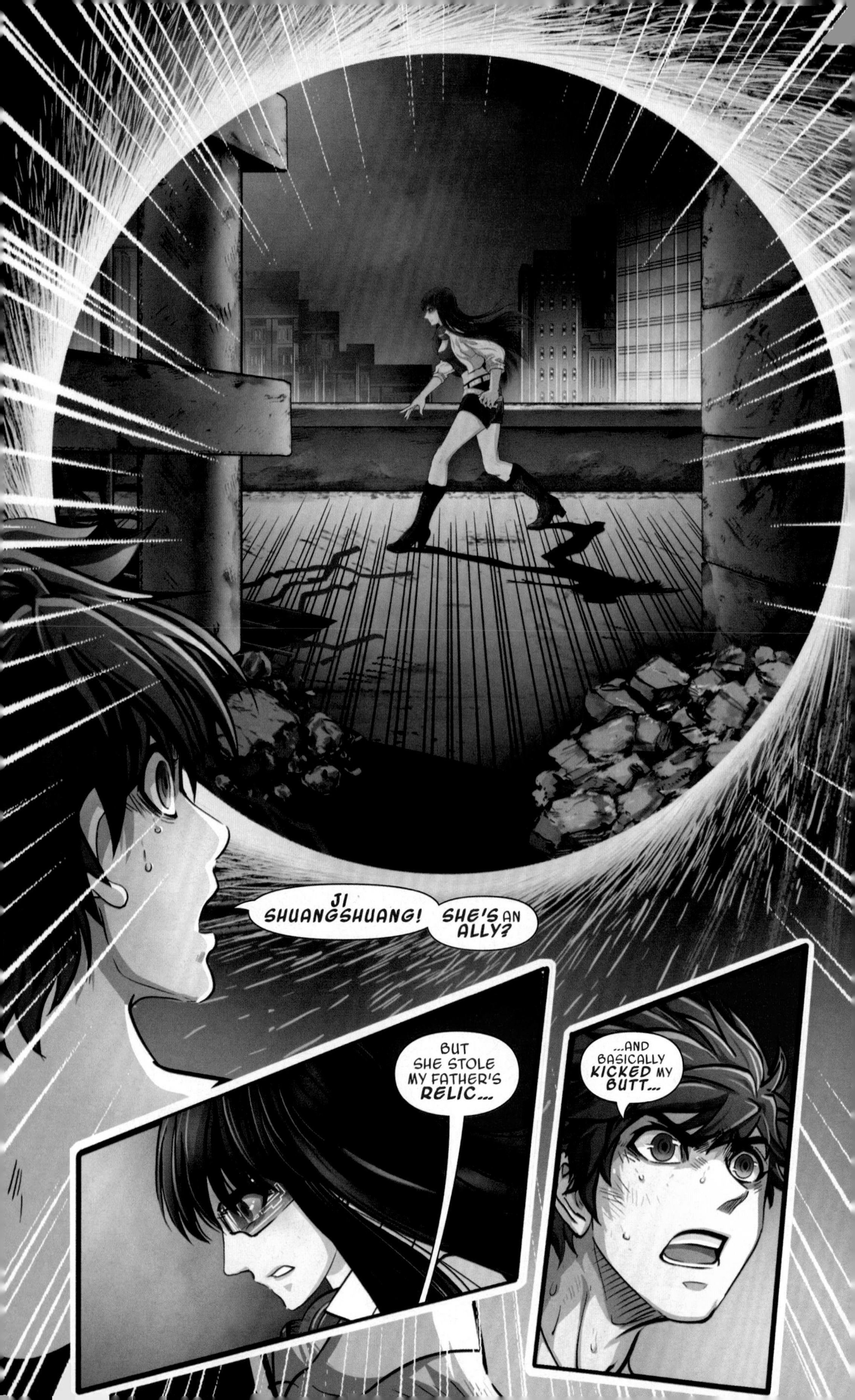
JI SHUANGSHUANG!
SHE'S AN ALLY?
BUT SHE STOLE MY FATHER'S RELIC...
...AND BASICALLY KICKED MY BUTT...

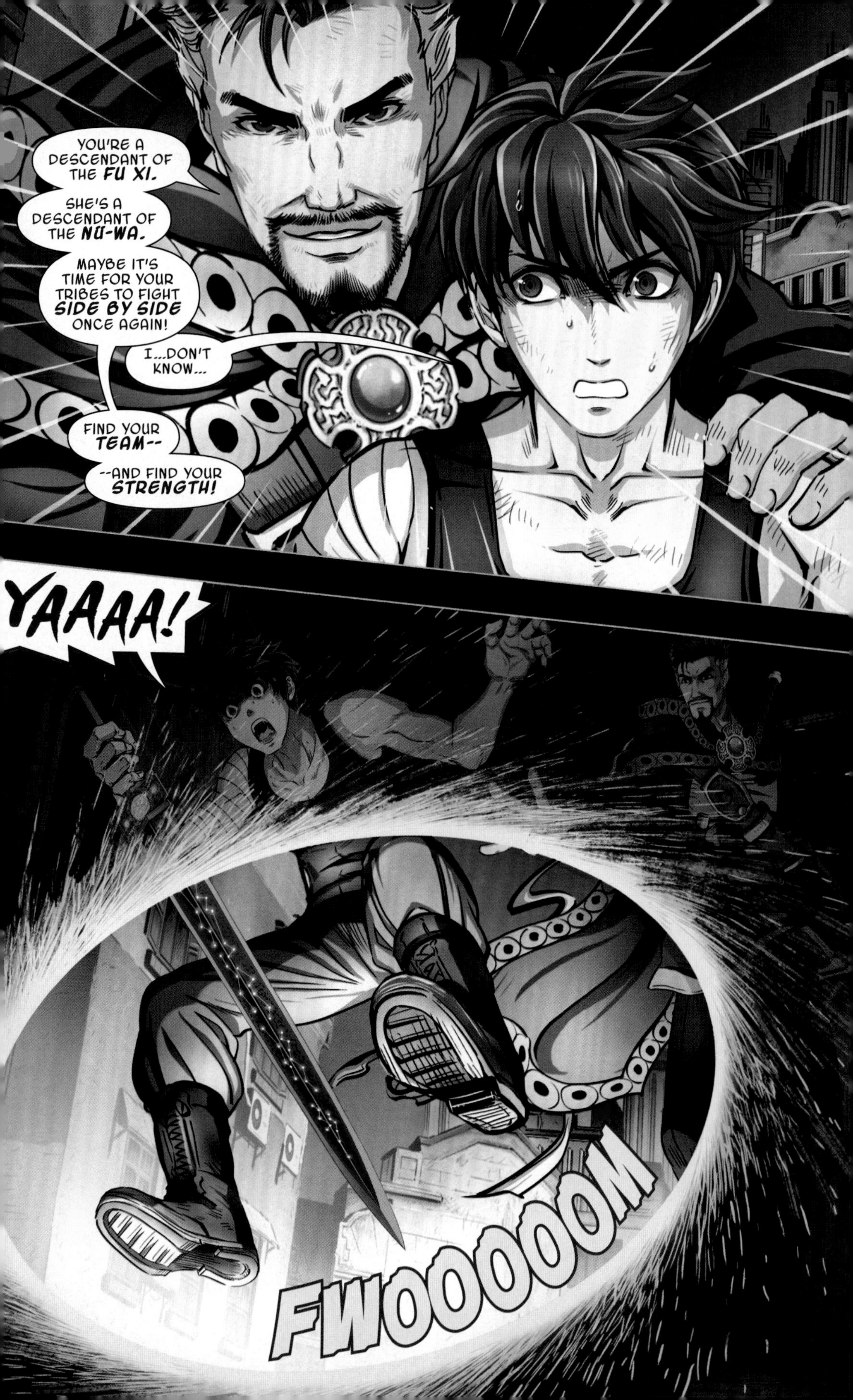
YOU'RE A DESCENDANT OF THE FU XI.
SHE'S A DESCENDANT OF THE NÜ-WA.
MAYBE IT'S TIME FOR YOUR TRIBES TO FIGHT SIDE BY SIDE ONCE AGAIN!
I...DON'T KNOW...
FIND YOUR TEAM--
--AND FIND YOUR STRENGTH!
YAAAA!
FWOOOOOOM

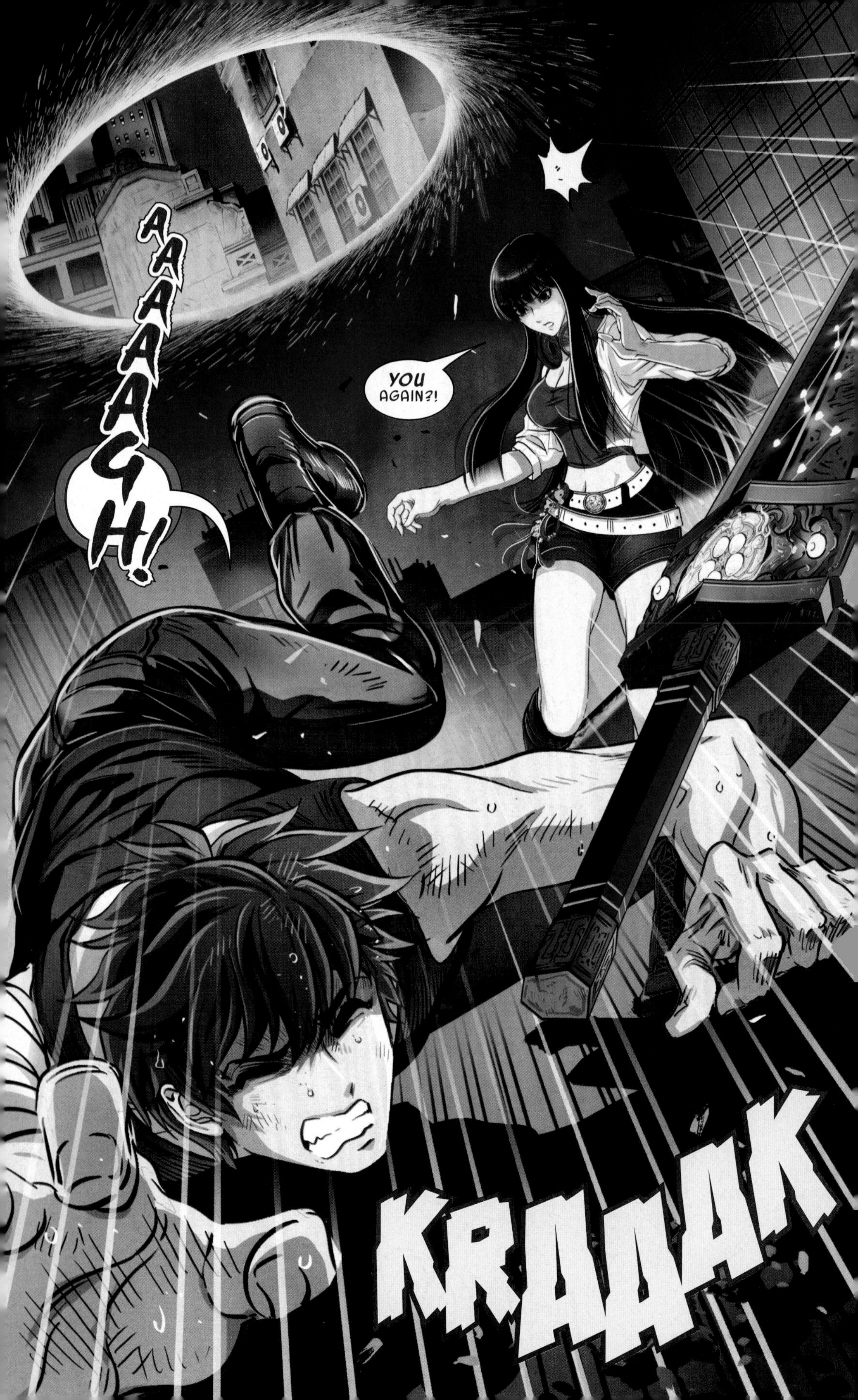
AAAAAAGH!
YOU AGAIN?!
KRAAAK

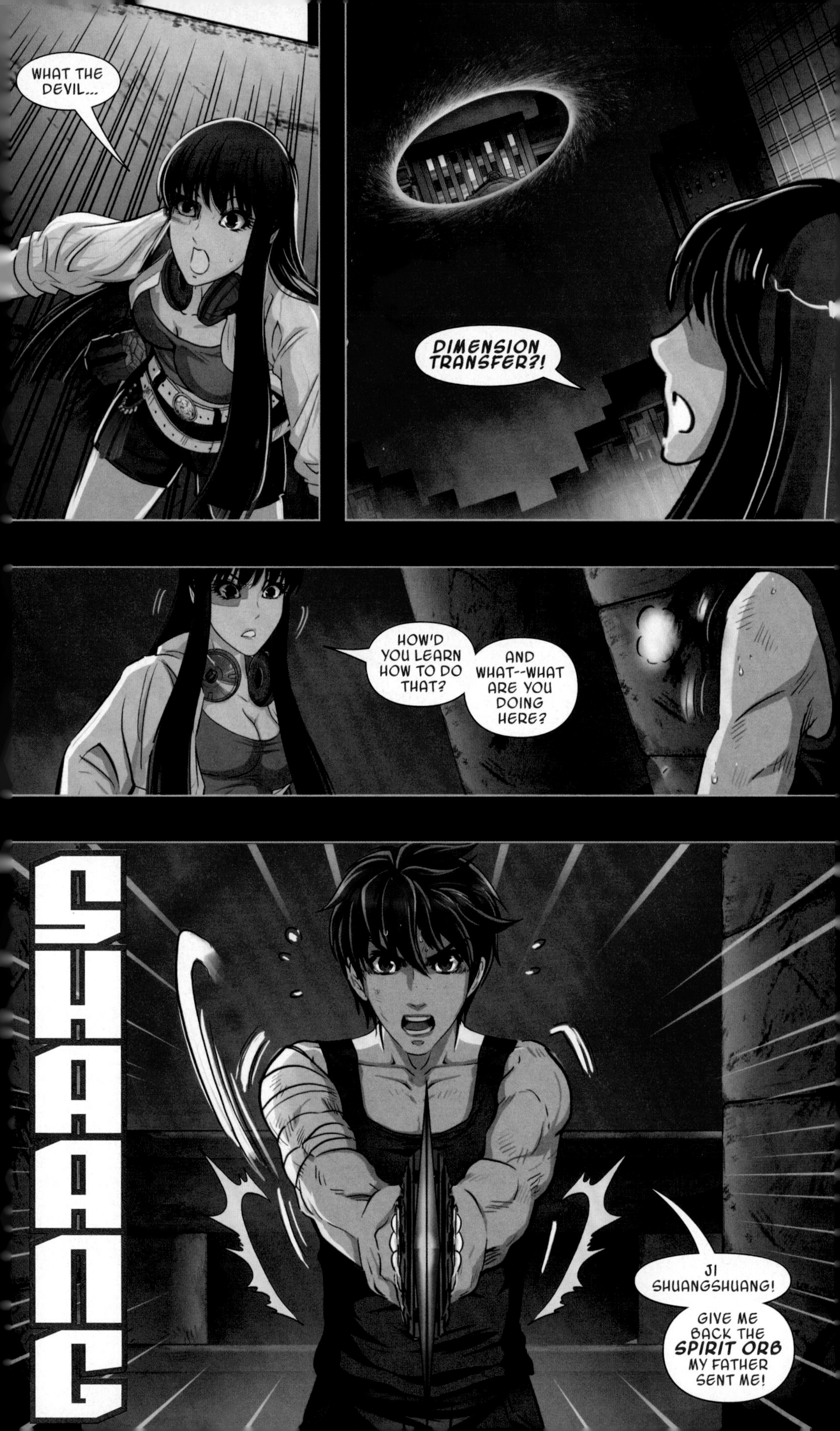
WHAT THE DEVIL...
DIMENSION TRANSFER?!
HOW'D YOU LEARN HOW TO DO THAT?
AND WHAT--WHAT ARE YOU DOING HERE?
SHAAANG
JI SHUANGSHUANG!
GIVE ME BACK THE SPIRIT ORB MY FATHER SENT ME!

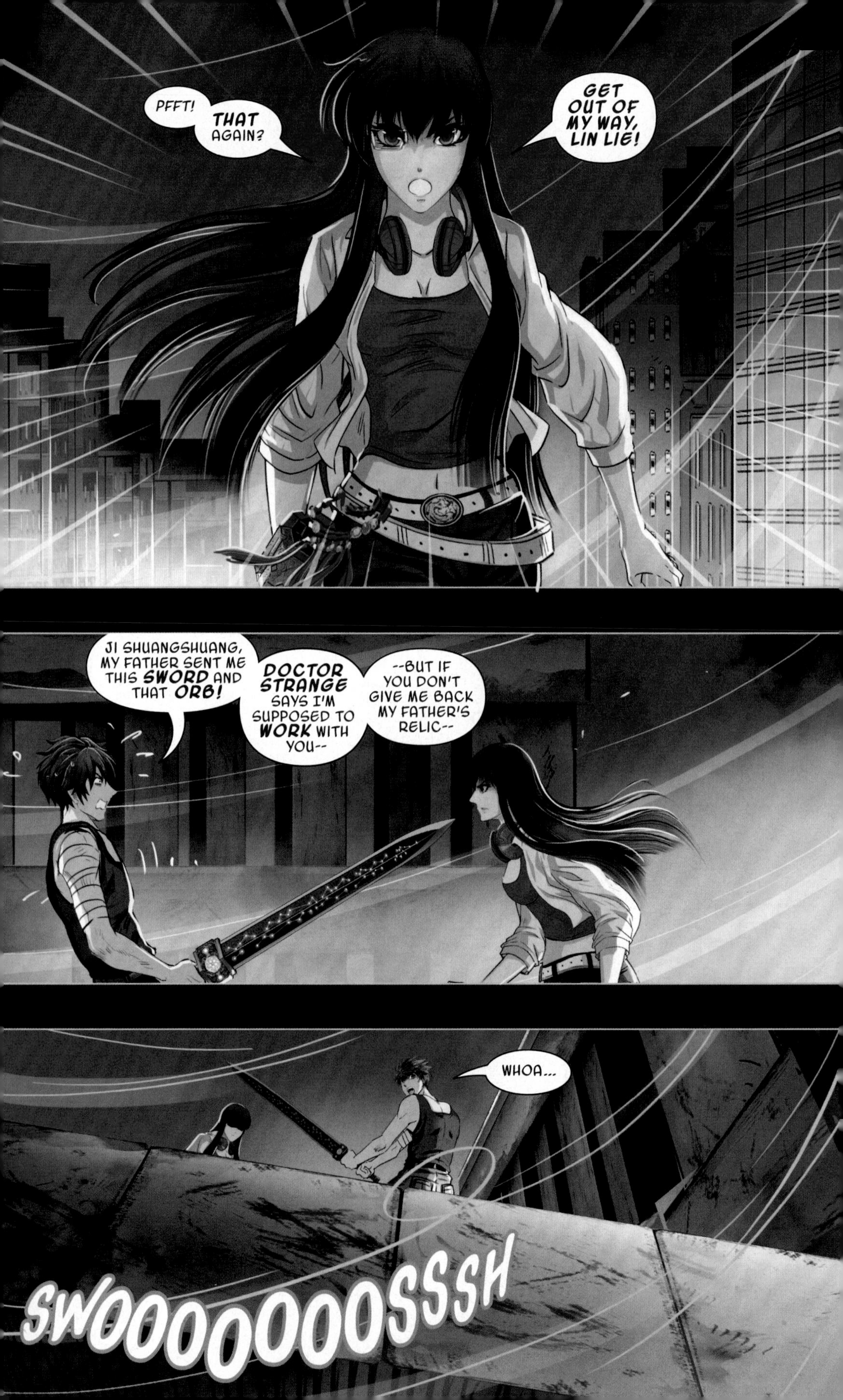
PFFT! THAT AGAIN?
GET OUT OF MY WAY, LIN LIE!
JI SHUANGSHUANG, MY FATHER SENT ME THIS SWORD AND THAT ORB!
DOCTOR STRANGE SAYS I'M SUPPOSED TO WORK WITH YOU--
--BUT IF YOU DON'T GIVE ME BACK MY FATHER'S RELIC--
WHOA...
SWOOOOOOOOSSSH

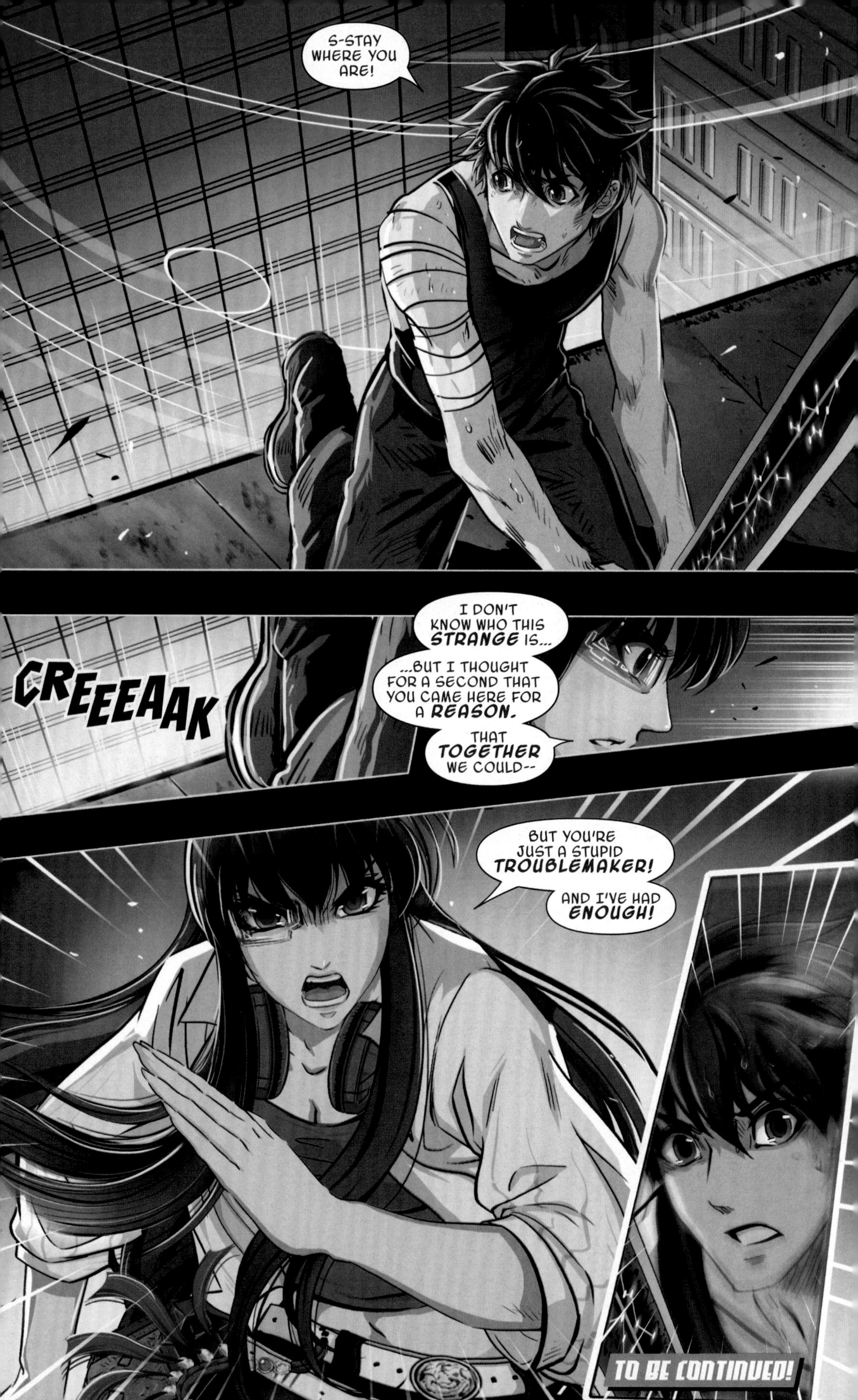
S-STAY WHERE YOU ARE!
CREEEAAK
I DON'T KNOW WHO THIS STRANGE IS...
...BUT I THOUGHT FOR A SECOND THAT YOU CAME HERE FOR A REASON.
THAT TOGETHER WE COULD--
BUT YOU'RE JUST A STUPID TROUBLEMAKER!
AND I'VE HAD ENOUGH!
TO BE CONTINUED!

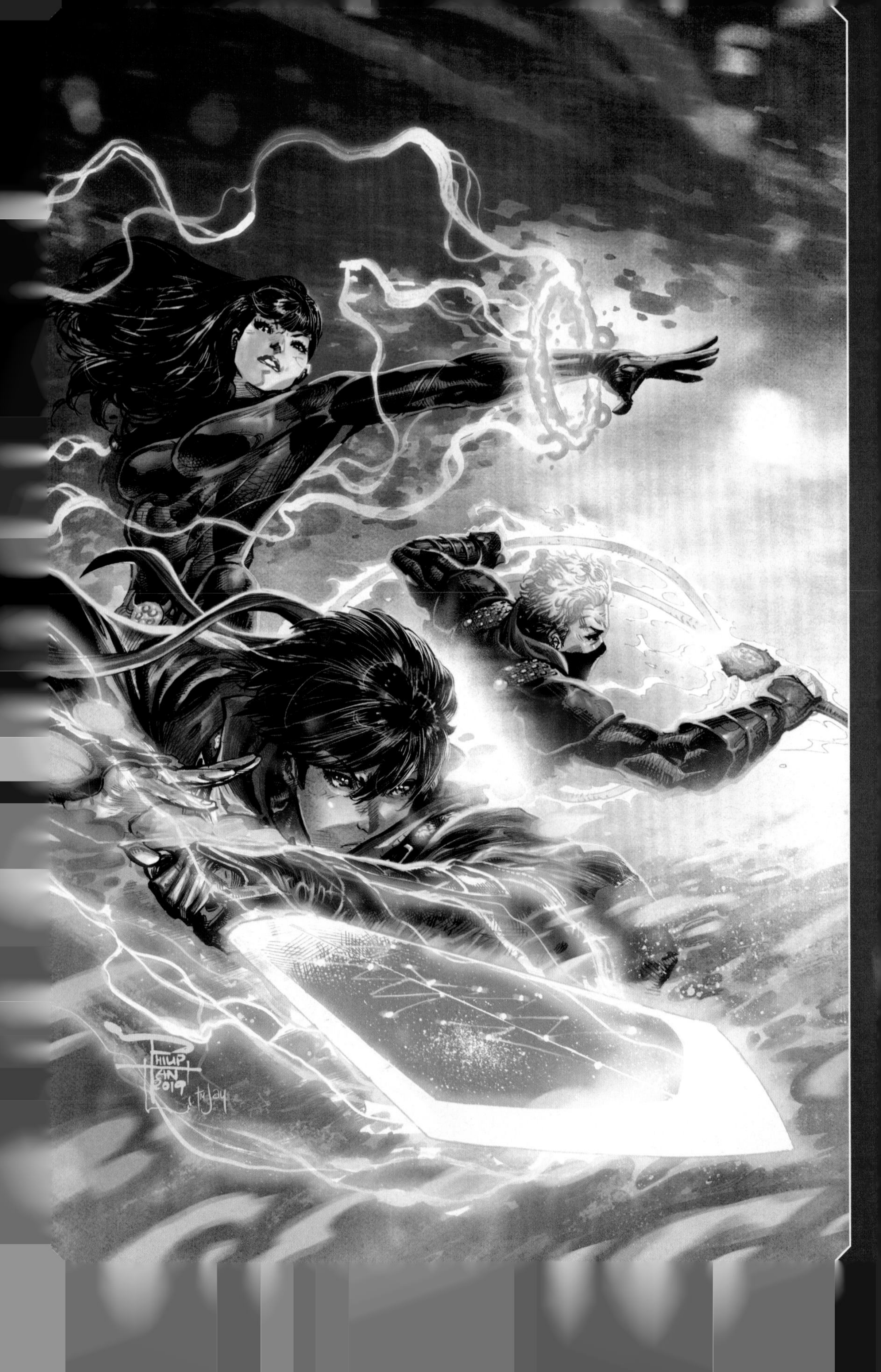

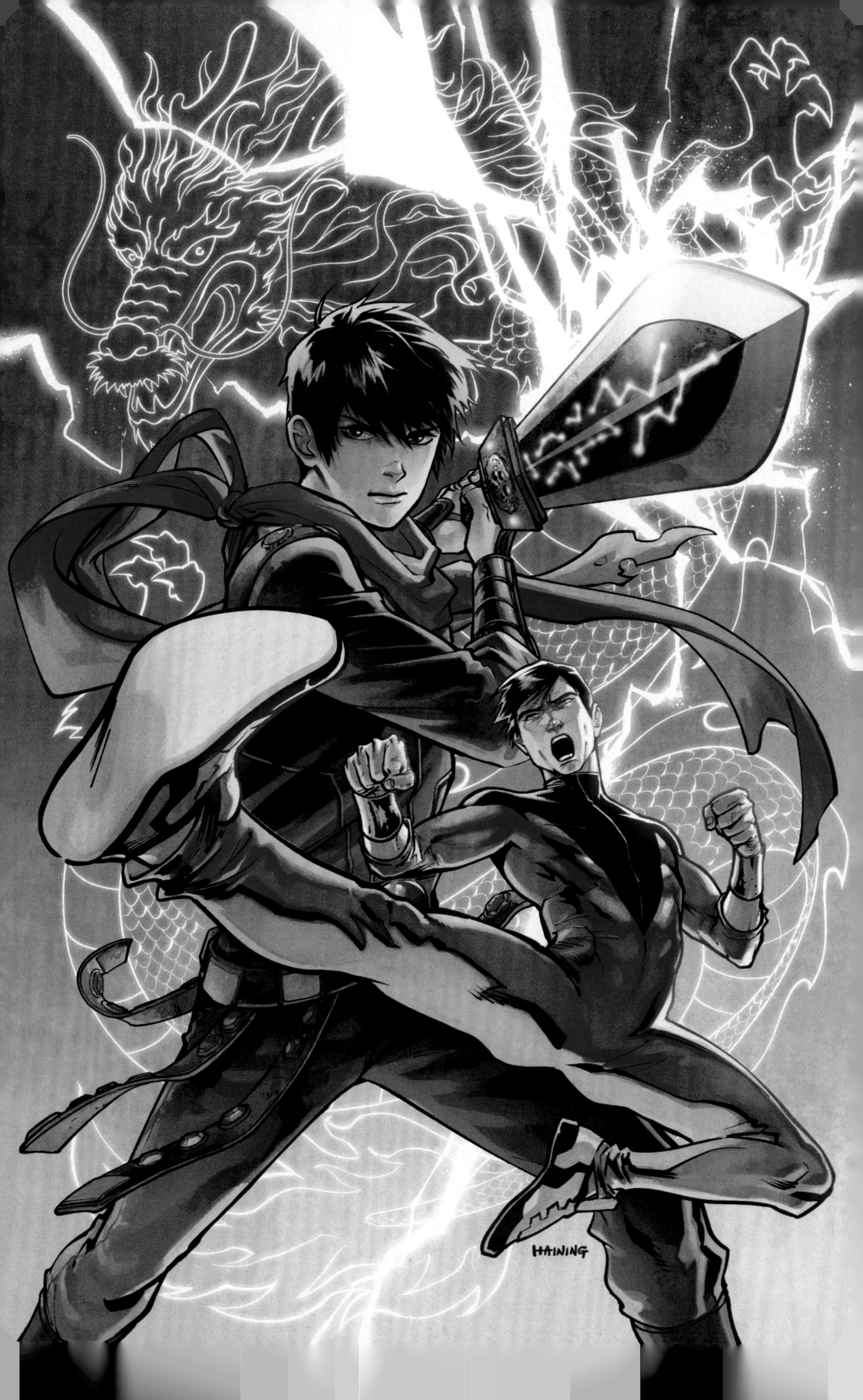
HAINING

Sword Master 001
variant edition
rated T+
$3.99 US
direct edition
MARVEL.com

series 3

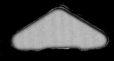

SWORD MASTER

三皇斗战士

林烈

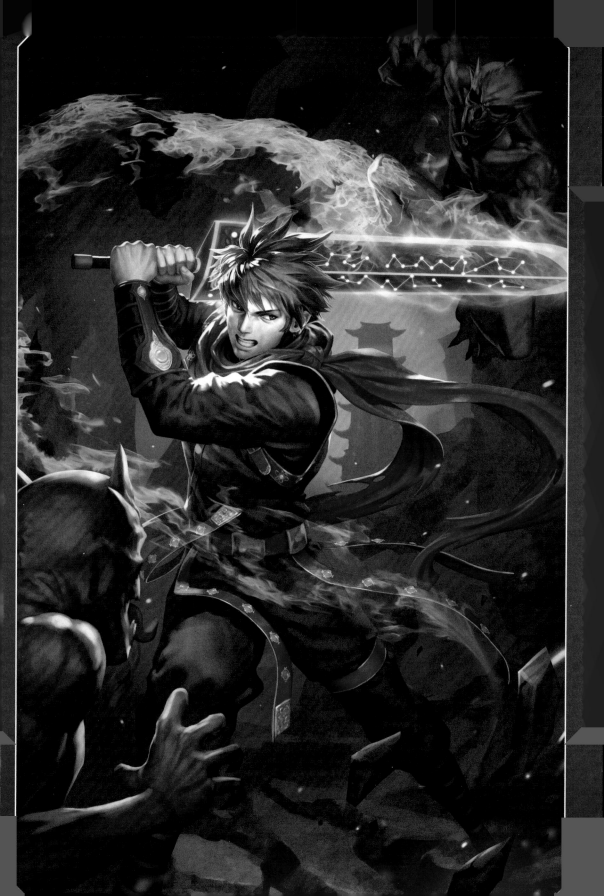

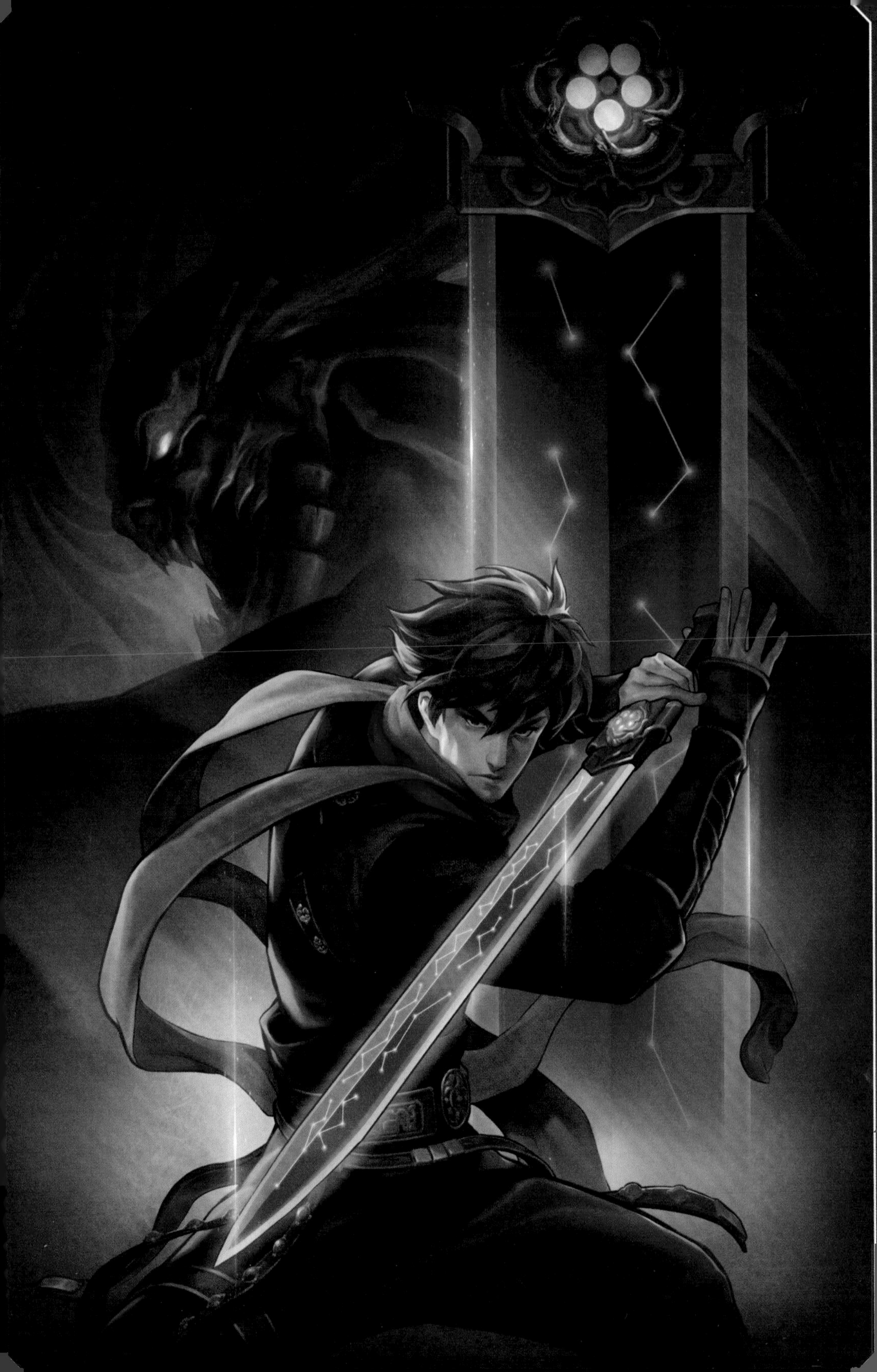

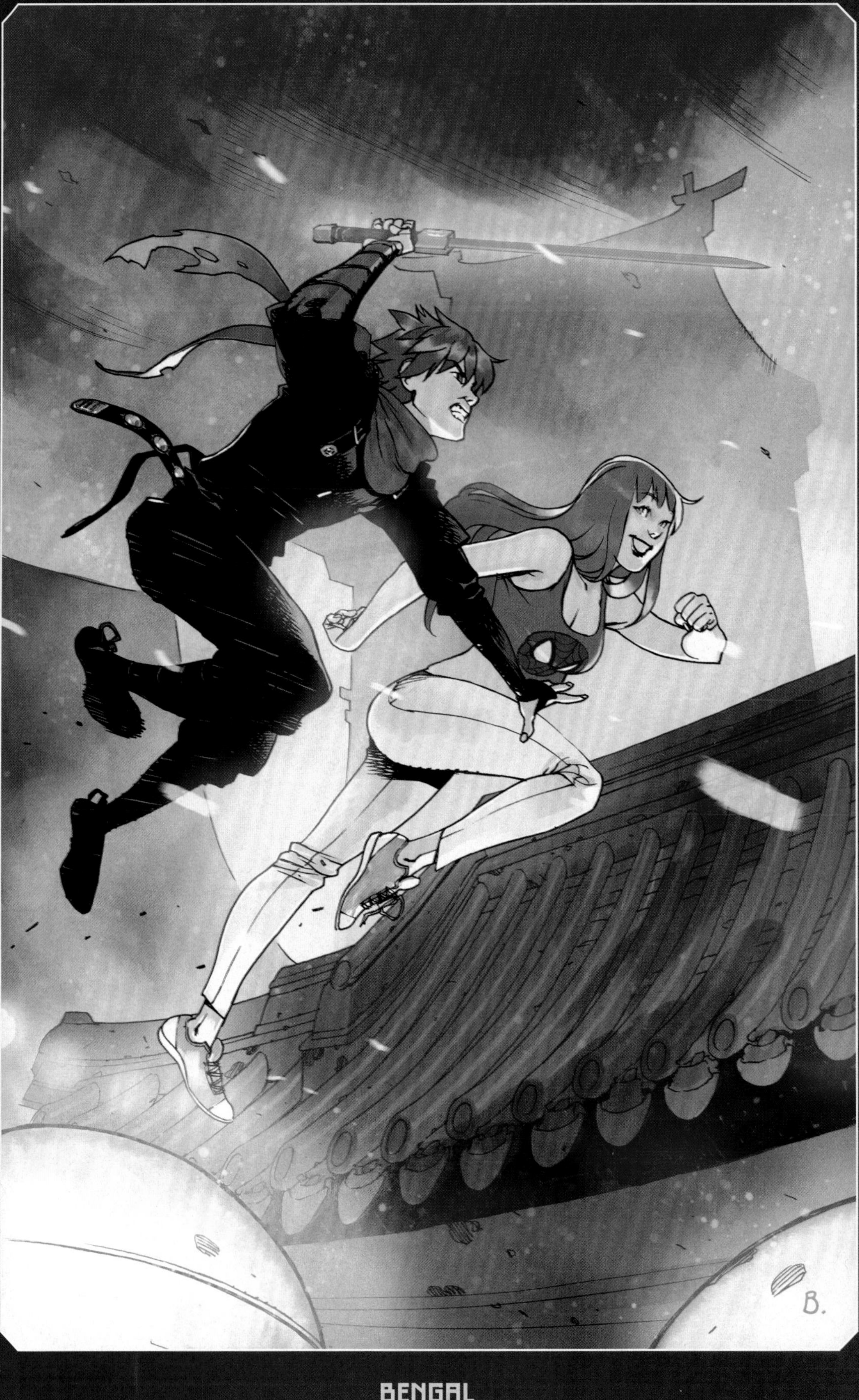
B.

BENGAL
#4 MARY JANE VARIANT